AF574890

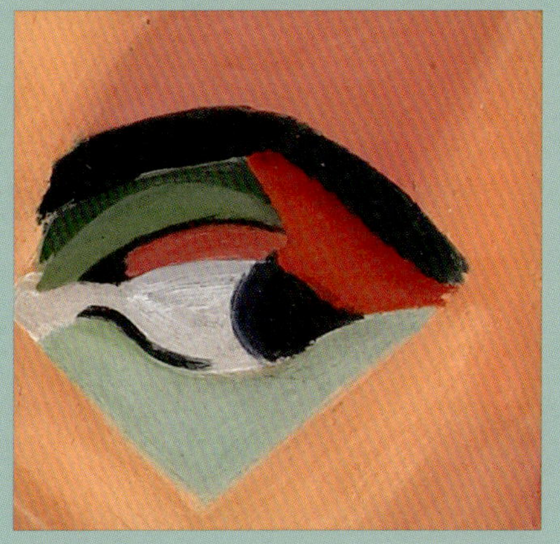

"Place absorbs our earliest notice and attention, it bestows on us our original awareness; and our critical powers spring up from the study of it and the growth of experience inside it. It perseveres in bringing us back to earth when we fly too high. It never really stops informing us, for it is forever astir, alive, changing, reflecting, like the mind of man itself. One place comprehended can make us understand other places better." —Eudora Welty

The Missis

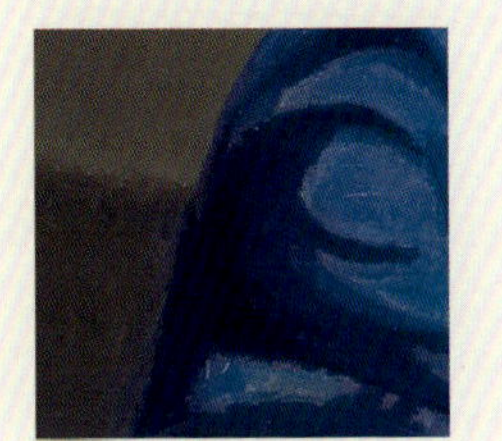

sippi Story

Patti Carr Black

Robin C. Dietrick, Editor

Mississippi Museum of Art, Jackson

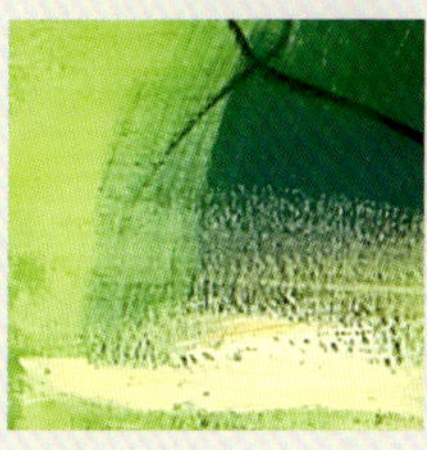
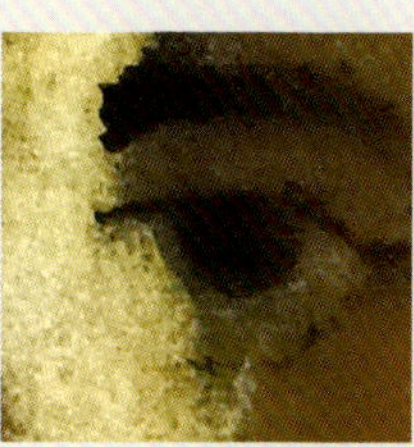
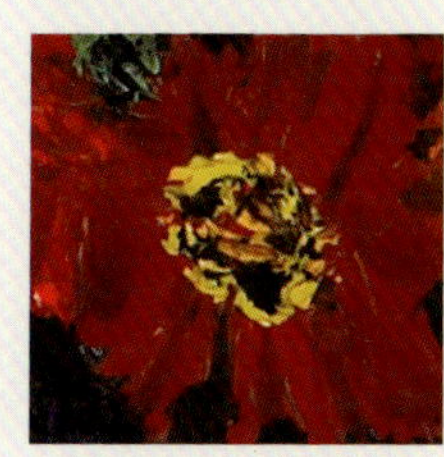
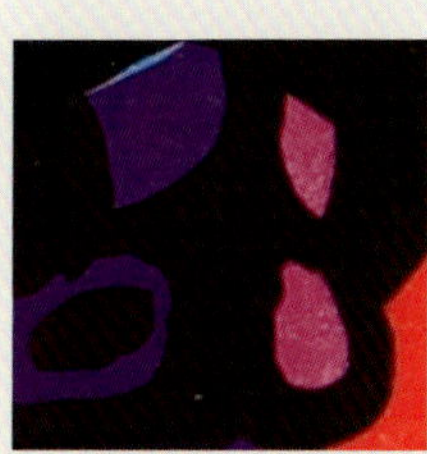

The Mississippi Story is published on the occasion of the grand opening of the Mississippi Museum of Art's new facility at 380 South Lamar Street in downtown Jackson, Mississippi, and in conjunction with the exhibition *The Mississippi Story*, opening June 9, 2007. *The Mississippi Story* exhibition is guest curated by Patti Carr Black and organized by the Programs Department of the Mississippi Museum of Art.

The Mississippi Museum of Art gratefully acknowledges the support of The Chisholm Foundation and The Phil Hardin Foundation, without which this book and *The Mississippi Story* exhibition would not have been possible.

The Mississippi Museum of Art and its programs are sponsored in part by the city of Jackson and the Jackson Convention & Visitors Bureau. Support is also provided by funding from the Mississippi Arts Commission, a state agency, and in part by the National Endowment for the Arts, a federal agency.

Edited by Robin C. Dietrick.
Copyedited by Kathy L. Greenberg.
Photography by Bill Jackson, Gil Ford Photography unless otherwise noted.
Designed by John A. Langston.
Printed in Canada by Friesens.

Library of Congress Cataloging-in-Publication Data

Black, Patti Carr.
The Mississippi story / Patti Carr Black ; Robin C. Dietrick, editor.
p. cm.
Issued in connection with an exhibition opening June 9, 2007, Mississippi Museum of Art.
Includes index.
ISBN 1-887422-14-5
1. Art, American--Mississippi--Exhibitions. I. Mississippi Museum of Art. II. Title.
N6530.M7B634 2007
709.762'07476251--dc22

2007011119

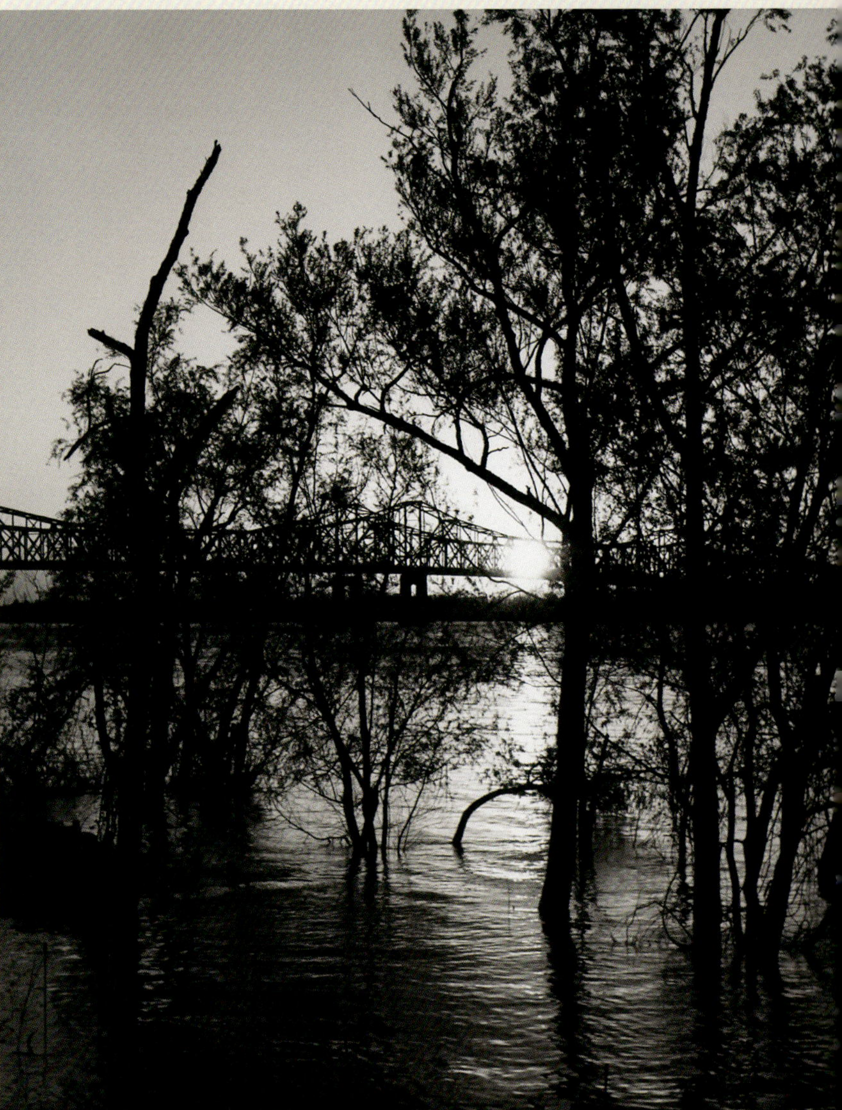

Bill Aron
(born 1941), *Mississippi River at Natchez*, 1991.
silver halide print,
20 x 16.

Contents

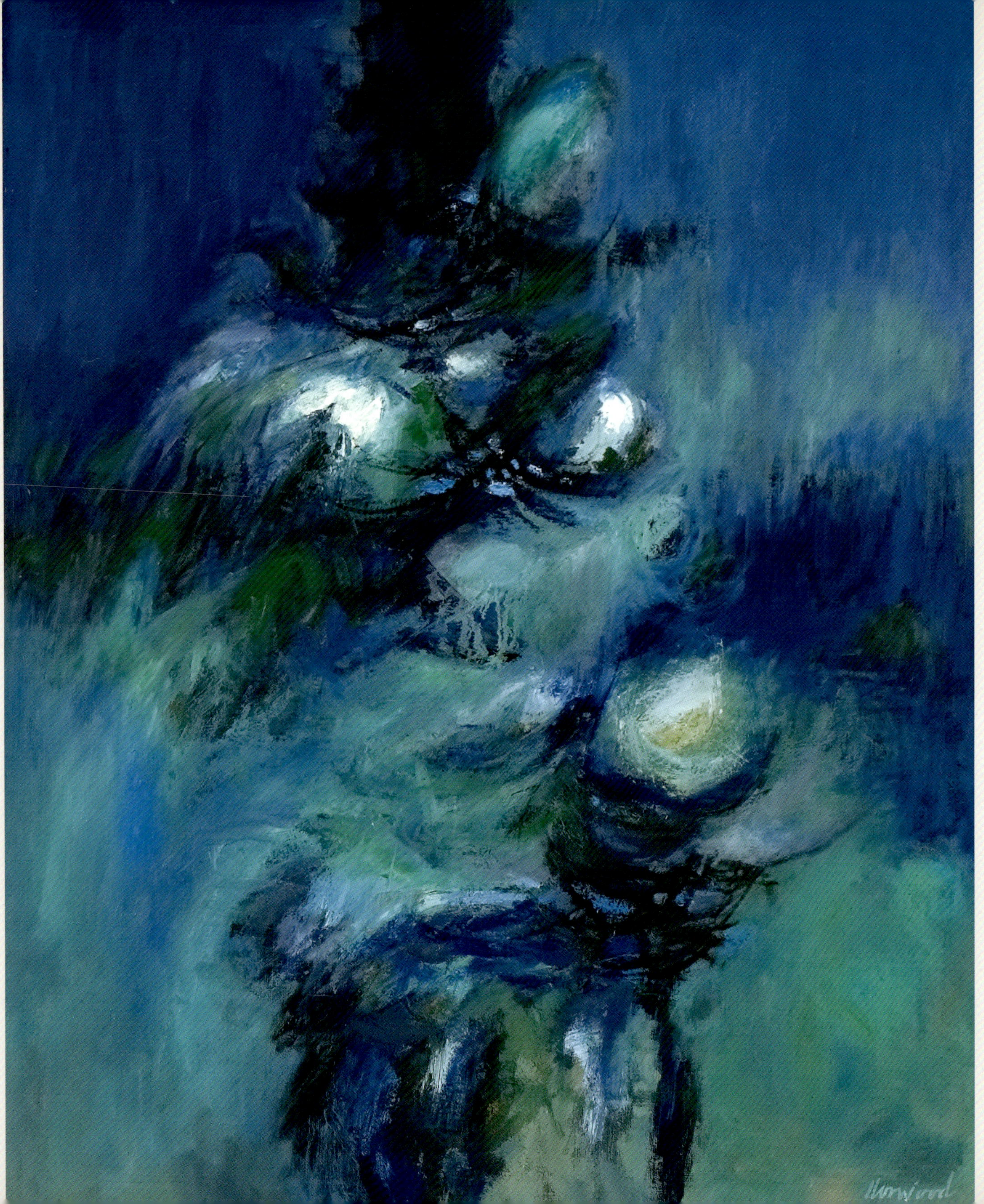

The Story of the Mississippi Museum of Art

The Mississippi Art Association, forerunner of the Mississippi Museum of Art, came into existence at 2:30 p.m. on Friday, October 27, 1911. The State Fair Association had requested artist Bessie Cary Lemly of the Belhaven College faculty, and founder of Jackson's Art Study Club in 1903, to organize an exhibition of local art for the state fair. The artists who participated in the 1911 State Fair were so enthusiastic about the outcome that they quickly organized the Mississippi Art Association (MAA), which allowed them to exhibit artwork regularly for public viewing. Members of the MAA included artists and supporters of the arts, all of whom were originally members of the Art Study Club.

The sole purpose of the MAA, at first, was to hold exhibitions at the state fair. Later, shows were held in any available space: the YWCA, the City Auditorium, the Public Library, and the Governor's Mansion, among others. Aileen Phillips Shannon, the artist who first taught Marie Atkinson Hull, followed Bessie Lemly as president, and in 1916 Marie Hull was elected to the position. During these early years, the MAA and Art Study Club lobbied the Mississippi legislature to introduce art classes to the public schools. Success came when Central High School of Jackson became the first public school in the state with an art education program and Mississippi State College for

< **Malcolm Norwood** (born 1928), *Promise of Fulfillment*, 1963. oil on canvas, 50 x 40.

Women (later Mississippi University for Women) became the first college to add art to its curriculum.

The MAA established a permanent art collection in 1911. Taking Marie Hull's suggestion, members initiated the purchase award system for the annual state fair exhibition. Bettie McArthur, head of Mississippi University for Women's art department, won the first purchase award for her painting *The Poplars of St. Legare*. It became one of the first additions to the collection. In 1926 the organization was incorporated and a charter secured, signed by Bessie Cary Lemly, Mrs. R. L. Hogue, and Martha Enochs. This step was inspired when the Gale family home at 839 North State Street (now called the Municipal Art Gallery) was presented to the city of Jackson. Although the MAA shared the house as a meeting place for various clubs, they were able to house their offices there, as well as the art collection.

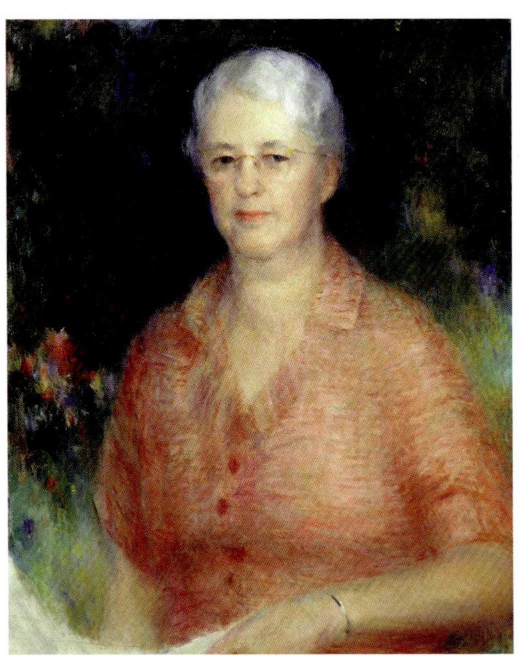

Karl Wolfe (1904–1984), *Portrait of Bessie Cary Lemly*, circa 1947. oil on canvas, 30 x 24

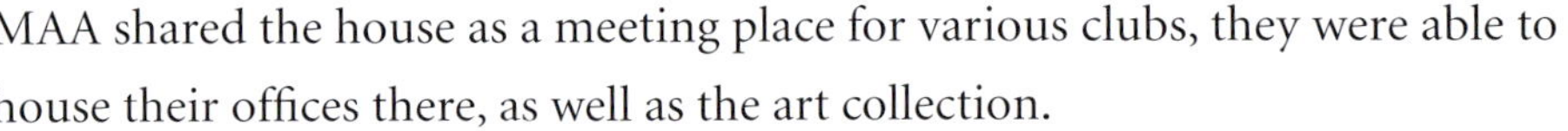

For the next fifty years, the MAA became increasingly active. An annual watercolor exhibition was established in 1931, complementing the annual oil exhibition. In the late 1930s Eudora Welty held a photographic exhibition there. Karl Wolfe, who was MAA president from 1940 to 1942, and William Hollingsworth worked on attracting nationally known artists to the juried exhibitions. In 1949 the first employee was hired: a woman who lived in the gallery, performed light housekeeping chores, and cared for the permanent collection. In 1951 the MAA re-filed for a charter of incorporation, having failed to file the required papers in due fashion. Joshua Green, attorney for the MAA, wrote the new charter.

Over the years, the organization added children's art, collegiate work, and Allison's Art Colony (a group that met several times a year from 1948 to 1963 at a spa in Madison County called Allison's Wells) to their exhibition agenda. Children's art classes, teacher-training workshops, scholarships for training, newsletters, contact with the state school system, and workshops sponsored at Allison's Wells furthered the MAA's commitment to their original purpose: "to raise the standard of appreciation among laymen, and to stimulate the production of the highest type of work from artists."

As the 1955 term president, Mrs. Morgan Jones made the first effort to secure an art museum for Jackson. She stated that it would be her main objective to work toward the realization of a full-fledged art institution. Subsequent officers also tried to meet that goal. As early as 1958 the MAA petitioned Jackson's city planning board to include an art gallery in the proposed new civic center. For the next twenty years the MAA worked toward constructing a museum building. A monumental effort of outreach, fund-raising, and consciousness-raising went into the effort. To assist in this endeavor, The Gallery Guild, Inc., was formed in 1965. In 1967 the MAA's first professional director, Louis Sedberry, was hired and occupied offices in the Municipal Art Gallery. Following Sedberry's directorship were Lowell Adams, John Craib-Cox, Michael Ogden, and Dan Matusiewicz as interim director.

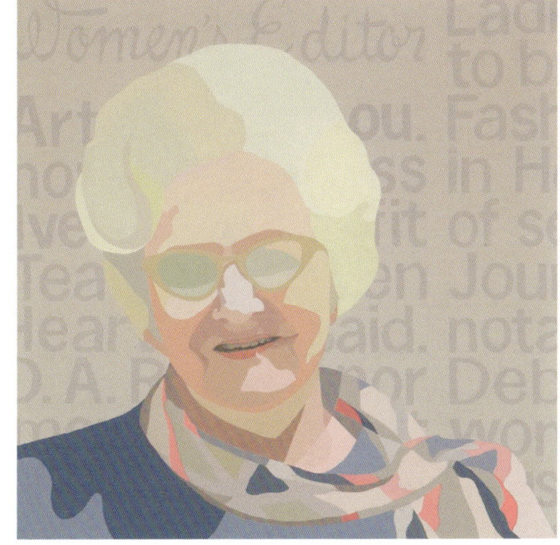

Merle Tennyson (now Merle Tennyson Montjoy) (born 1920), *Mary Alice, The Journalist*, 1971. acrylic on canvas, 24 x 24.

The Museum began to take definite form when the city announced that a cultural and educational complex would be built adjacent to the Jackson Municipal Auditorium. Tom Biggs of Jackson was selected as the architect. Jim Czarniecki was appointed first director of the new Mississippi Museum of Art, which would be housed in the complex. Dedication ceremonies for the new building were held on April 22, 1978, followed by two weeks of celebratory programming. When only national and international exhibitions were

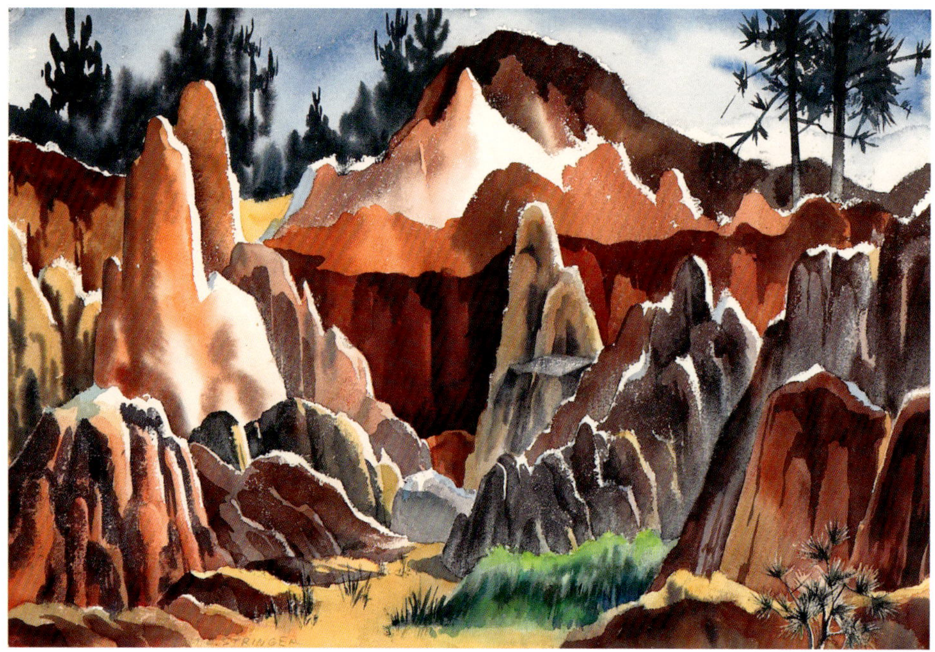

Mary Evelyn Stringer (1921–1995), *Gullies at Allison's Wells*, circa 1950. watercolor on paper, 10 x 15.

announced, the state's art community voiced its disappointment. Many felt that the Museum was made possible in large part because of the support of Mississippi artists; the Museum seemed to have deserted them. In response, in December 1978 the Museum created the short-lived Mississippi Gallery. The Mississippi Art Association's charter of incorporation was amended and the legal entity officially became the Mississippi Museum of Art on November 29, 1979.

Since its opening, the Mississippi Museum of Art has implemented many projects that include The Palette, a café that first opened in 1980; the Open Gallery (1983) that featured avant-garde work; the Impressions Gallery for children (1987-1997); satellite museums, introduced in 1989 (now the Museum's Affiliate Network of more than twenty-five locations around the state), the T. M. Hederman Memorial Endowment for Exhibitions (1986); and The Annie Laurie Swaim Hearin Memorial Exhibition Series (1992).

After Jim Czarniecki's resignation in 1983, Thad McLaurin and Marilyn Harris served as interim directors until Norman McCrummen III was appointed in 1984. His four-month tenure was followed by Alexander L. Nyerges, 1985-1992; Linda S. Sullivan, 1992-1995; Bill Loveless as interim director; Andrew Maass, 1996-2001; Jane Hiatt as interim director; and the Museum's current director Betsy Bradley, who began her tenure in December 2001.

In addition to a dizzying schedule of changing exhibitions, the Museum offers year-round educational programs for both children and adults and hosts The Scholastic Art Awards Mississippi Regional Competition as well as the biennial *Mississippi Invitational*. Adults can enjoy monthly programs such as "Unburied Treasures," which features art, music, and literature and "Jazz, Art & Friends," which celebrates the merging of artistic disciplines. The Museum also offers entertaining and educational programs associated with current exhibitions and audio tours of select exhibitions. Innovative educational areas are the "Closer Look Gallery" and its smaller counterpart, the "Family Corners." These spaces, located within the exhibitions themselves, offer visitors of all ages space to reflect on artwork and subjects found within the exhibitions.

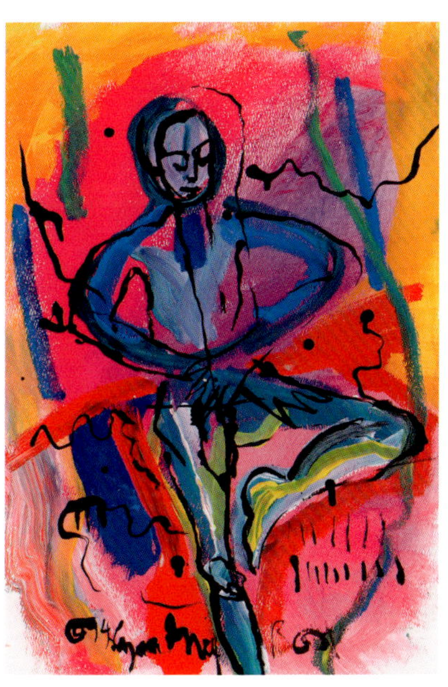

Lynn Green Root (1954-2001), no title, 1994. acrylic on paper, 18 x 12.

With its many programs, diverse exhibitions, and rapidly expanding permanent collection, the Museum outgrew its first permanent home at the Mississippi Arts Center. Planning for the current facility began in 2002, and in June 2007 the plans came to fruition with the opening of the new Museum in the Mississippi Arts Pavilion. The non-profit organization raised several million dollars from the community to fully fund renovations to the Arts Pavilion building and to support an endowment for its operation—a testament to the community's dedication to the Mississippi Museum of Art.

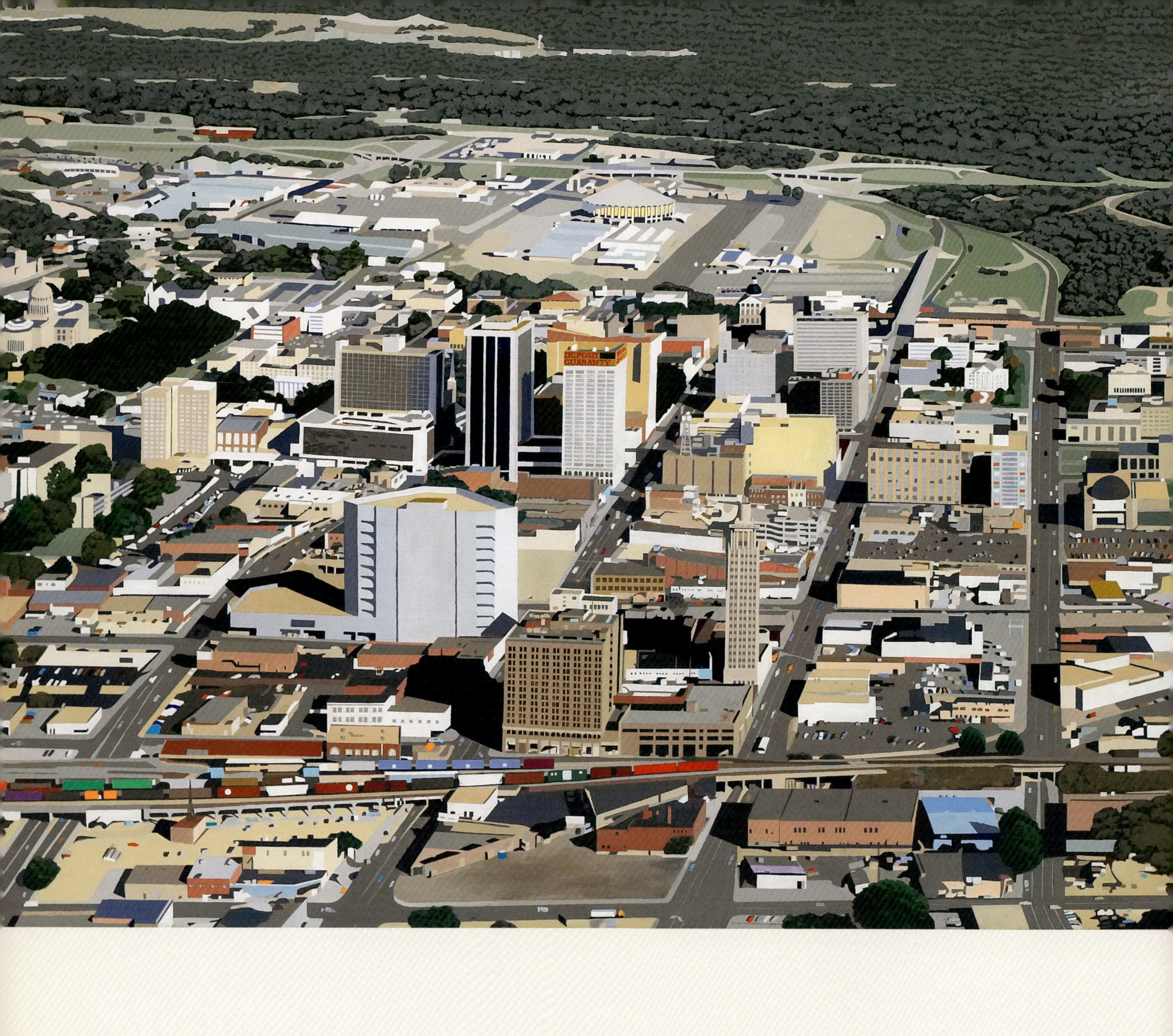
DEPOSIT
GUARANTY

Acknowledgments

Mississippians are most at ease when telling stories; thus, any artistic image seems to become one, whether its an abstract painting or a soulful blues progression. The Mississippi Museum of Art is pleased to present the “story” of visual arts in our state; and we are extremely grateful for the wisdom, research, care, and thoughtful writing of Patti Carr Black, who curated this groundbreaking exhibition and wrote the penetrating essay in this volume. Her previous work in *Art in Mississippi, 1720–1980* made her the obvious and wise choice for this work, and she does not disappoint the reader as she weaves carefully the threads that unite the images to our state and our people.

< **Carol Cole** (born 1943), *Jackson, MS, 1979*, 1979-1985. acrylic on canvas, 42 x 54.

To open our beautiful new facility, the Museum felt compelled to install its permanent collection in an exhibition that honors the place and the artists that formed this institution and gave it its identity. To the members of the Art Study Club who formed the Mississippi Art Association and the more than two hundred artists whose works appear in this exhibition; we extend our deepest gratitude for your commitment, your diligence, and your visions made concrete. To the past and current trustees, especially our chairman Jerry Host, I am most grateful for the guidance and determination and work, which have built a home worthy to hold Mississippi’s fine collection of art. The staff of this Museum has worked diligently to carry on our comprehensive services to the community while simultaneously turning a rectangular building into a museum of the highest quality. It is my honor to work with them daily, and my life is enriched by them—from the artistic team led by Daniel Piersol and including Beth Batton, Robin Dietrick, and Joanna Biglane to the educators Ivy Alley and Lianne Takemori who bring our collection of art into meaningful relationship with our audience every day, to the preparators who skillfully work their magic and transform walls into spaces of glory. L. C. Tucker, Melvin Johnson, and Wesley Hargon are masters of their trade and devoted to the loving care of the art they handle. Behind the scenes, the administrative and development teams, led by Mitchell Marcum and Jordan Perry, enable the operations of this museum to fulfill its mission; to Ann Harkins, Mindy Kunz, Maggie Lacey, Elizabeth Blanks, Annette French, Julia Stewart, James Steverson, Charles Moaton, and the ever faithful Nina Moss, I owe you my thanks.

Finally, this book has been lovingly handled as well. Robin Dietrick has edited the book and transferred its beautiful design by John Langston to the walls of the exhibition. Kathy Greenberg, our copyeditor, and Bill Jackson from Gil Ford Photography made the words and images sparkle. The support of the Phil Hardin Foundation and the Chisholm Foundation gave us the resources to produce what we think is a testimony to the richness of our legacy. To all of you, we thank you and wish for you the joy in reading this book that we have experienced in producing it.

Betsy Bradley
Director

Introduction

Since its inception, the Mississippi Museum of Art has served to educate visitors about the region's visual artistry. In 1911 members of the Art Study Club (which is still in existence) set out to create a state art museum. Their efforts resulted in an institution that has grown from holding small displays in a donated home to hosting international exhibitions. Today, with a full programming schedule and ever-expanding collection, the Museum has outgrown its first permanent home in Jackson. Its new location is at the fully renovated Mississippi Arts Pavilion, where space is dedicated specifically for the Museum's permanent collection of Mississippi art—the world's largest of its kind. The Museum has published *The Mississippi Story* in conjunction with an exhibition of the same title and with the grand opening of the new facility, opening June 2007. Art historian and Mississippian Patti Carr Black is both the guest curator of the exhibition and author of this book. Illustrated with over one hundred full-color reproductions, Black's essay explores the sense of place felt by Mississippians and the narrative output pervasive in the state's artistic accomplishments. In great detail, she examines Mississippi's time-honored practice of storytelling—one that emerges through writing, music, and art—and complements her scholarship with biographies of numerous regional artists.

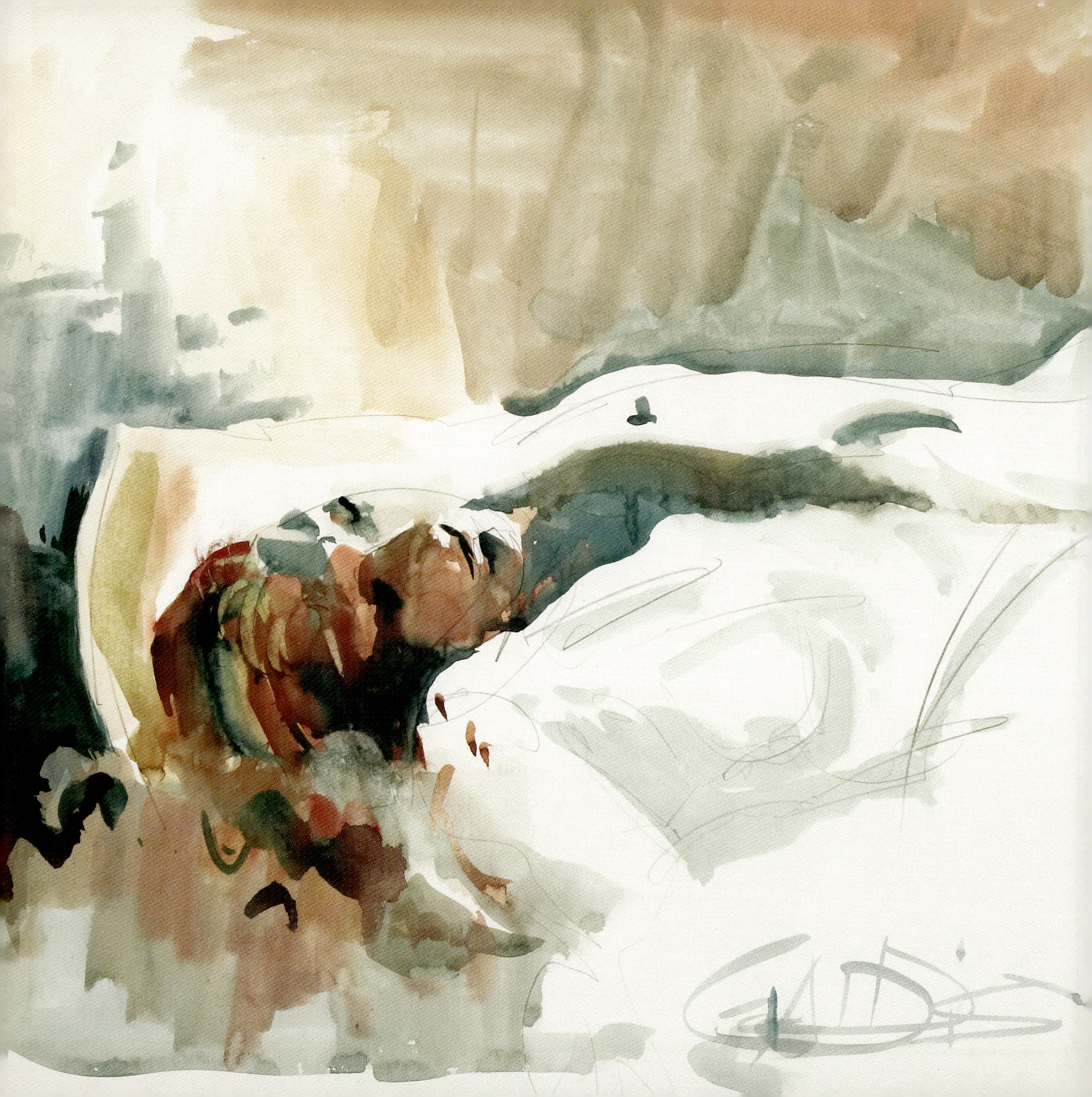

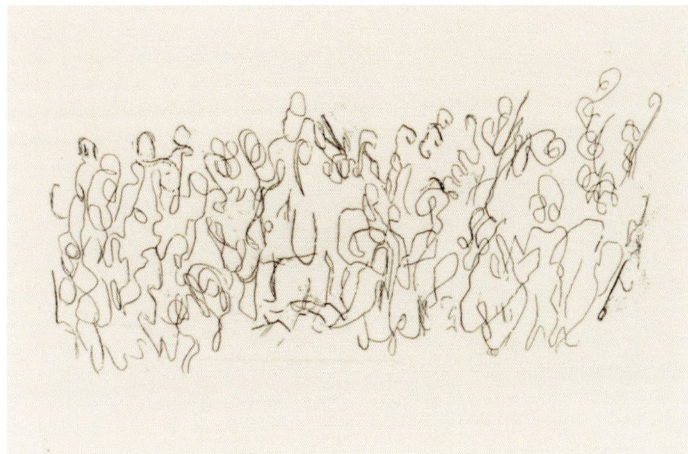

Elizabeth Pajerski (1915-2003), *Orchestra*, 1971. black and white etching, 15 x 17.

In *The Mississippi Story*, a broad variety of artwork is on view, its earliest an 1807 watercolor and the most recent completed two centuries later in 2007. Materials range from clay to oil to video and were made by artists from equally diverse backgrounds. Artwork by Mississippians or about Mississippi has been divided into four distinct categories: the influence of the land on the art, Mississippi's people as depicted in its art, life in Mississippi observed by its artists, and the exporting of Mississippi culture through its artists. The four sections of the exhibition work together to present the story of the state, its art, its history, and its people.

< **John Gaddis** (1929-1993), no title, no date. watercolor and graphite on paper, 18½ x 17½ (sight).

Mississippi's story continues to evolve, and the galleries will reflect that change in regular rotations of contemporary and past art. This publication documents only a portion of the artwork that will be shared with the public. We invite you to visit the Museum to experience the more than two hundred works that represent Mississippi's rich tradition of visual art.

Robin C. Dietrick
Curator of Exhibitions

The Mississi

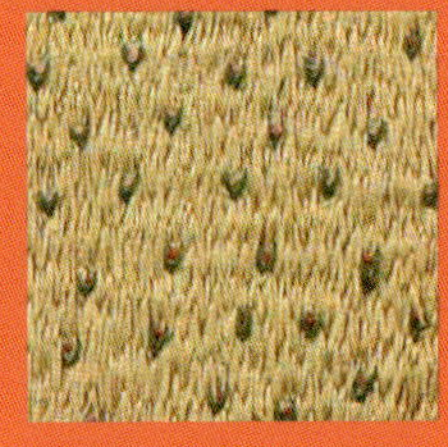

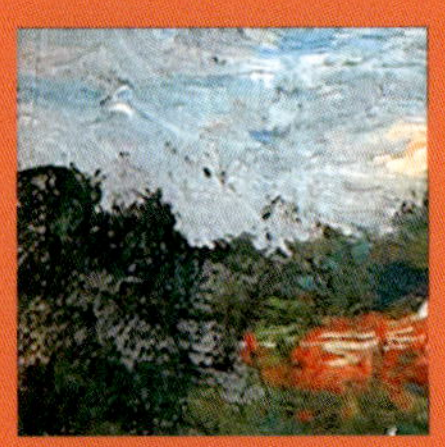

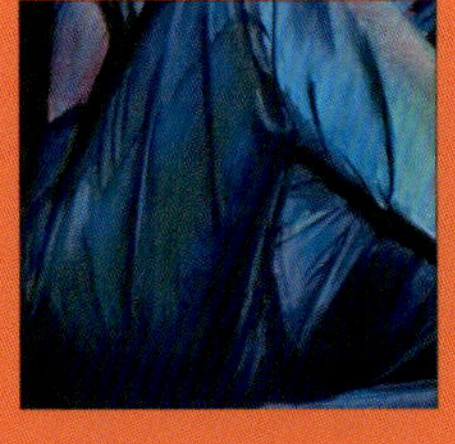

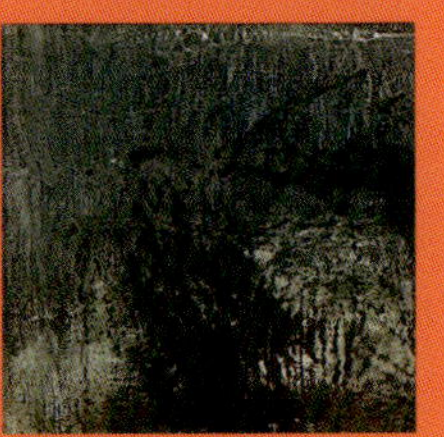

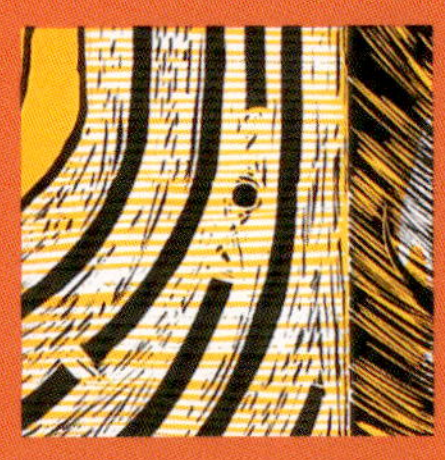

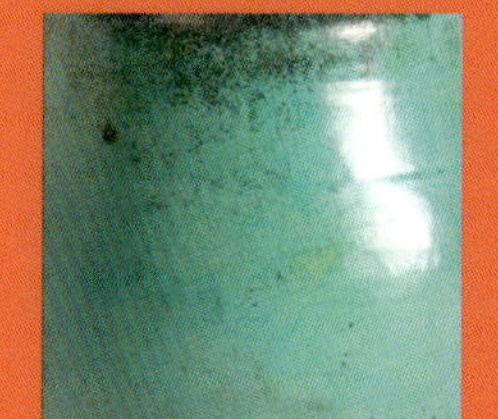

Patti Carr Black

ppi Story

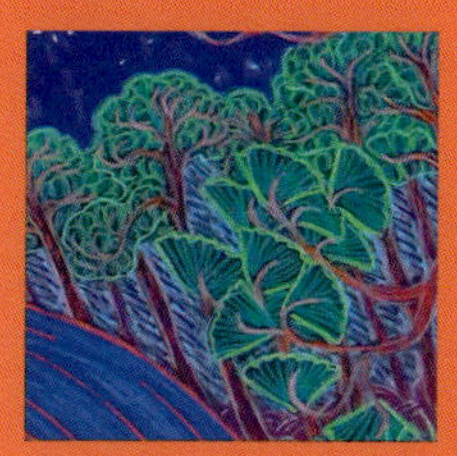

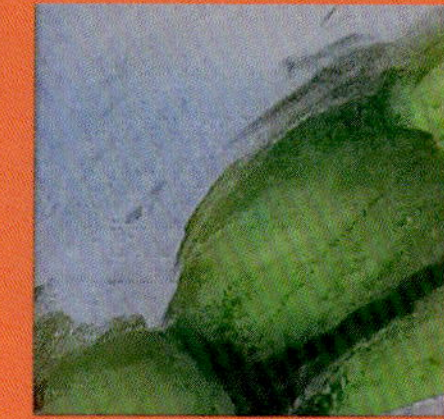

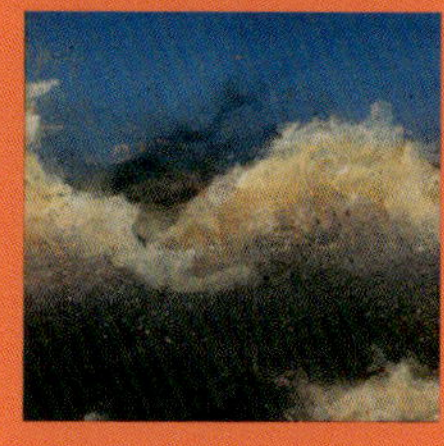

The garden smells of sun beating on tomatoes. The air is heavy as a touch, and it smells of hot okra and bean blossoms. It smells of earth, and it sings with insect voices.—Rebecca Hill

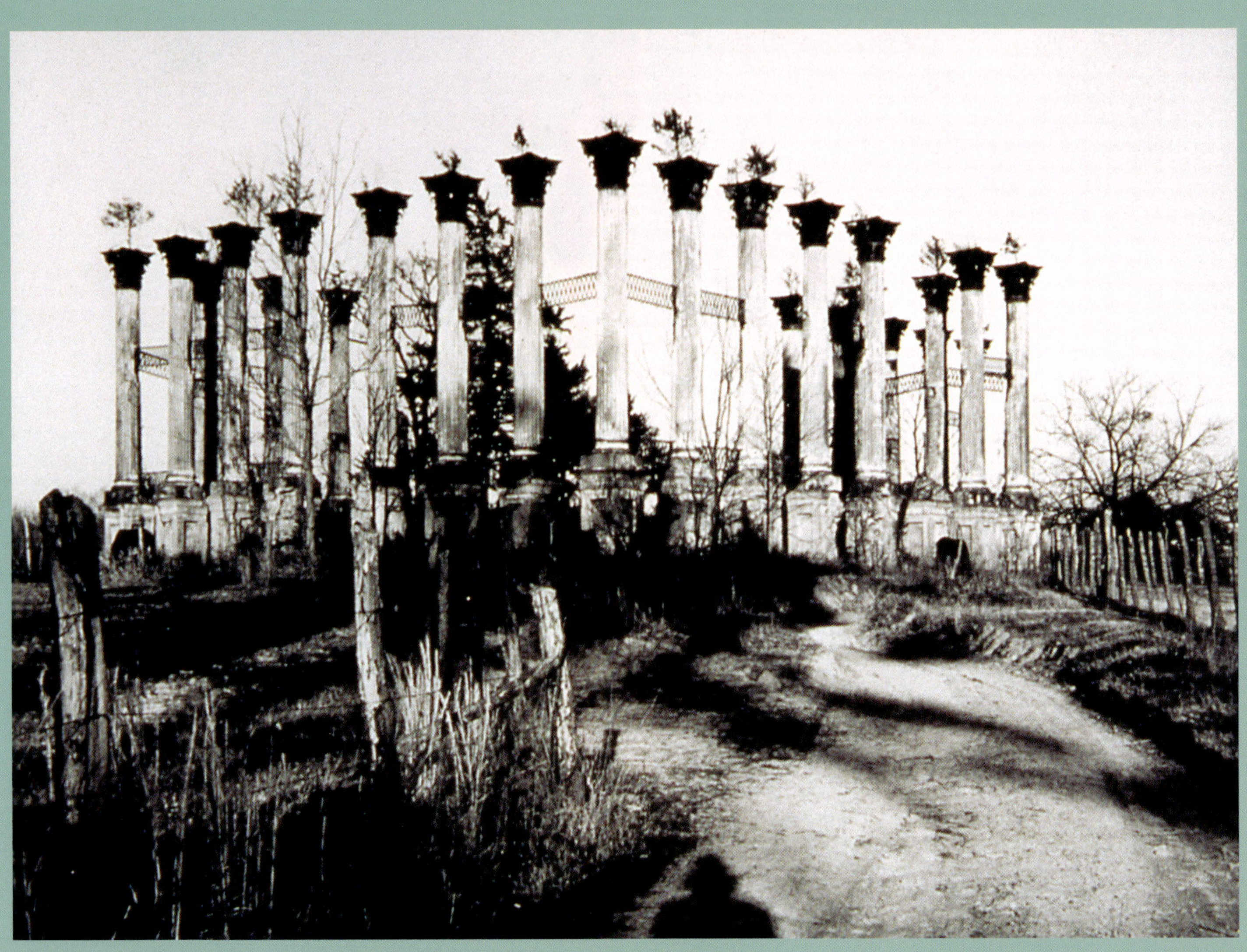

Eudora Welty wrote, "It seems plain that the art that speaks most clearly, explicitly, directly and passionately from its place of origin will remain the longest understood." The accompanying exhibition, composed primarily from works in the permanent collection of the Mississippi Museum of Art, explores art that is explicitly and passionately derived from Mississippi. The works exhibited here were produced within the state by artists who were native to or lived in Mississippi or by travelers who created a work about the state. In *The Mississippi Story*, the show's overall theme of place is presented in four sections: the influence of the land on the art, Mississippi's people as depicted in its art, life in Mississippi observed by its artists, and the exporting of Mississippi culture through its artists.

< Eudora Welty (1909-2001), *Ruins of Windsor, near Port Gibson*, post 1936. gelatin silver print, 10¾ x 13½ (sight). Copyright © Eudora Welty, LLC; Eudora Welty Collection—Mississippi Department of Archives and History.

To understand the pervasive effect of place on the art of Mississippi, consider the state's other great expressions of creativity: music, fiction, and memoir. Where else could one first hear Charley Patton's "High Water Everywhere" or Robert Johnson's "Cross Road Blues" but in the Mississippi Delta? Meridian's Jimmie Rodgers, "the father of country music," yodeled his way to fame and fortune with the lyrics for "Dear Old Sunny South by the Sea," "Mississippi Moon," and "Mississippi Delta Blues." Few would argue that William Faulkner and Welty are triumphant examples of the mastery of place in fiction, as in *Delta Wedding* or *The Sound and the Fury*, evoking an overwhelming sense of the places described. The genius of their work, of course, is that while it is filled with exquisite and accurate details of a specific landscape, the writing is born of great imaginative power and universal meaning. Memoir, of course, is largely an expression of place, and Mississippi writers have been unable to resist it: Ellen Douglas, Willie Morris, Elizabeth Spencer, and Larry Brown, among others.

The state's most provocative fiction writers have used place profoundly to focus their imagination and to visualize contextual background: again, Ellen Douglas of Jackson, Elizabeth Spencer of Carrollton; Larry Brown of Oxford, and Willie Morris of Yazoo City; Barry Hannah of Clinton; Lewis Nordan of Itta Bena; Ellen Gilchrist of Issaquena County; and Beth Henley of Jackson. These writers, like Faulkner, have taken "the artist in him in one hand and his milieu in the other and thrust the one into the other like a clawing and spitting cat into a croker sack." This is what makes art and place together vital and significant, and this is what our best visual artists also do.

Welty continued in her essay on place: "Painting and writing, always the closest two of the sister arts . . . have each a still closer connection with place than they have with each other; but a difference lies in their respective requirements of it, and even further in the way they use it—the written word being ultimately as different from the pigment as the note of the scale is from the chisel." *The Mississippi Story* invites viewers to examine the connection between place and the visual arts of the state, as well as Mississippi artists' requirements and uses of place.

Elements and Styles of Mississippi Art

In surveying Mississippi art, can it be said that there are common elements beyond the use of place in art? Is an analysis of Mississippi art as something apart an exercise in provincialism, or can it reveal that elements of culture profoundly affect elements of art? As represented by the Museum's collection, art in Mississippi seems to bear several common denominators that have influenced style.

While many Mississippi artists may have experimented with abstraction, hard edge, expressionism, op art, action painting, spatialism, and other movements that rejected a naturalistic portrayal of subject matter, most have steadfastly held to representational art. Many have appropriated impressionism, expressionism, cubism, fauvism, pointillism, and even surrealism as vehicles for representation. There have been few proponents of "the canvas freed from the portrayal of reality." Mississippi artists and audiences alike tend to view art from a literary point of view rather than an intellectual exercise or emotional expression involving only the intrinsic formal elements of art.

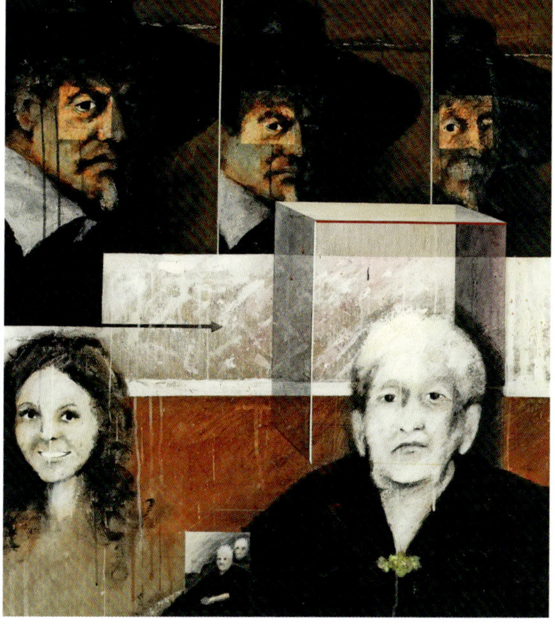

William Dunlap (born 1944), *Leona Winor is 100 Years Old*, 1971. polymer on linen, 54 x 47¾.

The narrative tradition is a powerful cultural phenomenon in Mississippi. While its influence is most apparent in the extraordinary literary output and the language of blues, country music, and gospel, it is also clearly abundant in Mississippi's visual arts. From the folk carvings of Willie Barton to the explicit stories of Ethel Wright Mohamed's textiles to the allusion-filled canvases of William Dunlap, Mississippi artists are telling a story. And photographers, our most peripatetic artists, are among the most compelling storytellers in Mississippi.

Again, it is fruitful to look to literature for explanations of this phenomenon. Literary scholar Hugh Holman wrote that "the Southerner has been noted for the particularity and the concreteness of his imagination." Mississippi visual artists seem to feel that representational art most clearly conveys the dimensionality and concreteness of life. Robert Penn Warren wrote about the

Southerner's "fear of abstraction." Perhaps to the visual artist in Mississippi the narrative impulse forbids the introspection of pure abstraction. Thomas D. Clark, a native Mississippian and distinguished historian, wrote that "one of the state's most distinctive personal traits [is the] enjoyment of folksy and humorous stories. Elements of these are laced throughout the literature of the state like golden threads." Artist William Dunlap said early in his career, "Writers have influenced me a lot more than painters. Everyone read, told stories, and talked incessantly, so the idea of making narrative art is something I've never questioned." Photographer Maude Schuyler Clay has stated, "The main reason I began taking pictures was to try and tell a story." Both Dunlap and Clay speak for generations of a visual tradition. Reynolds Price noted that the need to tell and hear stories is the second most important need after nutrition, and Mississippians have feasted at the narrative table.

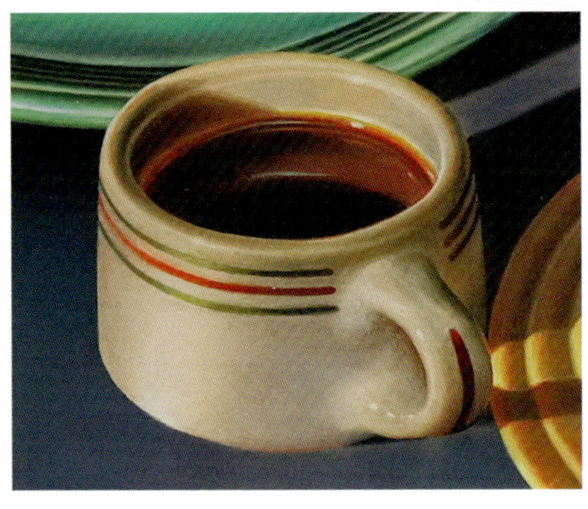

Glennray Tutor (born 1950), *Coffee Cup*, 1994. oil on prepared paper, 6¼ x 7¼ (sight).

Beyond the land itself, the entire range of Mississippi's material culture is a looming presence in its artwork. Southern artists, as with southern writers, excel in the evocation of the everyday world. The representation of details and incidental subject matter strengthens the concreteness of place. Glennray Tutor, a masterful painter of objects, asserted, "The subject matter is not something I have to go and find. It is something I experienced by living in the South and always have experienced. These are subjects that are around me and have an importance to me."

Another cultural influence in Mississippi is continuity, a sense of history or rootedness. Willie Morris observed that "Mississippi, well into the late twentieth century, retains much of its communal origins, and along with that a sense of continuity, of the enduring past and the flow of generational awareness, if you will, of human history." Mississippi visual artists may feel that cultural continuities are discarded in modernism's absolute sense of art. The apprehension of cultural continuity may be so strongly perceived and stamped so indelibly that some Mississippi artists have not wanted or could not find a way to express their relationship with place outside of concrete representation. For many Mississippi artists a strong sense of community may trump the self-referentiality of abstract expressionism, for representational art provides a clearer and more direct communication with others. In examining the sources of art, Eudora Welty went one step farther: into the emotional realm. She wrote that feelings are bound up in place: "Location . . . is the heart's field."

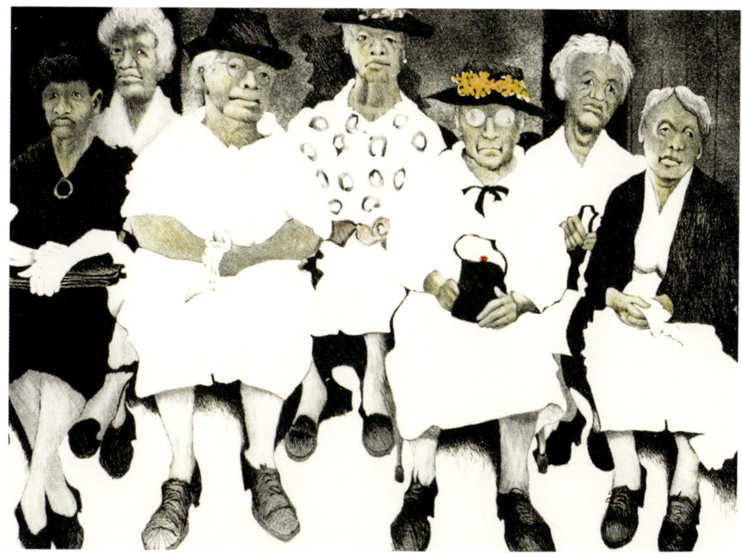

Dale Rayburn
(born 1942), *Sunday School Class*, 1976.
color etching, 19 x 24¼ (sight).

Art historians have cited as one influence the South's innate conservatism, a sense of inviolability, a resistance to things that uproot or change the status quo. Many Mississippi artists, however, have experimented widely in their choice of presentation. Yet another possible influence, largely unexplored except in the area of folk art, is religion. It may be that Mississippi's religious culture of widely shared values, beliefs, and outlook expresses itself, however subconsciously, on canvas. Faithful portrayals of the natural world, for example, would be expected in a culture infused with the evangelical tradition of "devotional celebration of God's handiwork." Religion, conservatism, and history may all exert themselves on Mississippi's art, but the visual evidence suggests that contact with place is the artist's main source of strength and identity. It follows, then, that traditional subject matter presented in representational form is an important aspect of the art.

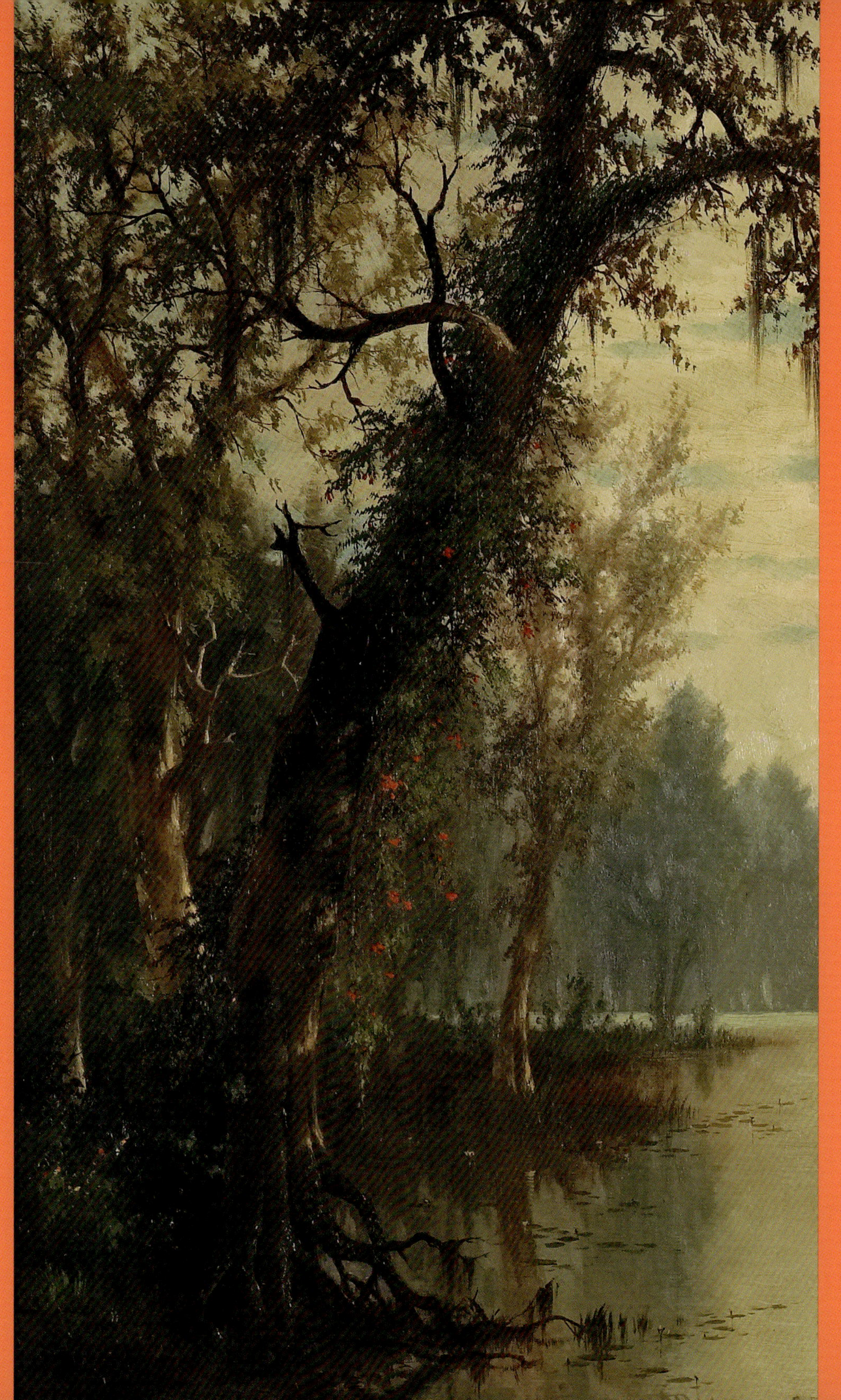

Joseph Rusling Meeker (1827-1889), *Day on the Yazoo*, 1885. oil on canvas, 24 x 14.

The Influence of the Land

In the years since the South's visual arts came to the attention of art historians, one fact has been noted by all: southern artists perceive nature as a dominant force and have a heightened awareness of nature, as well as a highly emotional response to it. Since the Civil War, landscape and various relationships to the land have been the dominant themes of Mississippi art. From nineteenth-century landscapes of the Gulf Coast to the regionalism of the 1930s to the myriad expressions of contemporary art, Mississippi artists—of whatever style, medium, and level of artistic training—overwhelmingly ratify the notion that they are deeply involved with landscape and nature, and more than that, with a specific landscape. That the landscape paintings of many Mississippi artists often seem symbolic—landscape removed from the processes of change and time, a kind of mythic place free from the preoccupations of modern human beings—suggests that a sense of nature may, in fact, override a sense of place.

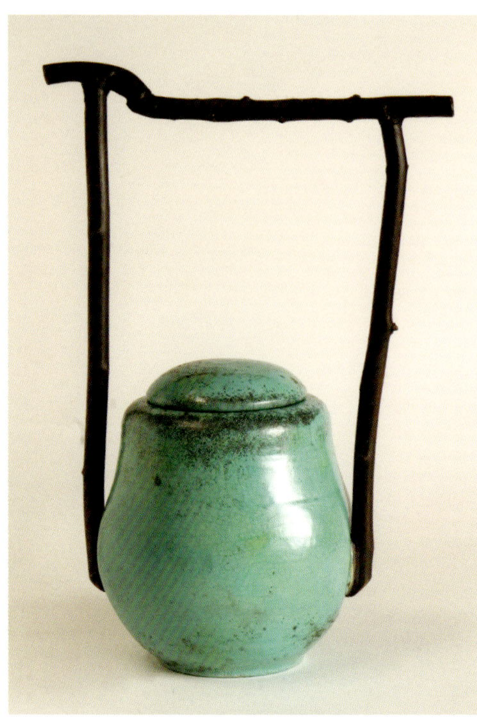

Obie Clark
(born 1948), no title, no date. ceramic, 15⅛ x 10⅜ x 5¾.

In a direct way the land itself has played a part in the creation of art, providing the actual materials for creating objects. The traditional Choctaw basket is made of swamp cane gathered in forays to Delta swamps, dyed with natural substances found in the woods, and woven by a member of the Choctaw Nation of northeast Mississippi. Biloxi potter George Ohr dug his clay from the Tchoutacabouffa River in Harrison County, and Peter Anderson at Shearwater Pottery in Ocean Springs foraged his clay near Lucedale. James Anderson has continued his father's tradition. Lee and Pup McCarty began making their pottery in Merigold with native clay from a ravine near Oxford, where William Faulkner directed them. Later they used clay from Shuqualak. Obie Clark of Taylor incorporates into his work his deep feeling for the natural world. He takes an item from nature and lets "natural design elements dictate the shape of the piece." On exhibit is a glazed pot with lid for which the artist used native twigs as handles. Reeds, grasses, and vines served as materials for folk baskets and other objects of art. Native trees provide the material for white oak baskets, fanciful woodcarvings, wood sculptures, and beautifully crafted furniture.

Mississippi's diversity of geophysical features has produced discrete sections of the state, and in turn subtle and not-so-subtle differences in social and cultural traditions, economics, and political attitudes. The land section is divided into those distinct areas, starting in the northwest corner with the Mississippi Delta, the Hill Country to the east, Jackson and the central area, River Country (the Old Natchez District), the Piney Woods to the east, and the Gulf Coast.

The Delta

A vaguely crescent-shaped area in the northwestern corner of the state, the Delta is a flat alluvial plain formed by the rich deposits of the Mississippi and Yazoo Rivers. For almost one hundred years after Mississippi became part of the United States, the Delta largely remained a dense wilderness. Heavy settlement came well after the Civil War, as swamps were drained, a levee system built, hardwoods cut, and railroad lines laid. With the richest soil in the state, the area became famous for its cotton production and the wealth it produced. Black labor sustained the system and fostered its seminal music, Delta blues. Today, rice and soybean fields and commercial catfish ponds vary the landscape.

The strong physicality of the laborers who built the Delta is captured in Leon Koury's bronze *Compress Worker*. Koury (1909-1993) was a Greenville native. His talent as a sculptor came to the attention of William Alexander Percy, who acted as a mentor in his early career and introduced him to nationally known sculptor Malvina Hoffman. Koury moved to New York to pursue training with Hoffman and remained in the East until his father's health pulled him home in 1961. He set up a studio in Greenville and became a colorful and influential figure in the art world there. Koury was primarily interested in the human figure and head, and he worked both in bronze and plaster. The

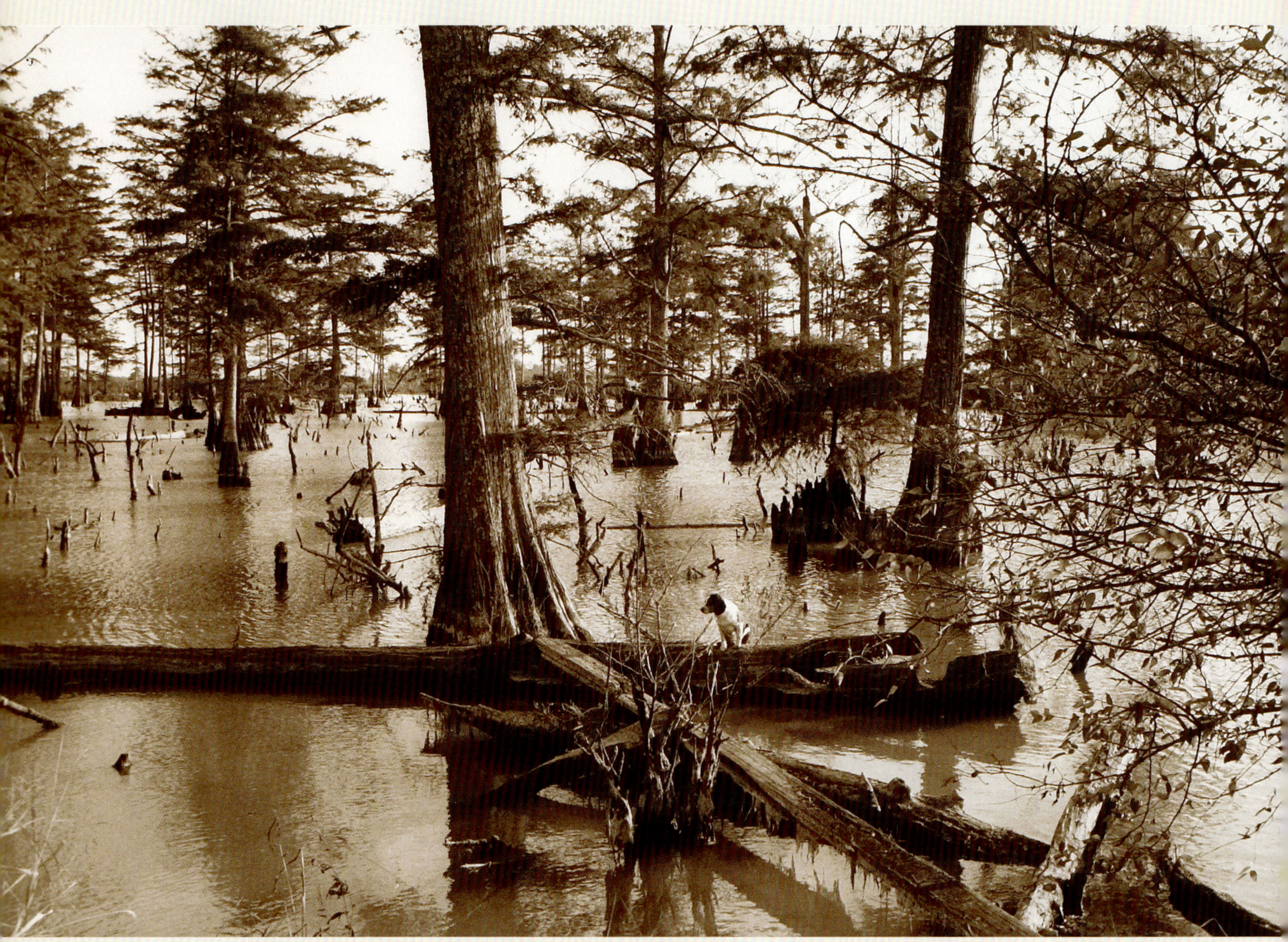

Greenville Arts Council selected him as the 1992 recipient for the Greenville Honors Its Own Award.

The Mississippi Museum of Art's earliest landscape of the Delta is *Day on the Yazoo*, painted by Joseph Rusling Meeker (1827-1889). A graduate of the National Academy of Design in New York, Meeker became enchanted with the bayous and swamps of the lower Mississippi River during his service on a Union gunboat. After the Civil War he settled in St. Louis, Missouri, and made painting excursions down the Mississippi River for many years, going all the way to New Orleans. Estill Curtis Pennington called Meeker "the foremost articulator of the romantic Louisiana landscape in the nineteenth century." He also worked in Mississippi, the Missouri River Valley, West Virginia, Minnesota, and the mountains of New Hampshire. His luminous painting of the Yazoo River, completed in 1885, shows Meeker's admiration for British painter J. M. W. Turner (circa 1775-1851), a master of light and tonality.

Maude Schuyler Clay's contemporary photograph of a Delta bayou is no less poetic. The fragile foliage of the cypress trees, the sturdy scalloped trunks reaching for the earth beneath the shimmering water, cypress knees, and fallen trees create a complexity of light and shadows at once beautiful and forbidding. Titled *Dog on a Log, Sandy Bayou, near Glendora, Tallahatchie County*, the photograph exhibited in *The Mississippi Story* is stunning with the dog's presence suggesting the quasi-taming of the Delta's roving streams and swamps. Born in 1953, Clay is a sixth-generation Delta native. She was raised in Sumner and studied at the University of Mississippi and the Memphis Academy of Art. Clay worked as assistant to her cousin, photographer William Eggleston, and later as a professional photographer in Manhattan. She worked in New York for twelve years before returning to Sumner in 1987 to raise a family with her photographer husband, Langdon, who was born in 1949 at New York City. Langdon Clay is a professional photographer who works worldwide and has made Sumner his home since 1987.

< Maude Schuyler Clay (born 1953), *Dog on a Log, Sandy Bayou, near Glendora, Tallahatchie County*, 1993. gelatin silver print, 16 x 20.

Originally working in color, Maude Clay turned to black-and-white photography as she moved deeper into the Delta landscape. The book *Delta Land*, published by the University Press of Mississippi in 1999, features many of her images. She received the Mississippi Institute of Arts and Letters photography award in 1988, 1992, and 2000, and she currently is working on a new series of low-light color portraits of family and friends. Her photographs are in the collection of the National Museum of Women in the Arts.

Cotton fields are historically the most associative image of the Mississippi Delta. Included in the exhibition is a circa 1907 panoramic photograph of a cotton field by John Calvin Coovert of Greenville, a 1980 photograph of a wagon load of cotton by Franke Keating of Greenville, and a contemporary close-up of Delta cotton bolls by photographer Bill Aron of Los Angeles. Other artworks also allude to cotton: Jane Rule Burdine's *Purnell and His Sister* stand in a cutover field of cotton at the end of the growing season; Rolland

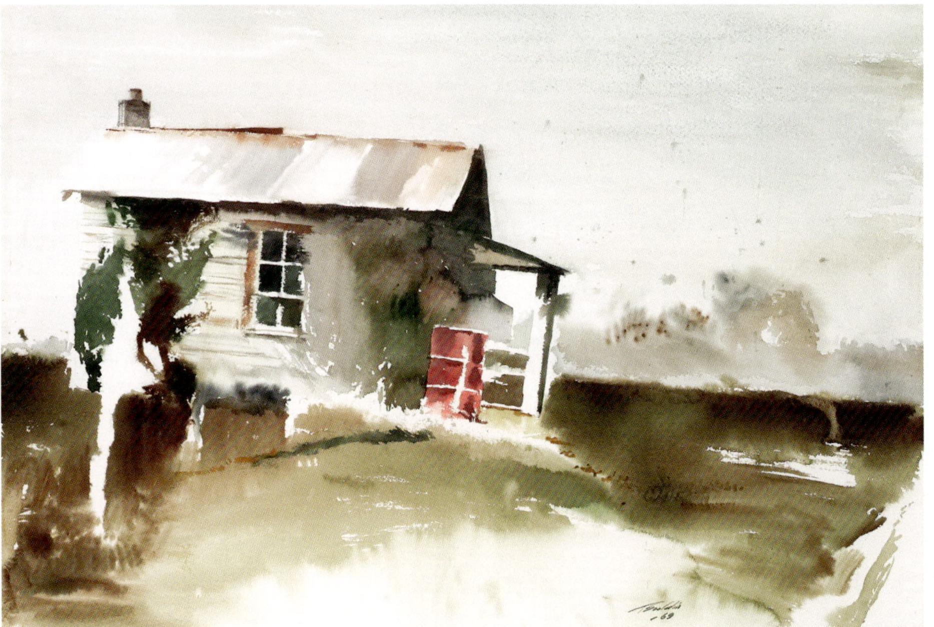

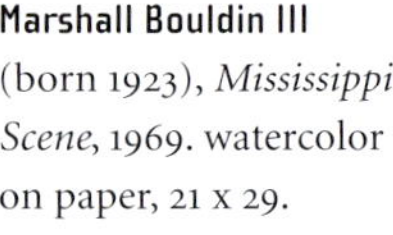

Marshall Bouldin III (born 1923), *Mississippi Scene*, 1969. watercolor on paper, 21 x 29.

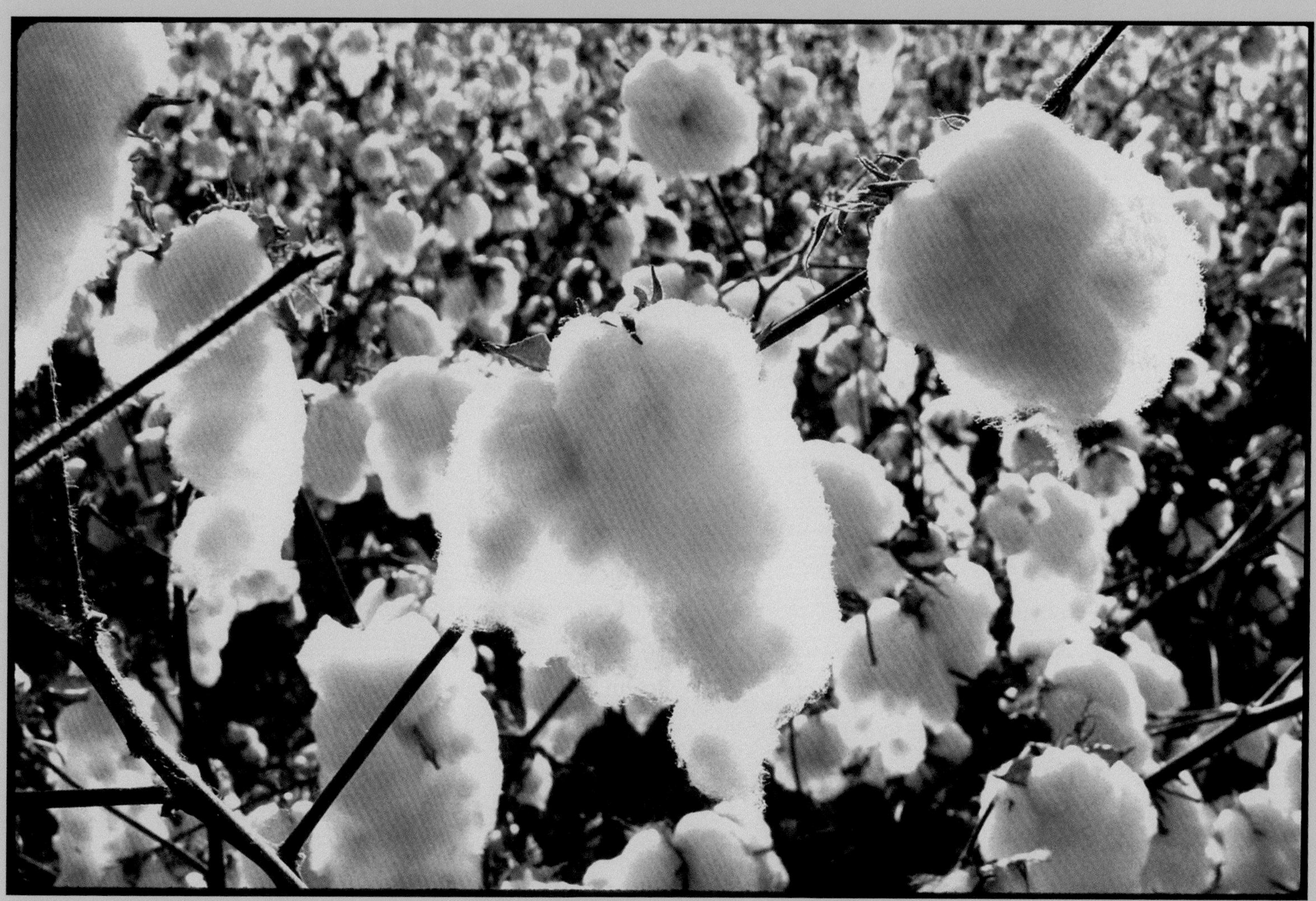

Bill Aron
(born 1941), *Cotton Field, Mississippi Delta,* 1991. giclée, 14½ x 20.

Christenberry is concerned with showing the slow decay of such structures using photography and detailed architectural models, Millsaps's soft gouache communicates serenity and life lived in *House with Yellow Flowers.* Millsaps was born in 1936, a native of Shaw and a graduate of Newcomb College with a master of arts degree from the University of Mississippi. She has been on the art faculties of Delta State University, Mississippi University for Women, and Millsaps College.

The closing image for the Delta section is *Time to Go Home,* a contemplative photograph of a horseman at sunset on the Mississippi River levee in Greenville. Photographer Franke West Keating was born in 1916 in Arkansas and has lived in Greenville all of her adult life. She and husband, Bern Keating, were nationally known photographers, on assignment around the world for America's leading magazines including *National Geographic, Life,* and *Smithsonian.* Along with many other books, the two collaborated on *Mississippi* (University Press of Mississippi, 1981), a rich photographic evocation of place. Bern and Franke Keating received Lifetime Achievement awards from the Mississippi Institute of Arts and Letters in 1995. Bern Keating died in 2004.

William Eggleston (born 1939) was raised in Sumner at the home of his grandfather, Judge J. A. May. He attended high school at Webb School in Tennessee, a military-style boarding academy, and moved to Memphis in the early 1960s. In Eggleston's words, he "matriculated at, and on occasion attended, Vanderbilt University, Delta State College, and the University of Mississippi." He began taking photographs at the age of ten in Sumner. He lists his first major influence as Henri Cartier-Bresson, but it was in color photography that he made his reputation

Eggleston began to experiment with color transparency film in 1965. In 1976 the Museum of Modern Art, New York, offered him a one-man show, the second exhibition of color photography in the museum's history. A monograph titled *William Eggleston's Guide* accompanied the exhibition. This exposure led

William Eggleston
(born 1939), no title, circa 1978. chromogenic color print, 14¾ x 9¾ (sight). © 2007 Eggleston Artistic Trust, courtesy Cheim and Read, New York. Used with permission.

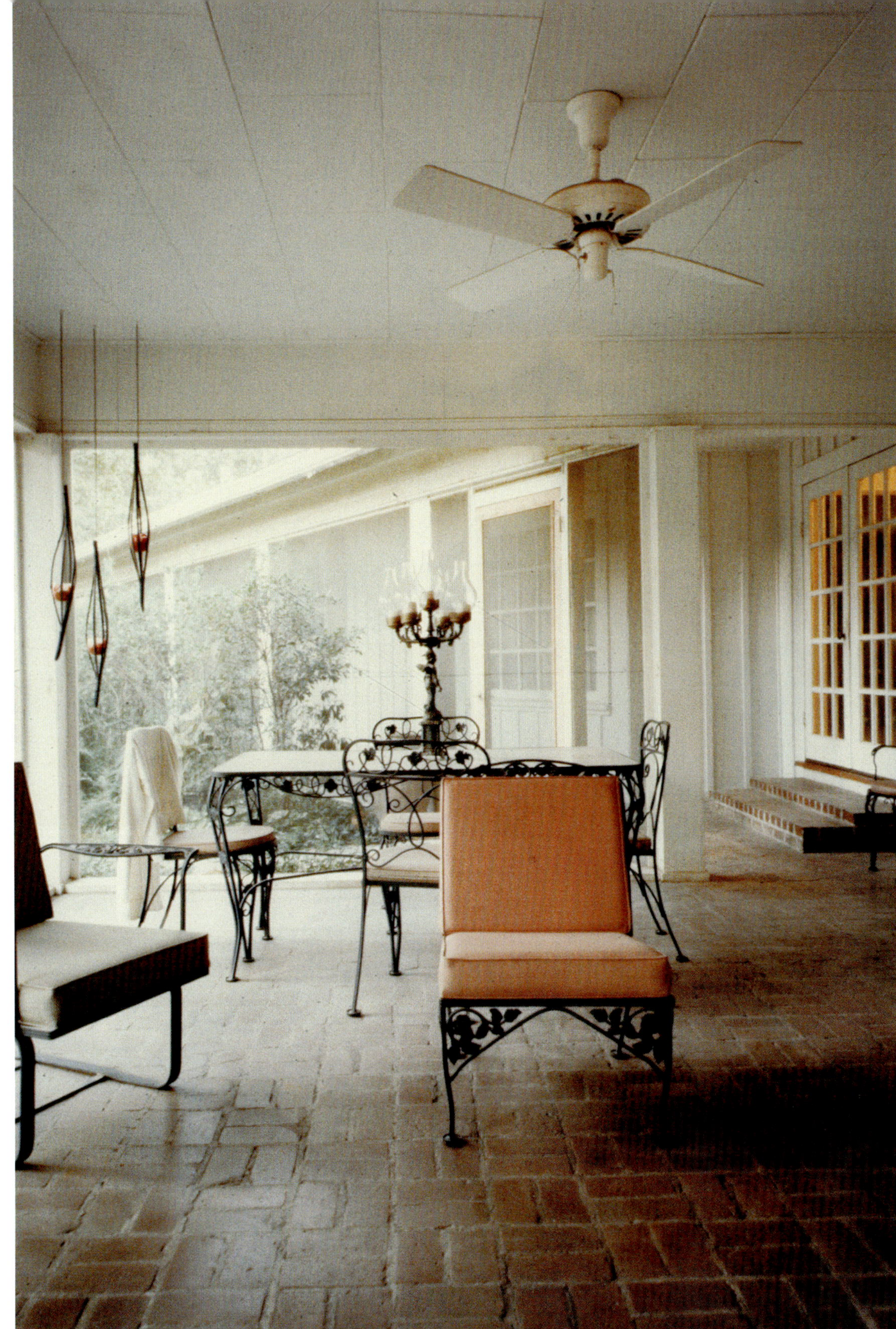

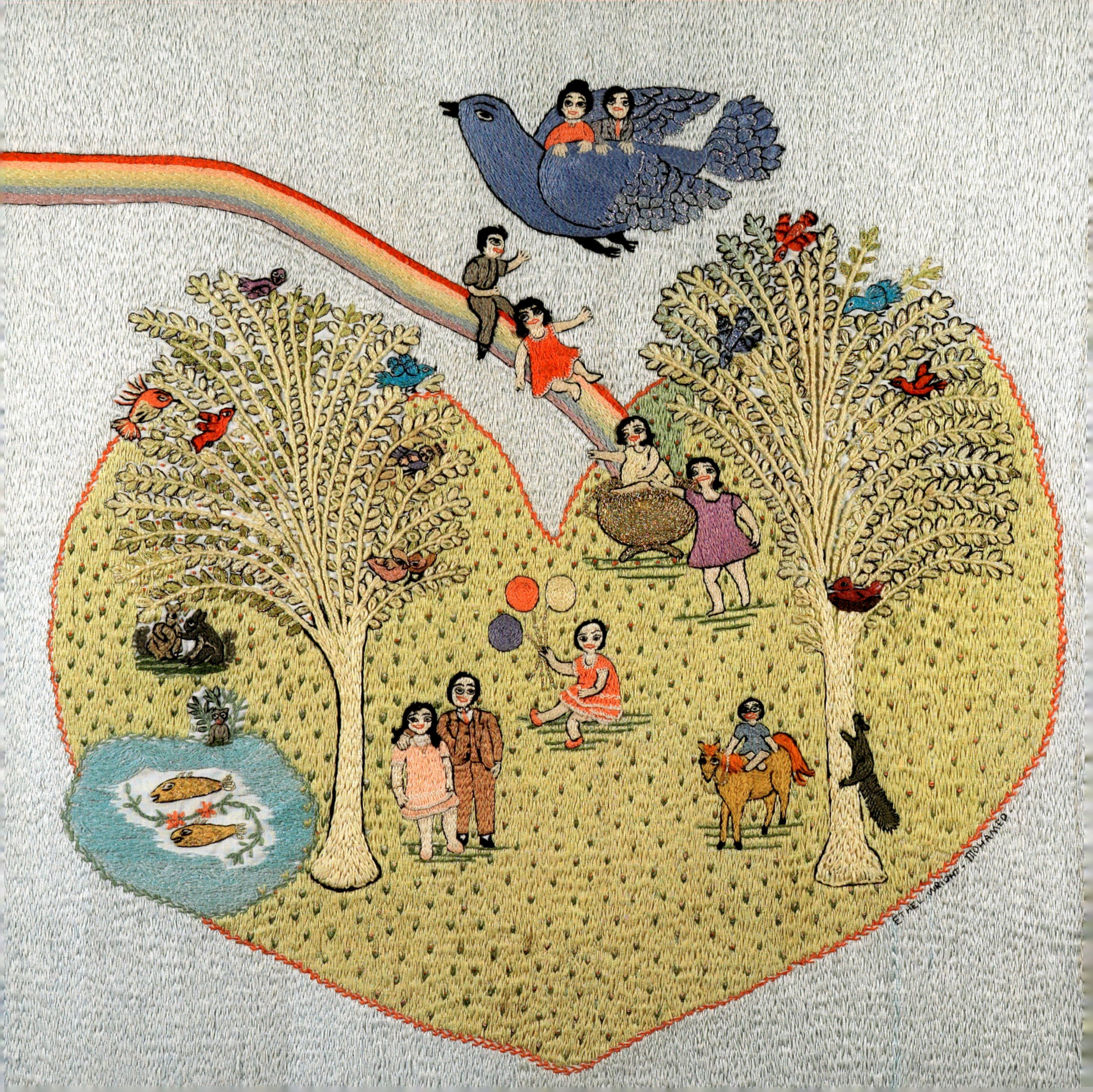
ETHEL WRIGHT MOHAMED

< Ethel Wright Mohamed (1906-1992), *The Blue Bird of Happiness*, circa 1979. silk and cotton, 25 x 25 (sight).

to Eggleston being called "the father of color photography." Since 1976, when he was commissioned by *Rolling Stone* magazine to photograph Plains, Georgia, Eggleston has photographed projects in many states, including California, Louisiana, Hawaii, Tennessee, and Mississippi. Throughout his career he has traveled extensively abroad, photographing projects in Kenya, Germany, Egypt, Great Britain, Russia, China, Japan, Italy, and Jamaica. From the beginning his work has been both controversial and honored. He has received many awards, including a Guggenheim Fellowship, National Endowment for the Arts fellowships, an award from the Photographic Society of Japan, the Spanish PhotoEspaña Award, the Gold Medal for Photography from the National Arts Club in New York, and the Getty Lifetime Achievement Award. Eggleston is also a musical composer and performer. One little-known credit is his role as Jerry Lee Lewis's father in the 1989 movie *Great Balls of Fire!*

Ethel Wright Mohamed (1906-1992) was born in Webster County and spent her adult life in Belzoni with her Lebanese husband, Hassam Mohamed. After her husband died in 1965, she began creating embroidered scenes from her childhood and years of marriage and motherhood. Her more than one hundred and twenty-five "memory pictures" constitute the most complete life story created in Mississippi art. Her work was first recognized publicly at the 1974 Festival of American Folklife, presented by the Smithsonian Institution in Washington. During her lifetime Mohamed's needlework was featured in numerous exhibitions at the Old Capitol Museum, the Renwick Gallery in Washington, D.C., the 1982 World's Fair in Knoxville, and the 1984 World's Fair in New Orleans. After her death her family opened Mama's Dream World, an exhibition space in Belzoni intended to present Mohamed's works in crewel embroidery.

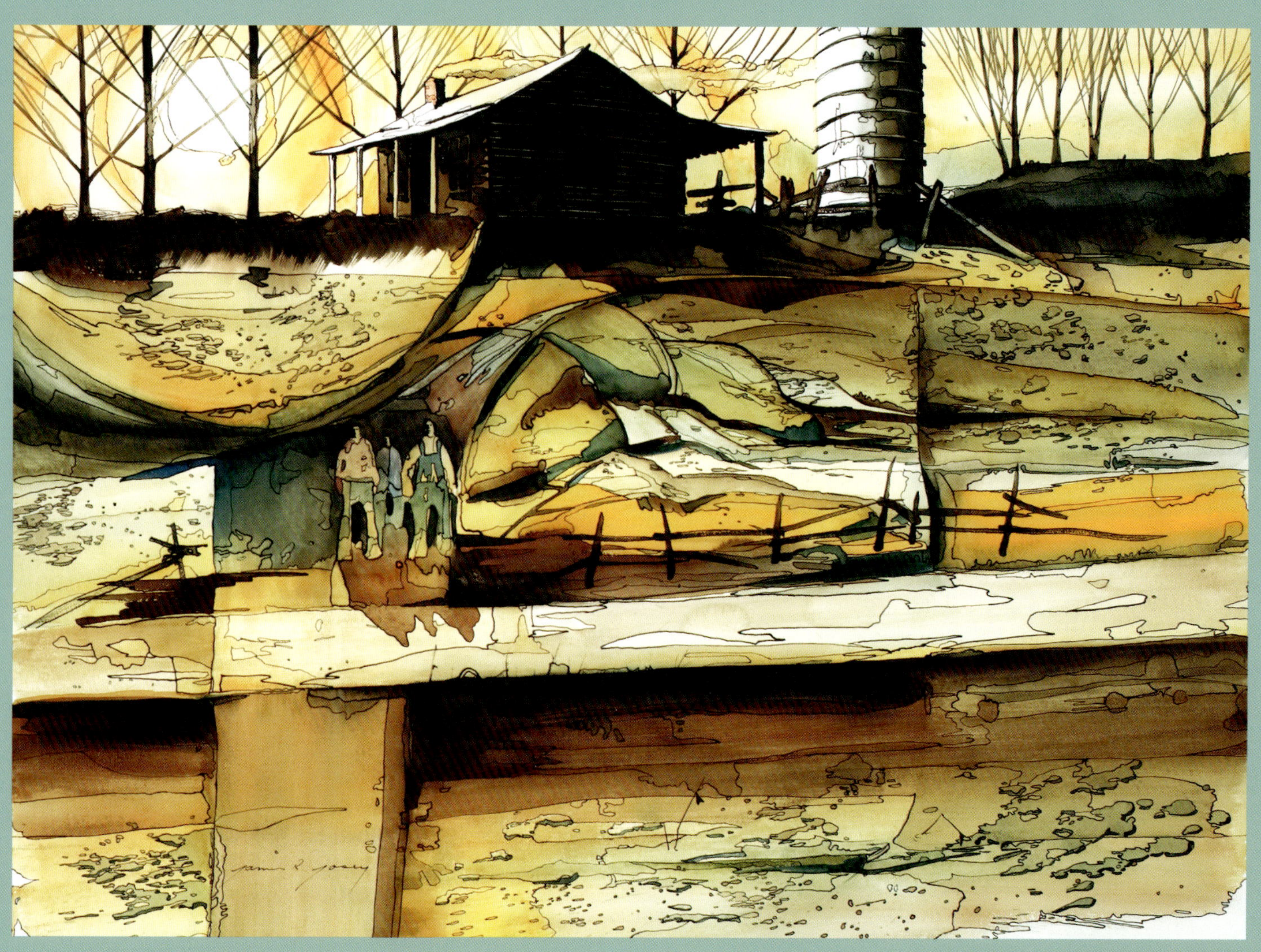

James Josey
(born 1945), *Off to the Factory*, 1975. watercolor on illustration board, 22¼ x 30.

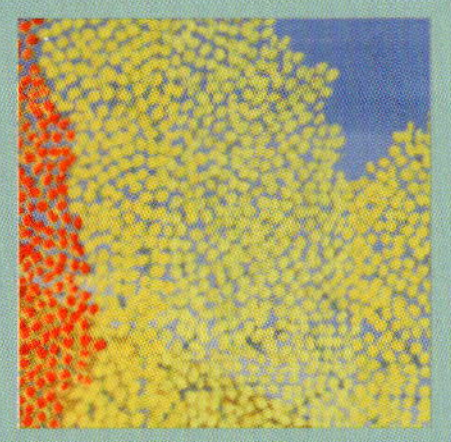

The Hill Country

In the northeast the red clay hills and Appalachian foothills attracted farmers looking for small acreages they could call their own and work themselves. The more ambitious farmers sought out the rich lands of the Tombigbee prairies, which supported cotton. Cotton quickly wore out the soil and small farmers had to switch to other crops or industry to maintain themselves. Some of Mississippi's most vital cities dot the area: Tupelo, Oxford, Grenada, Starkville, and Columbus. A number of Mississippi's most impassioned artists have come from the area.

Eugenia Summer, born in 1923 in Newton, is a quiet example of the tremendous influence that art academics have had on art appreciation and understanding in the state. Summer received her bachelor of arts degree from Mississippi University for Women (MUW), her master of arts degree from Columbia University, and joined the faculty of MUW in 1949. She subsequently studied in the summers at the Art Institute of Chicago, California College of Arts and Crafts, Seattle University, and Penland School of Crafts in North Carolina. She was one of the earliest and most successful artists in academe working in the modern idiom. The Precisionists influenced Summer in their painted themes derived from factories, oil fields, and industrial and mechanistic shapes. Her paintings were among the first pieces of nonobjective art

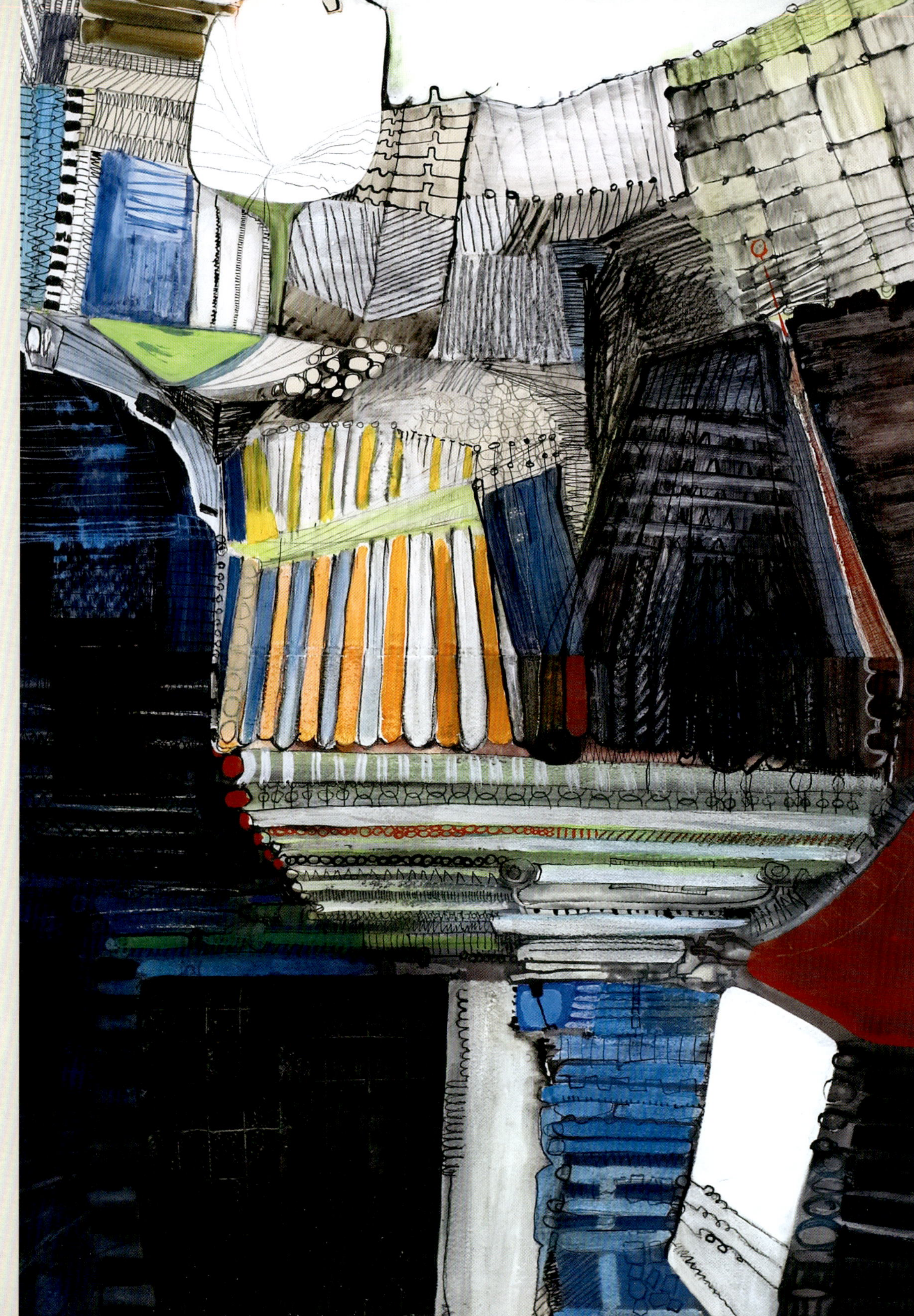

Eugenia Summer (born 1923), *Barricade*, no date. tempera and ink on paper, 35¼ x 23½ (sight).

acquired by the Mississippi Art Association (MAA), which provided the core of the Mississippi Museum of Art's current collection. *Barricade* (on exhibit) was acquired in 1968, the third of her paintings in the collection. It explores color juxtapositions and spatial relationships, using vaguely familiar industrial allusions. Summer was named dean of the Division of Fine and Performing Arts in 1982 and retired from MUW in 1987. The Fine Arts Gallery there was named for her in 2002. A major influence to the thousands of young women who attended her classes, Summer was honored with the Alumnae Achievement Award and the Honored Artist Award by the Mississippi State Chapter of the National Museum of Women in the Arts.

Born in 1944 in Webster County, William Dunlap is a landscape artist of national renown. He has worked in paint, monoprints, and multimedia installations that elaborate on the idea of the American landscape. The Corcoran Gallery of Art commissioned his *Panorama of the American Landscape* in the winter of 1984-1985, and it has been widely exhibited and acclaimed. Dunlap painted it as a contemporary response to the historical cycloramas of the nineteenth century. His work speaks passionately of place and the power of symbolism. Languid landscapes incorporate myriad subtle messages to the viewer: a serene countryside marred by human folly, chaos among placidity, the juxtaposition of the benign and the destructive. Memory and history strongly inform his contemporary vision. His work, layered with literary allusions, homage to other artists, historical events, private history and, above all, what he calls "charged places," has been called "narrative landscape." One of the most popular of Dunlap's iconic images is the dog in *Flat Out Dog Trot*, which was commissioned for the 1998 Jubilee!JAM poster. It has the characteristic ominous clouds over a bucolic landscape, all seen—as Dunlap perceives our modern propensity—from the windshield of a car going sixty miles an hour on the interstate.

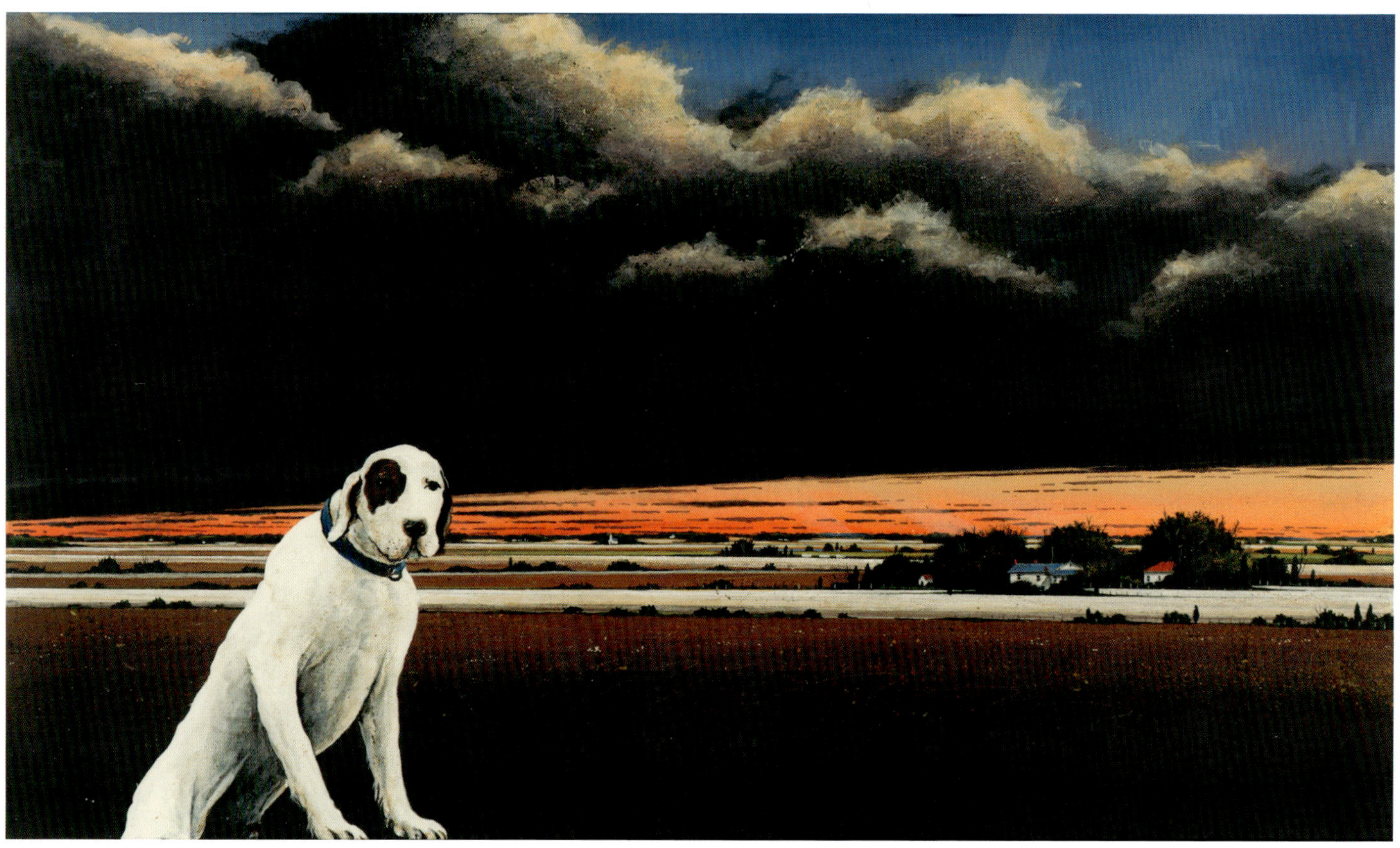

William Dunlap (born 1944), *Flat Out Dog Trot*, 1998. mixed mediums on canvas, 36 x 60.

Dunlap's work has brought him awards and fellowships from the Rockefeller Foundation, Wallace Foundation, Andy Warhol Foundation for the Visual Arts, Danforth Foundation, Virginia Commission for the Arts, and Mississippi Institute of Arts and Letters for visual arts. In recent years he has added to his schedule an active lecturing career and curating major international exhibitions through the Meridian International Center in Washington, D.C. He works tirelessly as an arts advocate and received an Emmy for his work as a television art commentator. His work is in major collections: Metropolitan Museum of Art, Corcoran, Ogden Museum of Southern Art, numerous corporations, and the U.S. State Department, which has placed his work in American embassies around the world. The University Press of Mississippi recently published a survey of his paintings titled *Dunlap.* The artist maintains studios in Mississippi, Virginia, and Florida.

James Josey was born in Florida and raised in West Point, Mississippi. He graduated from Mississippi State University with three degrees but decided to pursue art, working in Jackson during the 1970s. A successful watercolorist, he now lives in Corpus Christi, Texas. His painting *Off to the Factory* observes the cultural transformation in Mississippi that began after World War II. Small farmers still living on their homesteads turned to industry for their livelihood. Eventually, the farms were sold and workers moved to the towns and cities in the area. North Mississippi was one of the first places in Mississippi to experience the shift from agriculture to industrialization.

The first folk artist in Mississippi to garner national attention was Theora Hamblett of Oxford. Her memory and visionary paintings gained the attention of New York gallery owner Betty Parsons. She in turn introduced Hamblett's work to the museum world, and the Museum of Modern Art in New York acquired the artist's canvas *The Vision* in 1954. This news electrified art collectors in Mississippi and her work became some of the most marketable art there. Before Hamblett's death in 1977, she held numerous solo exhibitions in the state and at Memphis Brooks Museum of Art. *The Vision* was chosen for the World's Fair in Brussels, and in 1975 the University Press of Mississippi published *Theora Hamblett's Paintings.* The Mississippi Art Association acquired *Walking, Meditating in the Woods* in 1966. It shows her characteristic use of vivid, primary color, an almost pointillistic brush stroke, and mystical allusions, indicated by the white-clad figure.

This section ends with one of Eudora Welty's most famous images, *Home by dark, Yalobusha County*, photographed before 1935. During the Depression years Eudora Welty worked for the Works Progress Administration and trav-

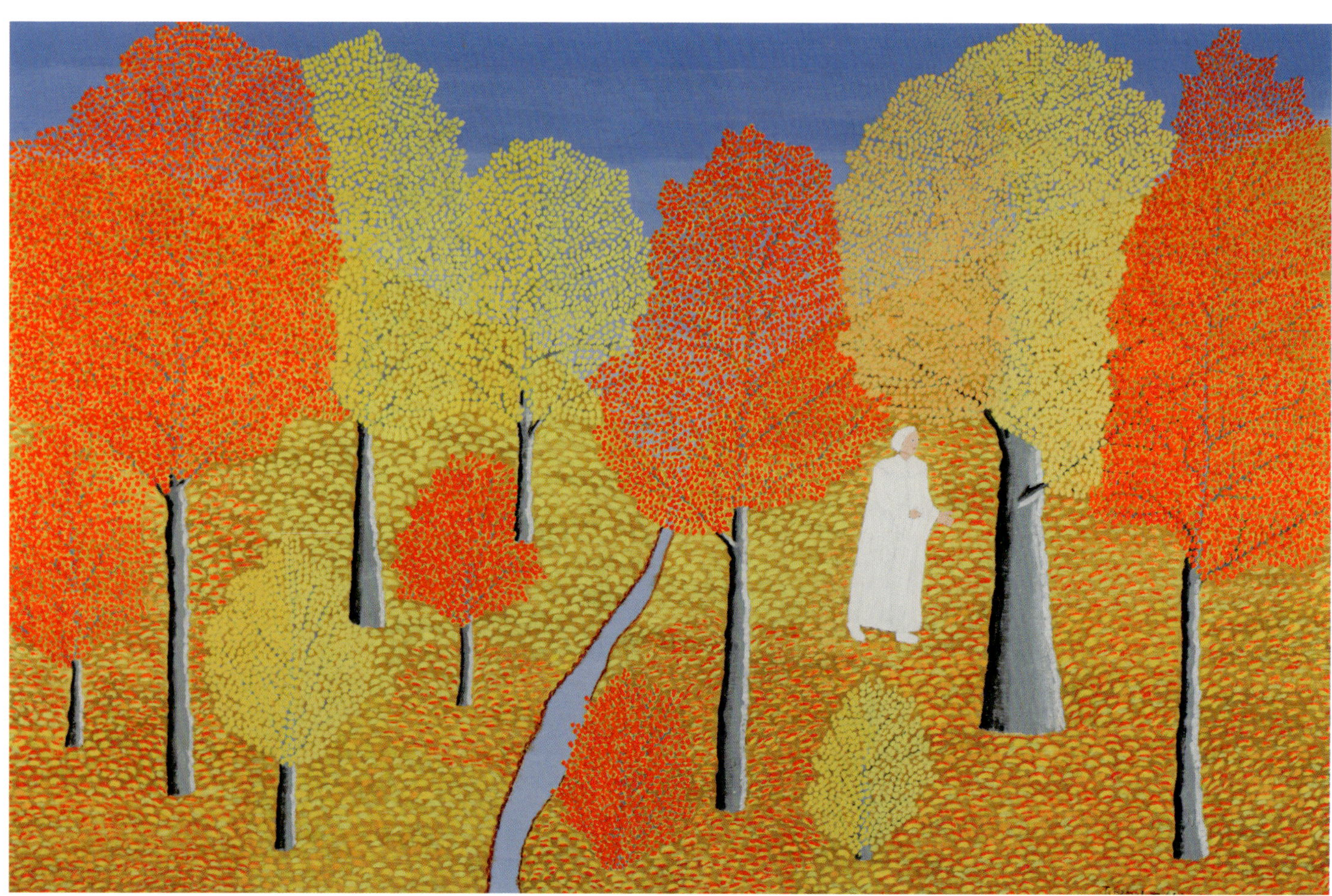

Theora Hamblett (1893-1977), *Walking, Meditating in the Woods*, 1963. oil on canvas, 31 x 43.

eled the state. She took photographs on her own initiative. In this work a black family, dressed it seems for Sunday activities, is in a wagon on a dusty Mississippi back road, perhaps heading home from church. Welty said, "a good snapshot stops a moment from running away"; but her photographs do more than that. Welty was an intense observer and worked "to catch something as I came upon it, something that spoke of the life going on around me." She was the most prolific and sensitive recorder of Mississippi in the 1930s.

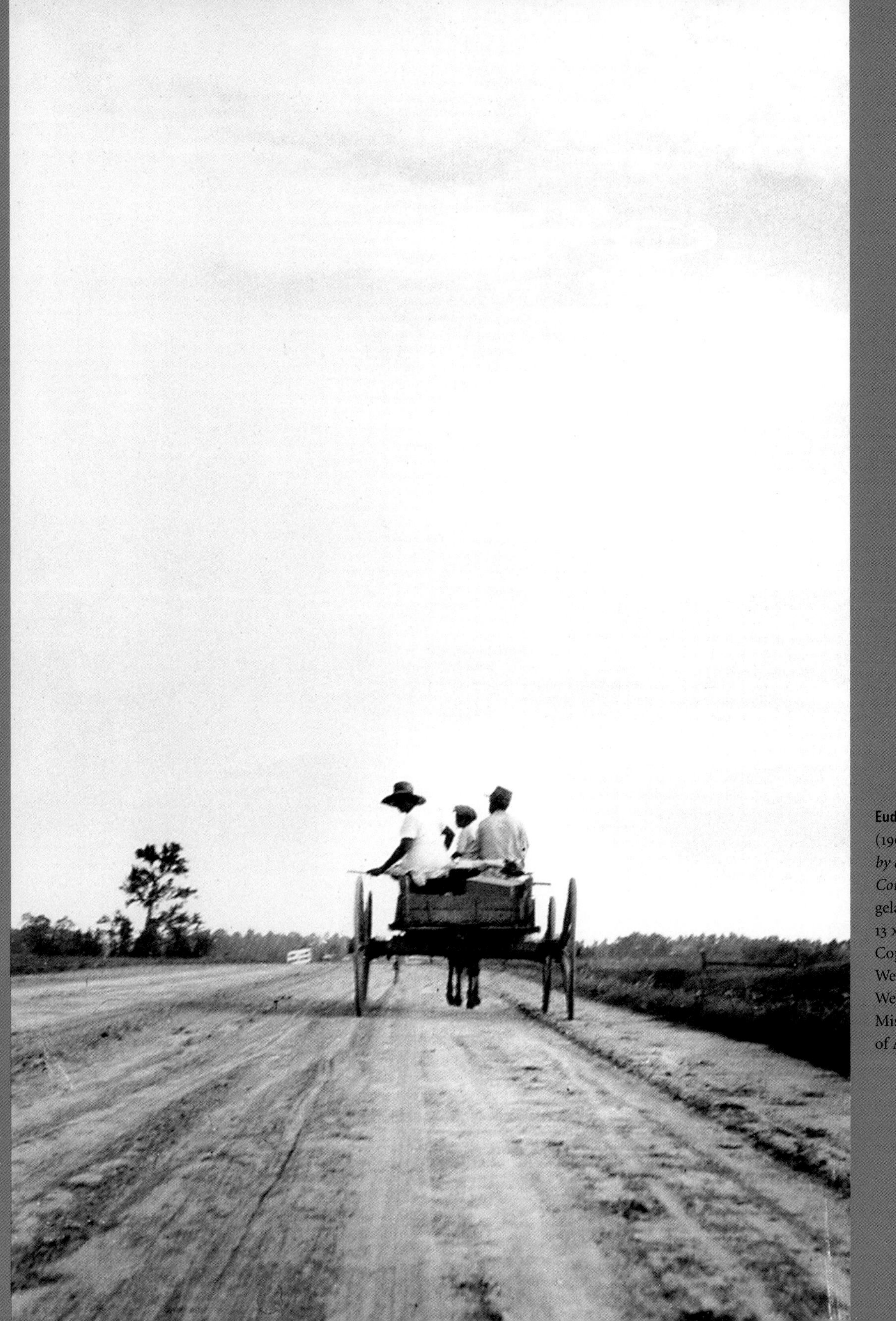

Eudora Welty
(1909-2001), *Home by dark, Yalobusha County*, prior to 1935. gelatin silver print, 13 x 8¼ (sight).

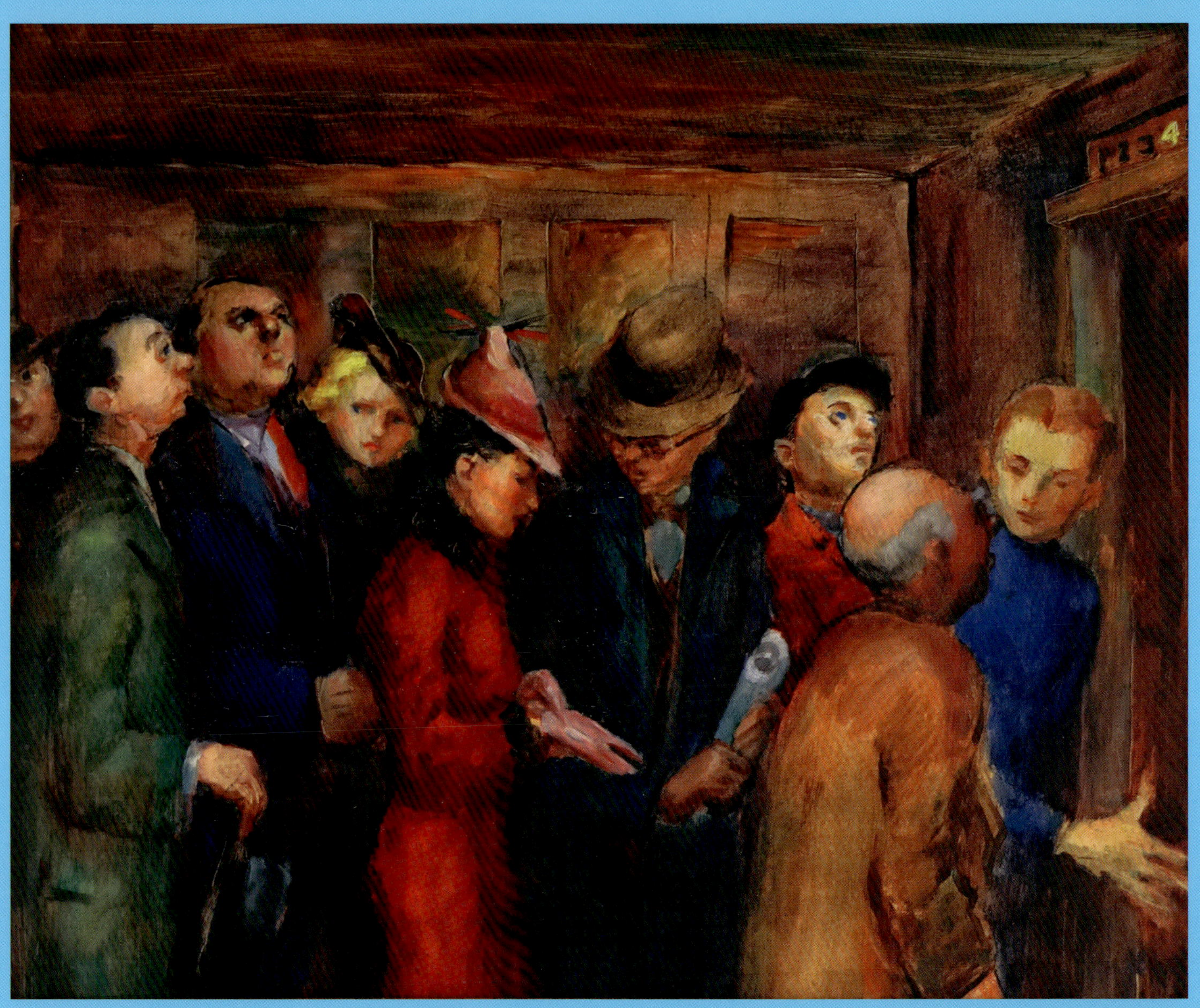

William Hollingsworth (1910-1944), *Elevator, Tower Building*, no date. oil on board, 24 x 28.

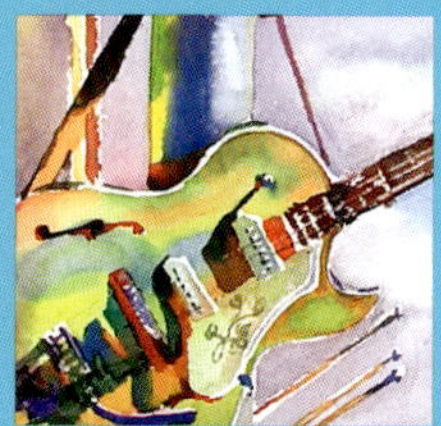

Jackson and the Central Prairie

When Mississippi became a state, two-thirds of it was still Indian land. Anticipating removal of the Choctaws and Chickasaws, the legislature decided that the capital should be placed close to the geographic center of the state. The new site was named after Andrew Jackson and opened for state government in December 1822. At the outbreak of the Civil War in 1861, Jackson was Mississippi's fourth largest town, following Vicksburg, Natchez, and Columbus. By the first decade of the twentieth century, however, Jackson had become the financial, educational, and cultural center of Mississippi.

Jackson is home to the University of Mississippi Medical Center and the Mississippi College School of Law. It is also the hub of five liberal arts institutions: Jackson State University, Belhaven College, Millsaps College, Tougaloo College, and Mississippi College. The art departments of these schools have always attracted talented artists to their faculties. Among the most acclaimed was William Hollingsworth (1910-1944), a native Jacksonian who founded the art department at Millsaps College in 1941. Hollingsworth graduated from the Art Institute of Chicago and brought home to Jackson in 1934 fellow student Jane Oakley as his wife. He became Mississippi's preeminent landscape artist, painting the countryside in Hinds and Madison Counties, cityscapes in Jackson, and small-town scenes around the central area of Jackson. He was

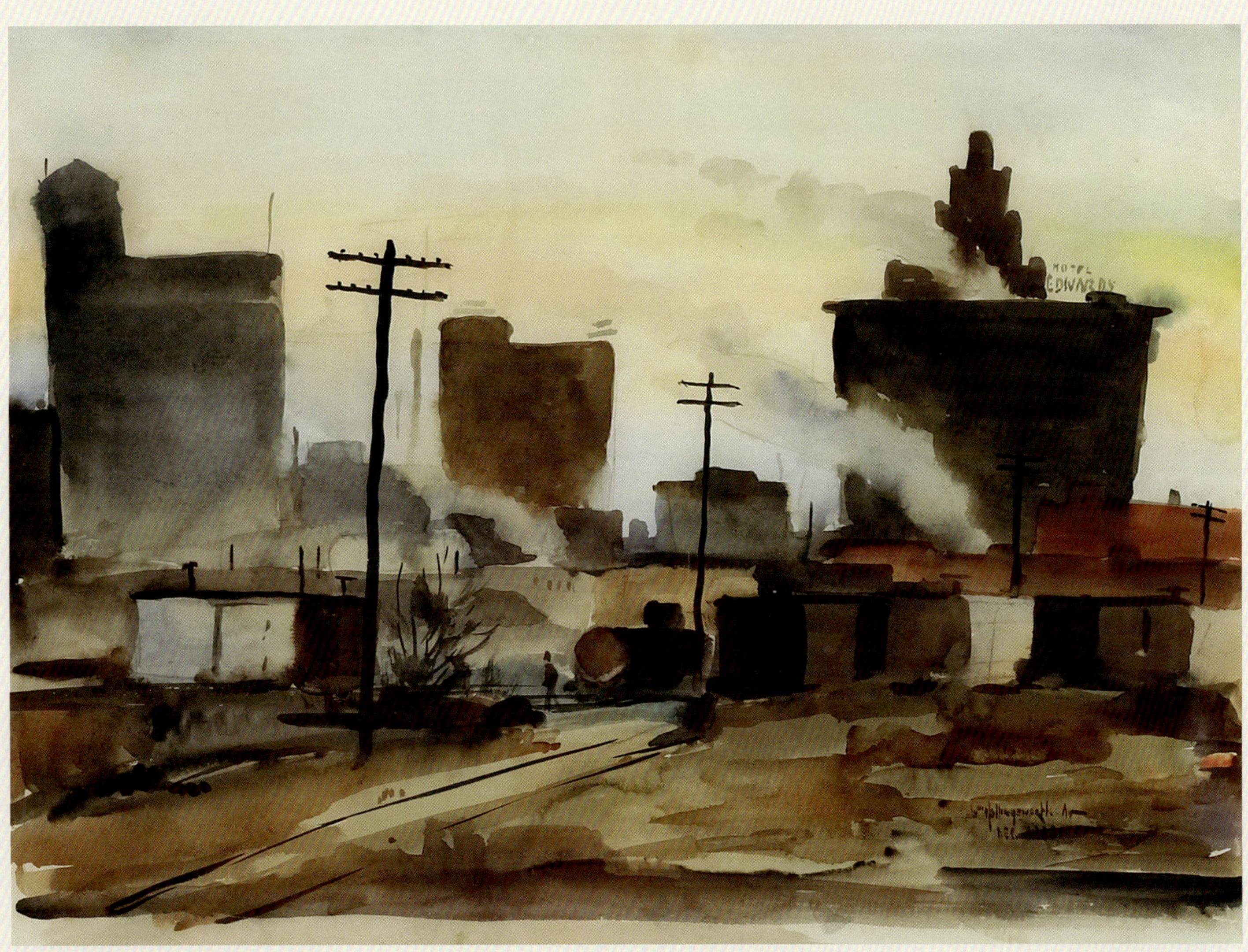

William Hollingsworth (1910-1944), *Before the Sun*, 1939. watercolor on paper, 17 x 22 (sight).

especially drawn to black culture and painted a large number of genre scenes in black communities. His body of work altogether presents a close look at the Depression's effect on central Mississippi. Eudora Welty, his friend and contemporary, wrote, "All might have been a phenomenon to his [Hollingsworth] eyes—all Mississippi. He loved the violet spaces hanging beyond the last ridge, the rich red gullies, the loneliness of telephone poles marching away, the hush of snow, the warm streaming lights of city rain. . ." The 1939 watercolor *Before the Sun* finds him in the early morning hours catching the activity on Jackson's railroad tracks. *Crossroad* is a portrait of Negro quarters "across the track" somewhere in Jackson. Equally adept in watercolor, oil, and pencil, his liquid, loose style gave a lyrical feeling to his paintings, and of all the painters in Mississippi, Hollingsworth was the most attentive to the details of ordinary life.

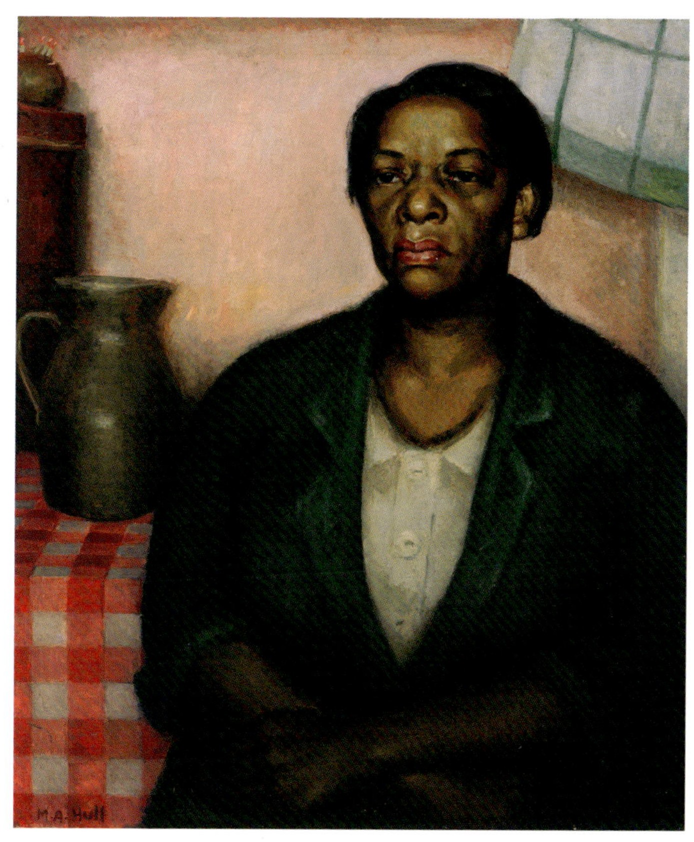

Marie Hull (1890-1980), *Melissa*, 1930. oil on canvas, 30 x 25.

Marie Atkinson Hull (1890-1980) was one of the most influential and respected artists in the state for seven decades. Born in Summit, she moved to Jackson to attend Belhaven College and graduated in 1908. Over the next several years she studied at the Pennsylvania Academy of the Fine Arts and at the Art Students League of New York. She married architect Emmett J. Hull in 1917 and became a lifelong citizen of Jackson. She was one of the original

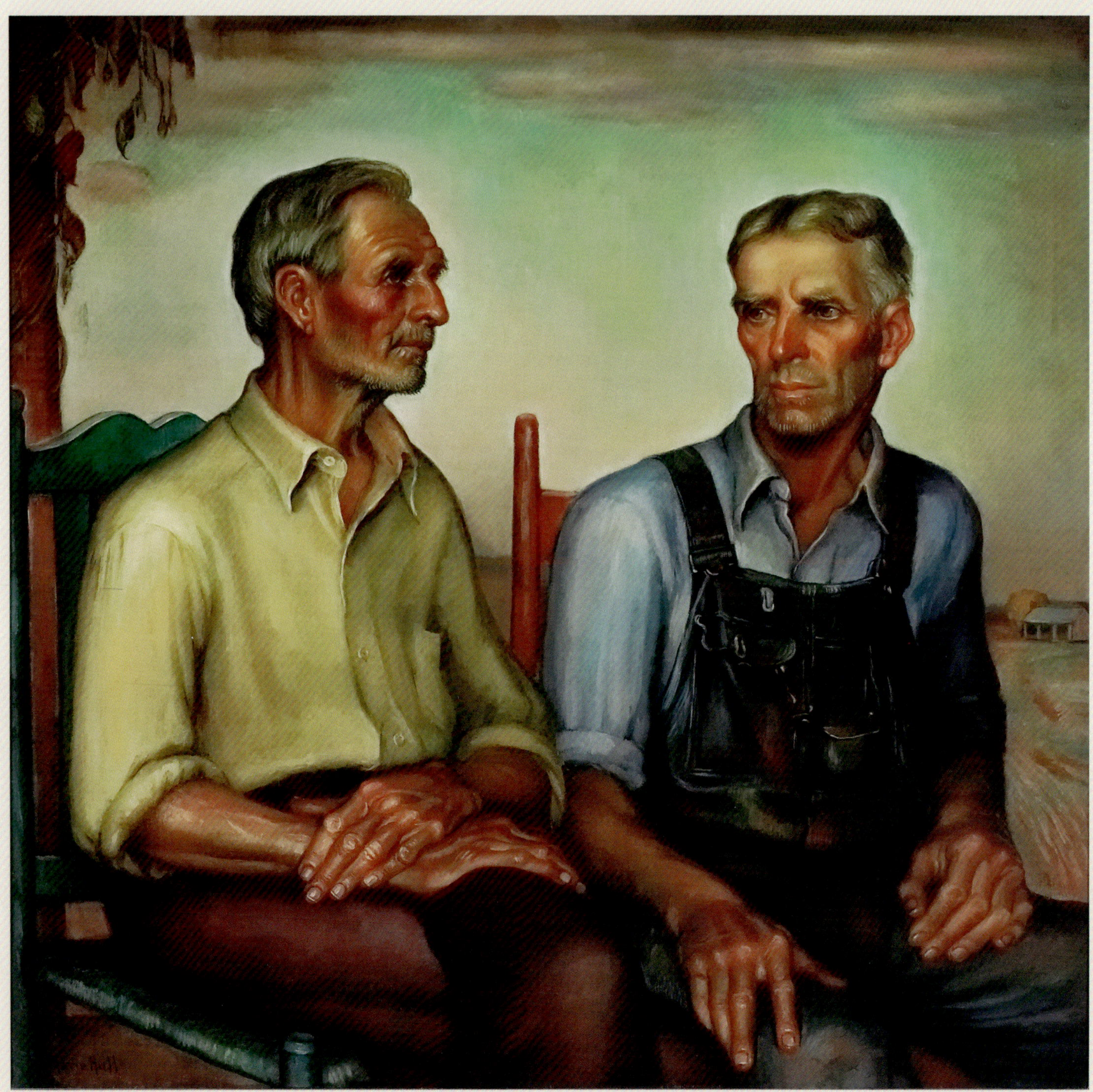

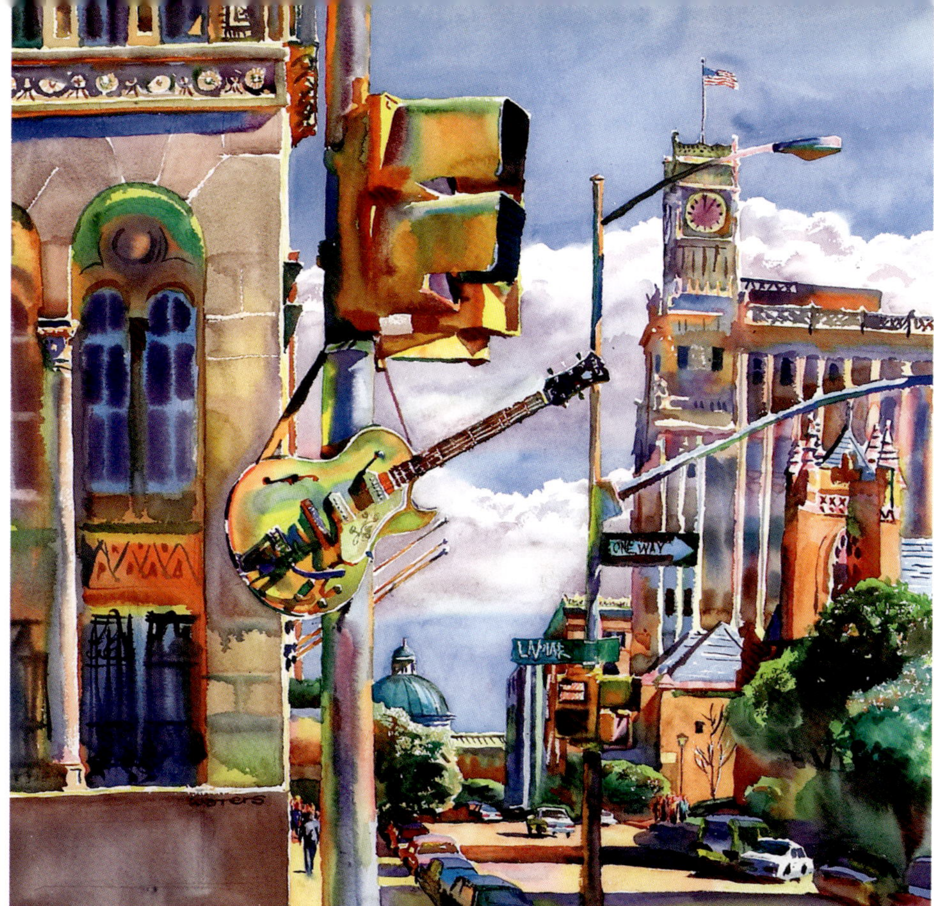

Wyatt Waters (born 1955), *High Notes*, 1999. watercolor on paper, 29 x 29 (sight).

members of the Mississippi Art Association (1911) and lived to see the opening of the Mississippi Museum of Art, for which she had worked and campaigned. Always open to new ways of presentation, her long career was filled with high energy and a fluent ability to master many different painting styles and genres, including landscape, still life, and portraiture. She was a passionate teacher, a tireless promoter of art in the state, and the mentor of several generations of artists. Hull's body of work ranges from realism to impressionism, expressionism to nonobjective and even hard edge. Her portrait of Melissa is an example of her virtuosity and eloquence in portraiture.

< **Marie Hull** (1890-1980), *Sharecroppers*, 1938. oil on canvas, 40 x 40¼.

Wyatt Waters came from a much later generation. He was born in Brookhaven in 1955 and grew up in Florence and Clinton. He received his bachelor and master of arts degrees from Mississippi College and moved to Jackson after his marriage. In 1989 he moved back to Clinton, where he built his studio, and has taught at Millsaps College and Mississippi College. Waters is Mississippi's most productive and constant chronicler of the built environment. He has set up his easel on location throughout the state and captured a wide variety of scenes in vivid watercolor. His subject matter includes churches, homesteads, rural scenes, and city streets. His palette, created in sunshine, is distinctive. Waters has referred to it as "magnified hues." Many vanished buildings have been preserved in his art because he "began working ahead of the wrecking ball." He has published these scenes in several books, including *Another Coat of Paint*, *Painting Home*, and *An Oxford Sketchbook*. On exhibit is *High Notes*, a painting of downtown Jackson commissioned for the 1999 Jubilee!JAM poster. The building seen in the painting is the Lamar Life Building on Capitol Street in downtown Jackson.

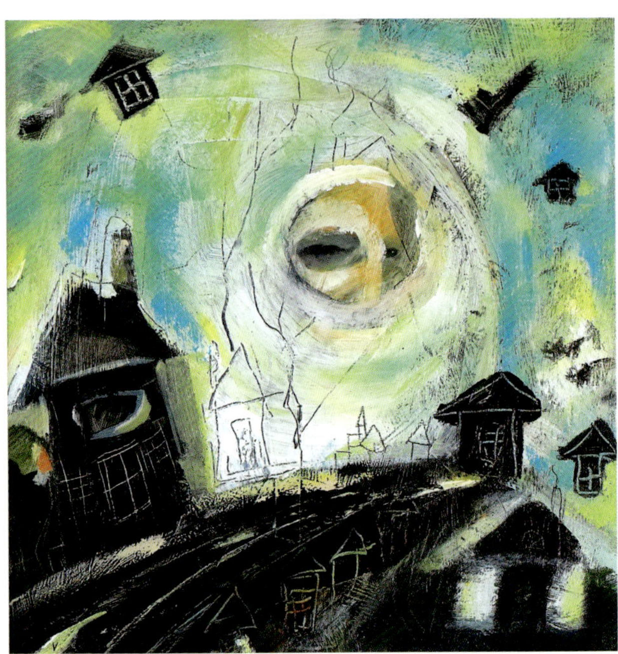

Vidal Blankenstein (born 1958), *Night Moon*, 2005. mixed mediums on board, 12 x 11½.

One of the newest acquisitions in the Museum's landscape collection is *Night Moon*, a mixed mediums painting by Vidal Blankenstein, who has described it as the memory of "the full moon over Poplar Boulevard." Born in 1958, Blankenstein is a native of Natchez. She is a graduate of Louisiana Tech University in Ruston and now an advertising executive and well-known artist in Jackson. Using a variety of techniques—painting, collage, sgraffito, and drawing—she has produced a fantastical somnambulistic night landscape of the well-known Belhaven neighborhood.

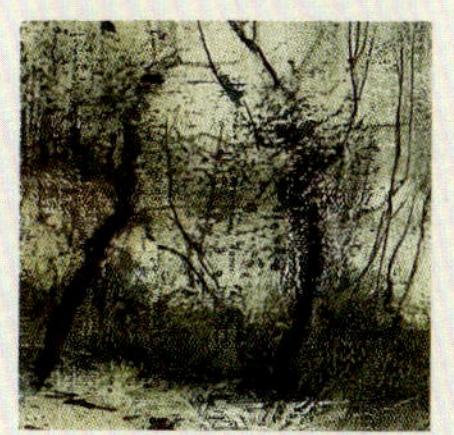

The Piney Woods

The dense growth of pine trees in the southeastern corner of the state attracted the naval stores industry as early as the eighteenth century. Pine resin and tall trunks for masts furnished the early sailing ships from France, Spain, and England, which in turn claimed the land that became Mississippi. Herdsmen first thinly settled the Piney Woods, as they preferred forests for hunting and the open range for their livestock. The area's prosperity came late in the nineteenth century, when lumbermen from northern states came down to cut and mill the abundant timber resources. The railroads made distribution possible. After the lumber boom, the area began its diversification, building the major cities of Laurel, Hattiesburg, Picayune, Brookhaven, and McComb. The Lauren Rogers Museum of Art in Laurel was born with a gift from a family of timber entrepreneurs; Hattiesburg, a well-situated railroad town, is the home of the University of Southern Mississippi and William Carey College.

In the 1960s a trio of artists living in or around McComb dominated the state's art scene, in large measure for their willingness to experiment with contemporary art styles. Ruth Miller Atkinson Holmes (1909-1981) was born in Hazlehurst; Bess Phipps Dawson (1916-1994) was a native of Tchula; Halcyone Barnes (1913-1988) hailed from Dallas, Texas. The three got together when they studied art at Southwest Mississippi Junior College in Summit

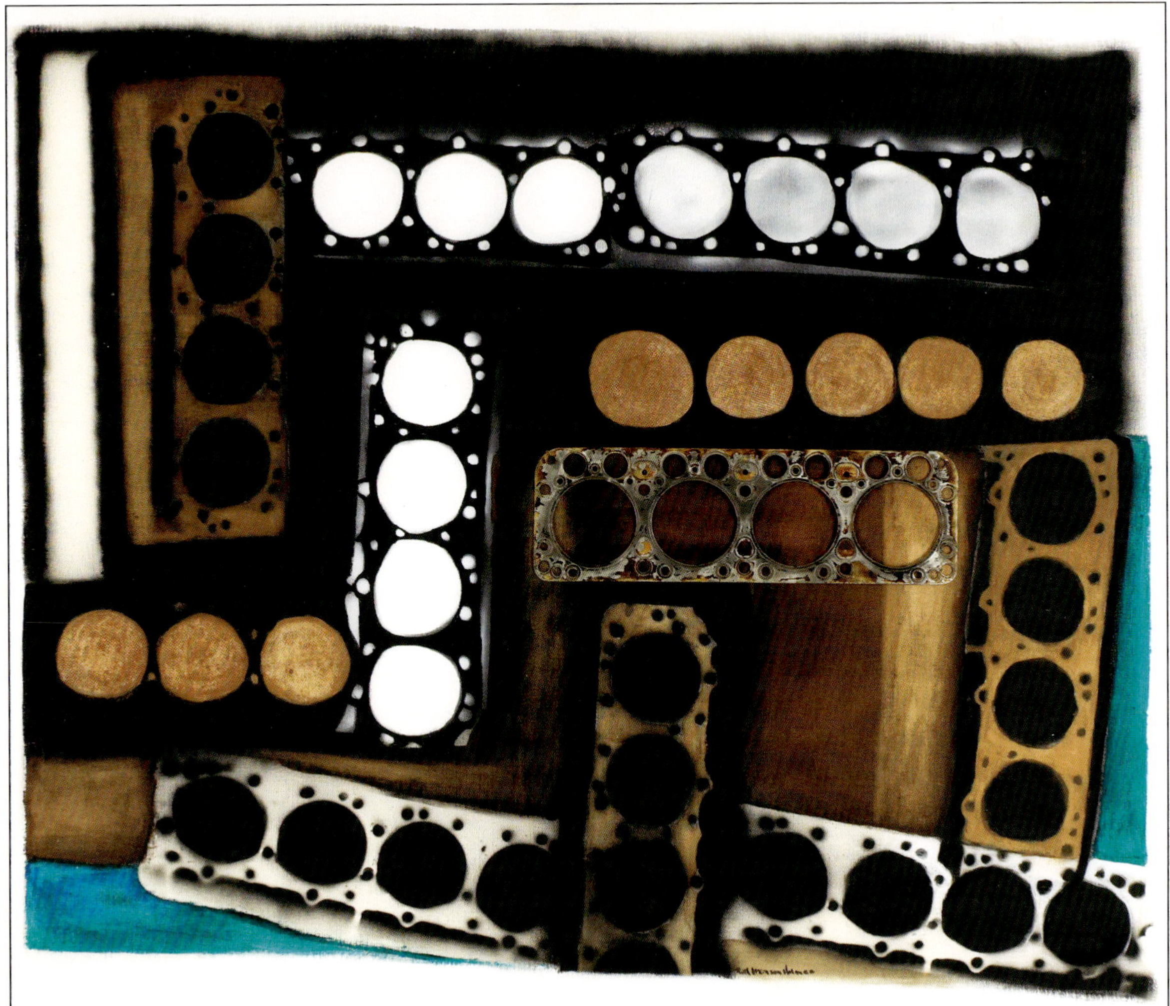

Ruth Atkinson Holmes (1909–1981), *For the Space Age*, 1965. oil on canvas with found objects, 48 x 54.

under Roy Shultz of Kentwood, Louisiana. Shultz introduced them to abstract expressionism and encouraged them to experiment. "It wasn't long before we had abandoned magnolias and shacks," Bess Dawson explained. They did not, however, abandon place. Their work symbolizes the change in the southern area of Mississippi during that era. *For the Space Age*, painted in 1965, represents Ruth Atkinson Holmes. Construction had been underway for the NASA testing facility (now called the John C. Stennis Space Center), which opened

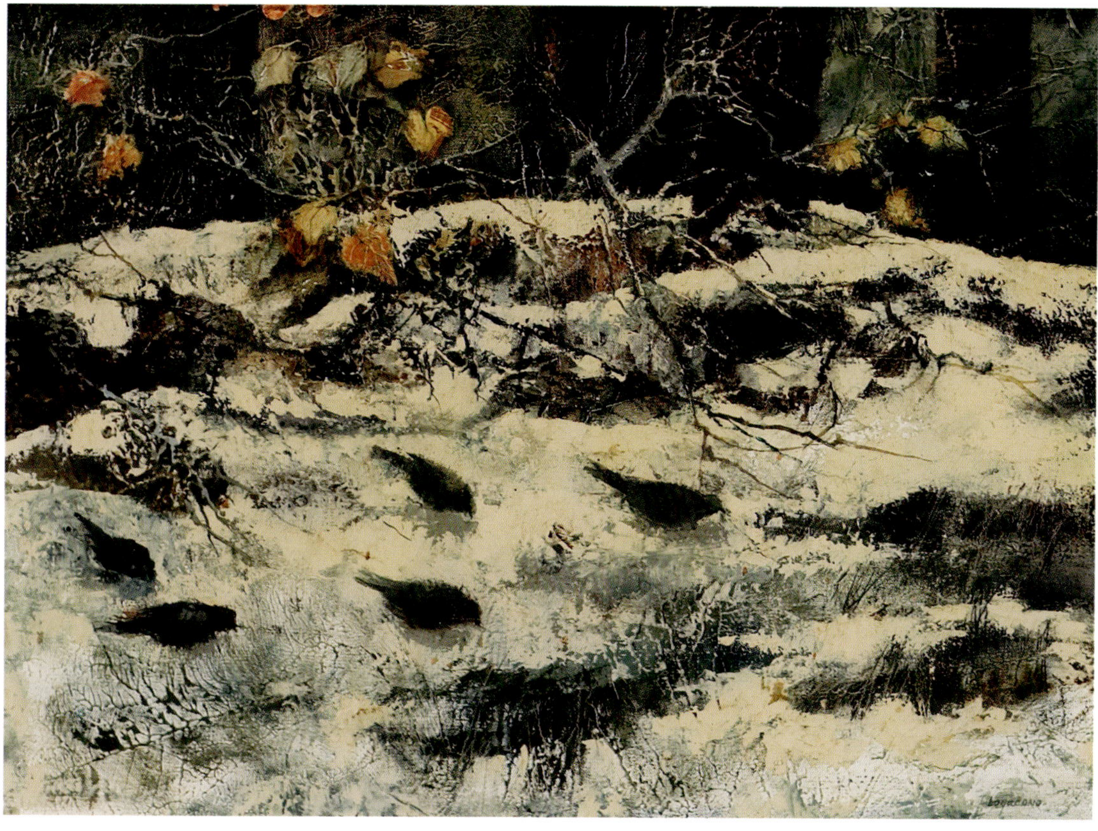

Mary Katherine Loyacono McCravey (born 1910), *Birds in Winter*, no date. oil on canvas, 18 x 24.

that year near Picayune. Such an installation represented a major shift in the area's concept of place. Holmes responded in kind. Her collage is bold, mechanistic, and enigmatic—all qualities that a space rocket testing facility might elicit.

Mary Katharine Knoblock Loyacono McCravey was a longtime art educator in Jackson, teaching in Jackson Public Schools from 1937 to 1968. Born in 1910 in Forest, McCravey graduated from Belhaven College in 1932 and in the summers studied at the University of Chicago, the Art Institute of Chicago, the University of Colorado, and art colonies in Rockport, Massachusetts, and Taos, New Mexico. McCravey worked in landscape, figurative work, and genre

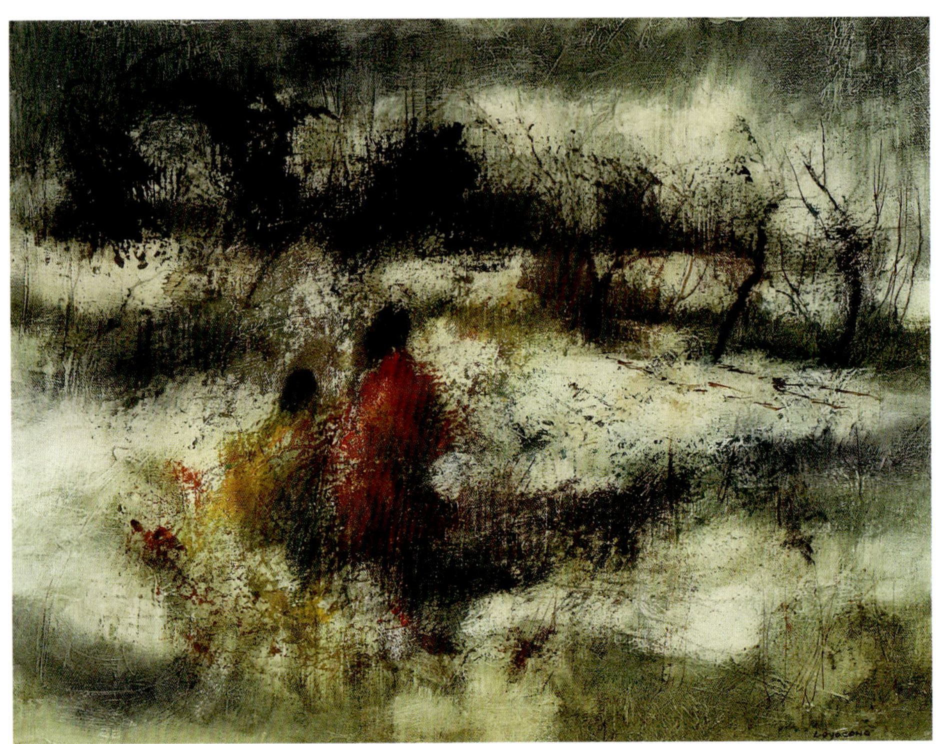

Mary Katherine Loyacono McCravey (born 1910), *Choctaws*, no date. oil on canvas, 16 x 20.

and developed a signature texture that distinguishes her work. Although impressionistic in approach, McCravey gave her art a physicality by working the surfaces of her paintings with thick layers of paint, scraping, and layering. Her early works were signed "Loyacono" until her marriage to W. D. McCravey in 1968. At that time she returned to Forest to live and continue painting. She preferred unspoiled landscapes, which she frequently peopled with figures engaging in some activity: picking blackberries, walking through the woods, wading in water. On exhibit are *Choctaws*, *Birds in Winter*, and *Landscape*, all of which are characterized by her impasto strokes, vivid color, and depictions of untrammeled nature. McCravey received the 2004 Governor's Lifetime Achievement Award.

River Country: Old Natchez District

Still a dominant geographical feature of the United States, the Mississippi River early on attracted European explorers and settlers who used it as the central artery of communication and commerce to link newly occupied lands. The French first explored and sparsely settled the Natchez area in 1714 but virtually abandoned the settlement in 1729 after an uprising ended in the Natchez Indian tribe's massacre. Great Britain and Spain successfully held Natchez and ceded it to the United States in 1783 and 1795, respectively. The rich alluvial soil, invention of the cotton gin, availability of slave labor, and coming of the steamboat all catapulted the Natchez District into great wealth and standing. Cotton planters, many of them educated and prosperous, came from older states and created a relatively refined society on the frontier. Cotton and the commerce and travel on the Mississippi River brought a diverse population to the river cities of Natchez, Vicksburg, Port Gibson, and Rodney.

The river country section opens with the earliest image of Mississippi in the collection: a watercolor sketch of the Mississippi River at Natchez. William Constable (1783-1861) and his brother sold their business in Brighton, England, to finance a journey to the United States in 1806. The brothers' extensive sightseeing trip took them down the Mississippi River. Constable made watercolor sketches "not as works of art but as a record of the aspects of scenes as

Robert Havell (1793-1878) after **John James Audubon** (1785-1851), *Finches and Tanager* from John James Audubon's *The Birds of America*, 1837. hand-colored aquatint and engraving on Whatman paper, 38 x 25½.

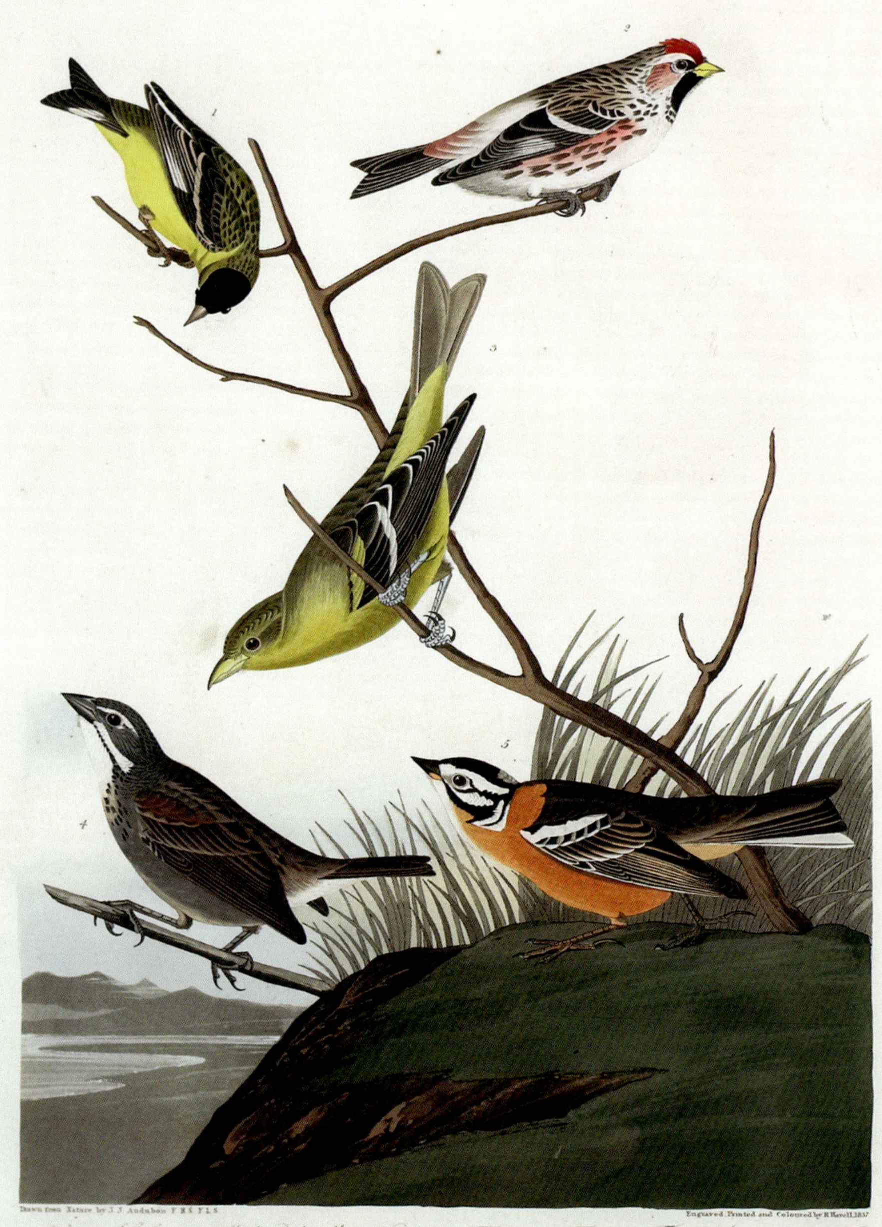

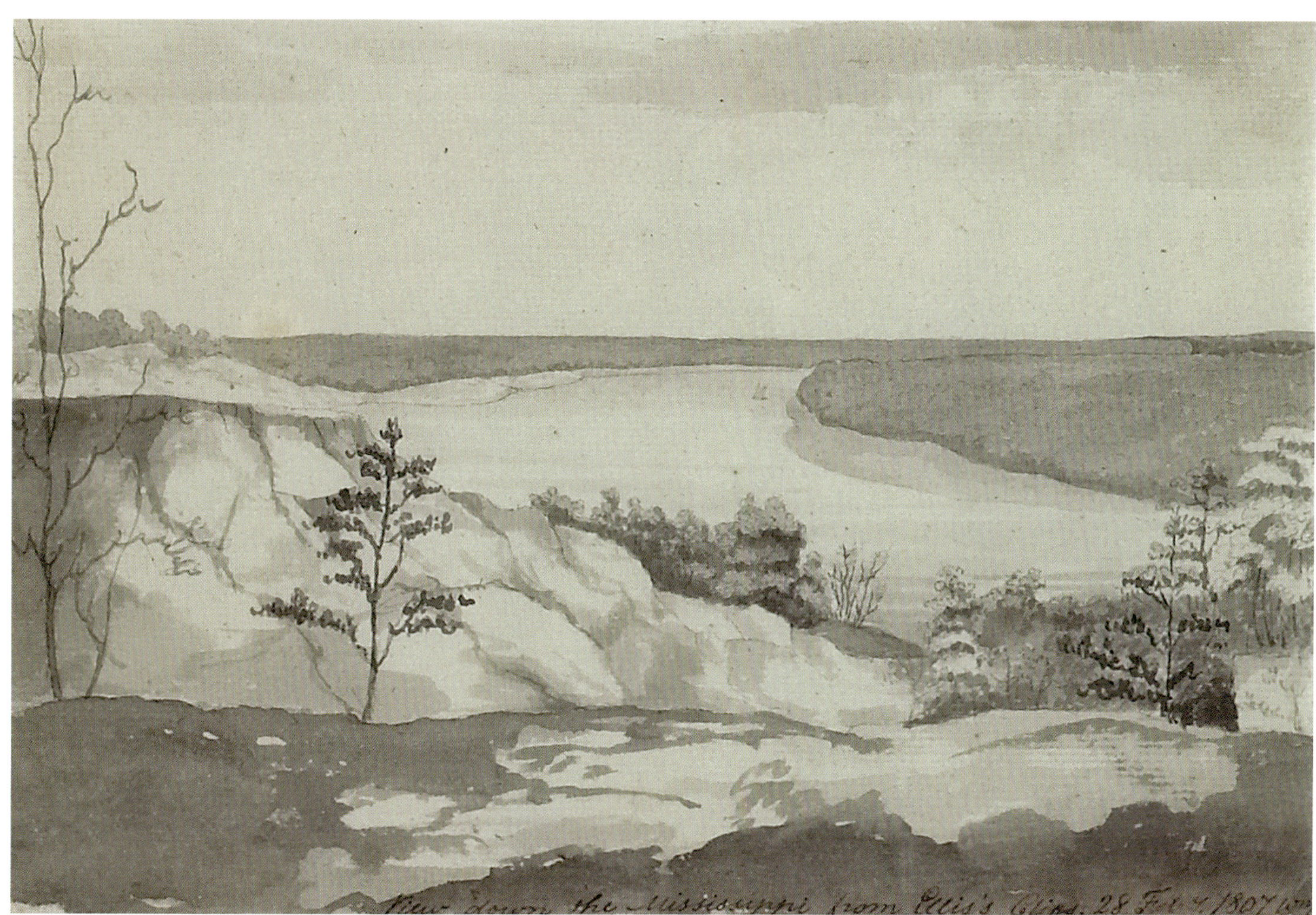

William Constable (1783-1861), *View Down the Mississippi from Ellis's Cliffs 28 Feby. 1807*, 1807. watercolor and graphite on paper, 6¾ x 9½ (sight).

they were . . . before the advent of man but long since passed away." The Museum acquired *View Down the Mississippi from Ellis's Cliffs 28 Feby. 1807* in 2000.

The naturalist John James Audubon (1785-1851) first traveled the Mississippi River by flatboat in 1820 on a mission to find new species of birds that he could paint. He lingered in New Orleans before returning to Natchez in the spring of 1822. Audubon announced his intention of making Natchez a permanent residence and brought his family from Kentucky. He opened a school for drawing and vocal music in Natchez. After learning oil painting from an itinerant artist he took up landscape and portraiture, but his major work was to sketch birds. His notes specify many of the drawings he made of birds in and around Natchez, including the towhee, chuck-will's widow, Carolina chickadee, wood thrush, the tyrant and gray crested flycatchers, blue-eyed yellow warbler, and several others that he spotted on the Mississippi River. After he and his son suffered a severe bout of yellow fever, Audubon decided to leave Natchez in October 1823. He continued to work on his bird project for fifteen years, traveling as far south as the Florida Keys, west to Texas, and north to Labrador, Canada. The exhibition presents an engraving from his *Birds of America* series in 1837, which illustrates an Arkansas siskin, mealy redpoll, Louisiana tanager, Townsend's finch, and buff-breasted finch.

The Mississippi River remained a favorite image of traveling artists for two centuries and became an important subject in the twentieth-century work of Caroline Compton (1907-1987) of Vicksburg. Compton earned her bachelor of arts degree from Sweet Briar College in Virginia and studied at Grand Central School of Art in New York. She returned home to work, using graphite, watercolor, woodblocks, and oils to record her native place—its houses, public buildings, people, landscapes, and waterfront. *The River at Vicksburg* was painted as it must have appeared in the day-to-day lives of those who lived and worked in the town but whose daily life did not take them to the waterfront. Much like in George Inness's *A Glimpse of the Hudson at Milton* (also in the Museum's collection), the mighty force of water is seen almost as a footnote to the land. The Mississipppi Museum of Art presented a major retrospective of Compton's work in 1999.

Another Vicksburg native, Andrew Bucci (born 1922) has won widespread recognition outside the state. He began studying with Marie Hull in the 1930s. After graduating in architectural engineering from Louisiana State University,

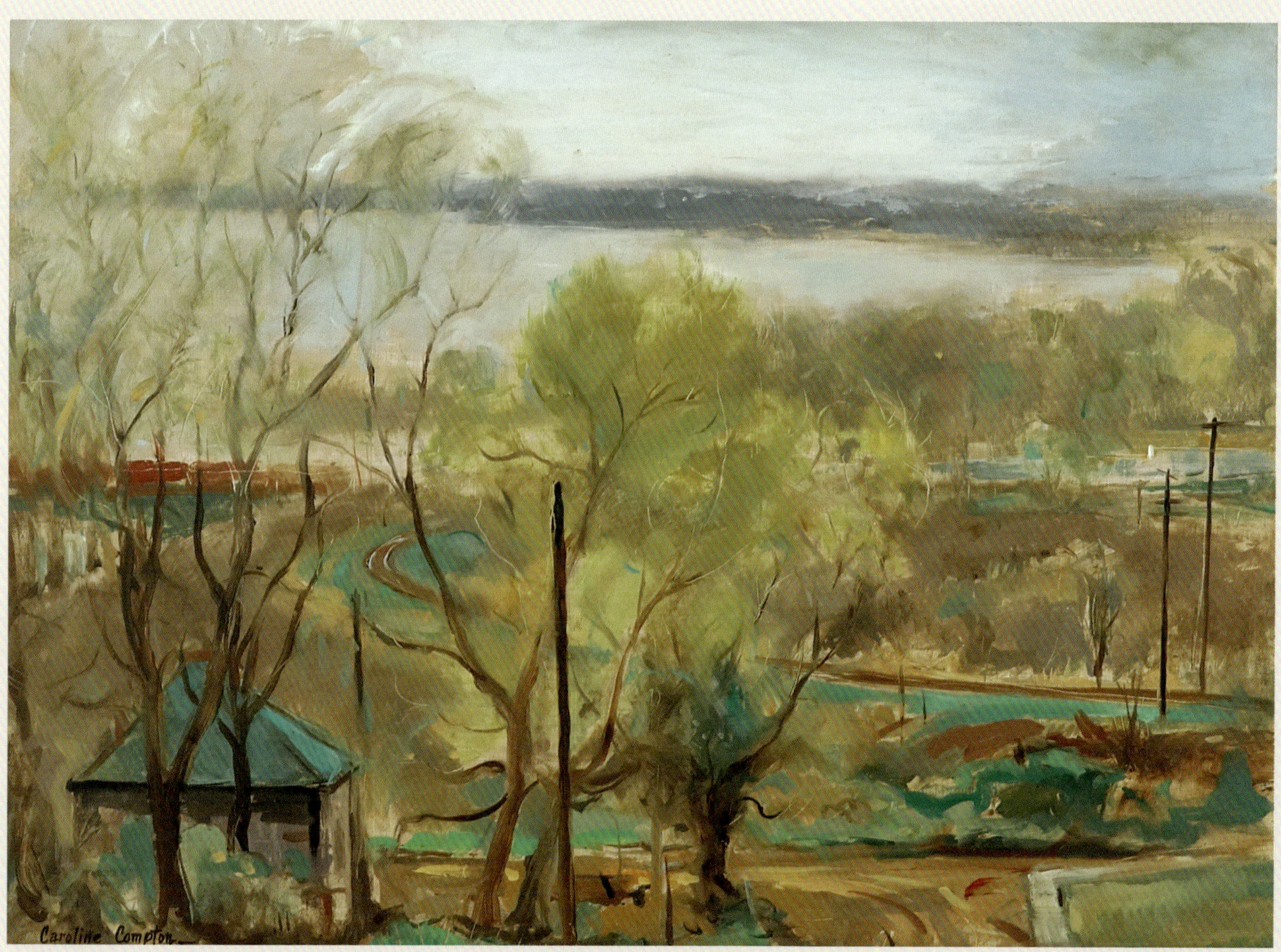

Caroline Compton
(1907-1987), *The River at Vicksburg,* no date.
oil on board, 18 x 24.

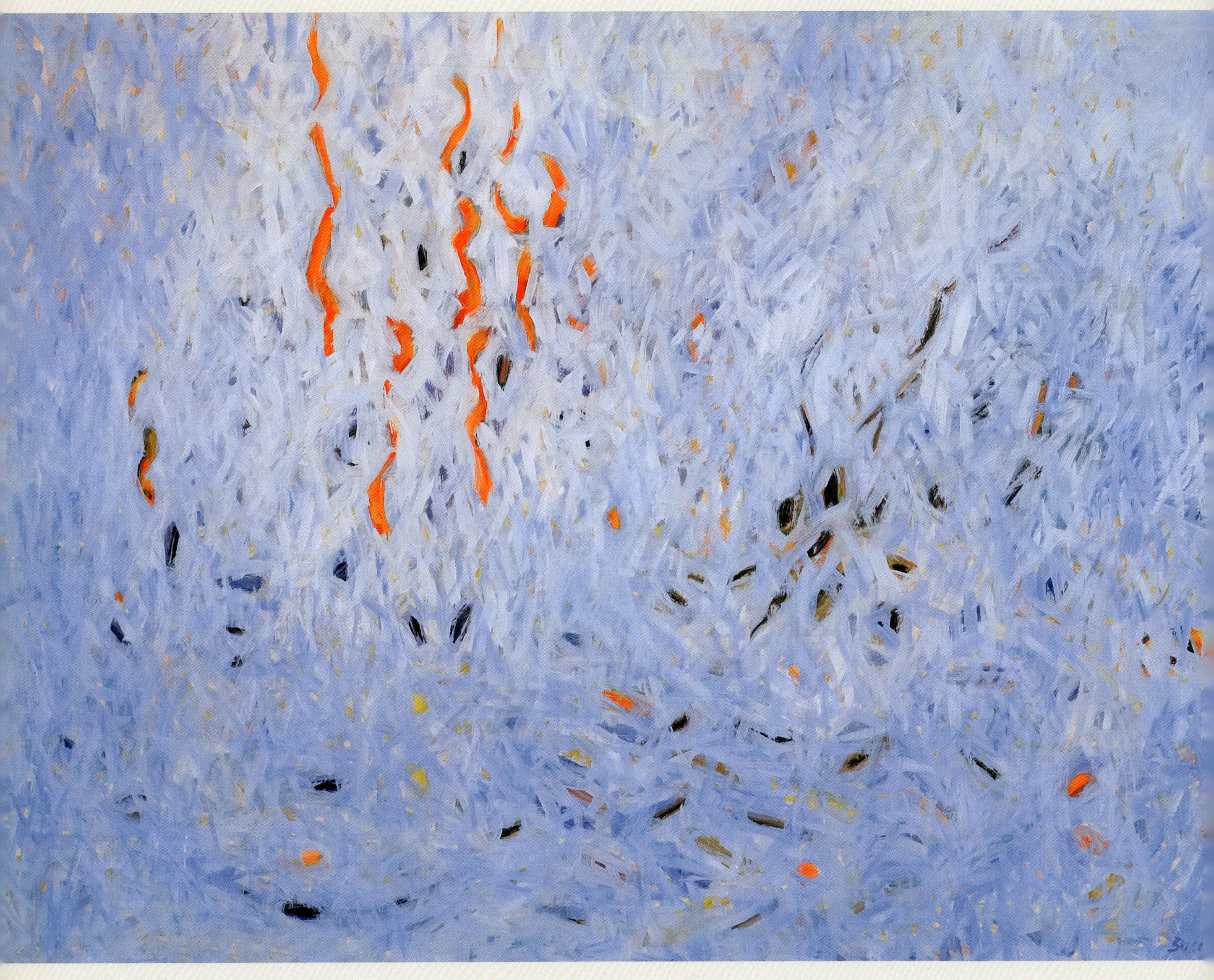

< **Andrew Bucci** (born 1922), *Fox Fire*, 1976. oil on board, 35 x 45.

Bucci served as a meteorologist in World War II, which allowed him to study at the Académie Julian in Paris. After the war he continued studying with Marie Hull and enrolled in the Art Institute of Chicago, where he received a bachelor of fine arts degree in 1952 and an M.F.A. in 1954. Bucci has spent most of his career in Washington, D.C., where he currently lives. He has exhibited often with the Society of Washington Artists and served as president of the Washington Watercolor Society. Bucci's paintings have been viewed throughout the South and East for over half a century, beginning with an exhibition presented by the Mississippi Art Association in 1947. Bucci was one of the first Mississippi artists to successfully use a nonobjective approach to his landscapes. His work is lyrical and inventive, embracing expressionism and its variations. His signature style is calligraphic, with flowing structural lines and delicate colors. The oil *Fox Fire* (1976) shows many of his characteristic attributes: soft colors, gestural strokes, an oriental aspect. (Fox fire is the luminescence of decaying wood, perhaps a memory of Bucci's childhood on the river.) His watercolors from the 1960s, influenced by Japanese woodblock prints, have been described as "subtle and translucent as haiku poems." Bucci's works are in the collections of the Ogden Museum of Southern Art, Lauren Rogers Museum of Art, Arkansas Arts Center, Memphis Brooks Museum of Art, Florence Art Gallery in South Carolina, Delta State University, Hinds Junior College, and Mississippi University for Women.

The river country was a favorite setting for Eudora Welty in both her fiction and nonfiction. *A Still Moment, The Robber Bridegroom, Asphodel, At the Landing,* and *Some Notes on River Country* were all set in the area. Similarly, many of her photographs recorded the Mississippi River ghost town of Rodney and surroundings. On view is one of her most popular images, *Ruins of Windsor, near Port Gibson* (1942), which also captures the photographer's shadow.

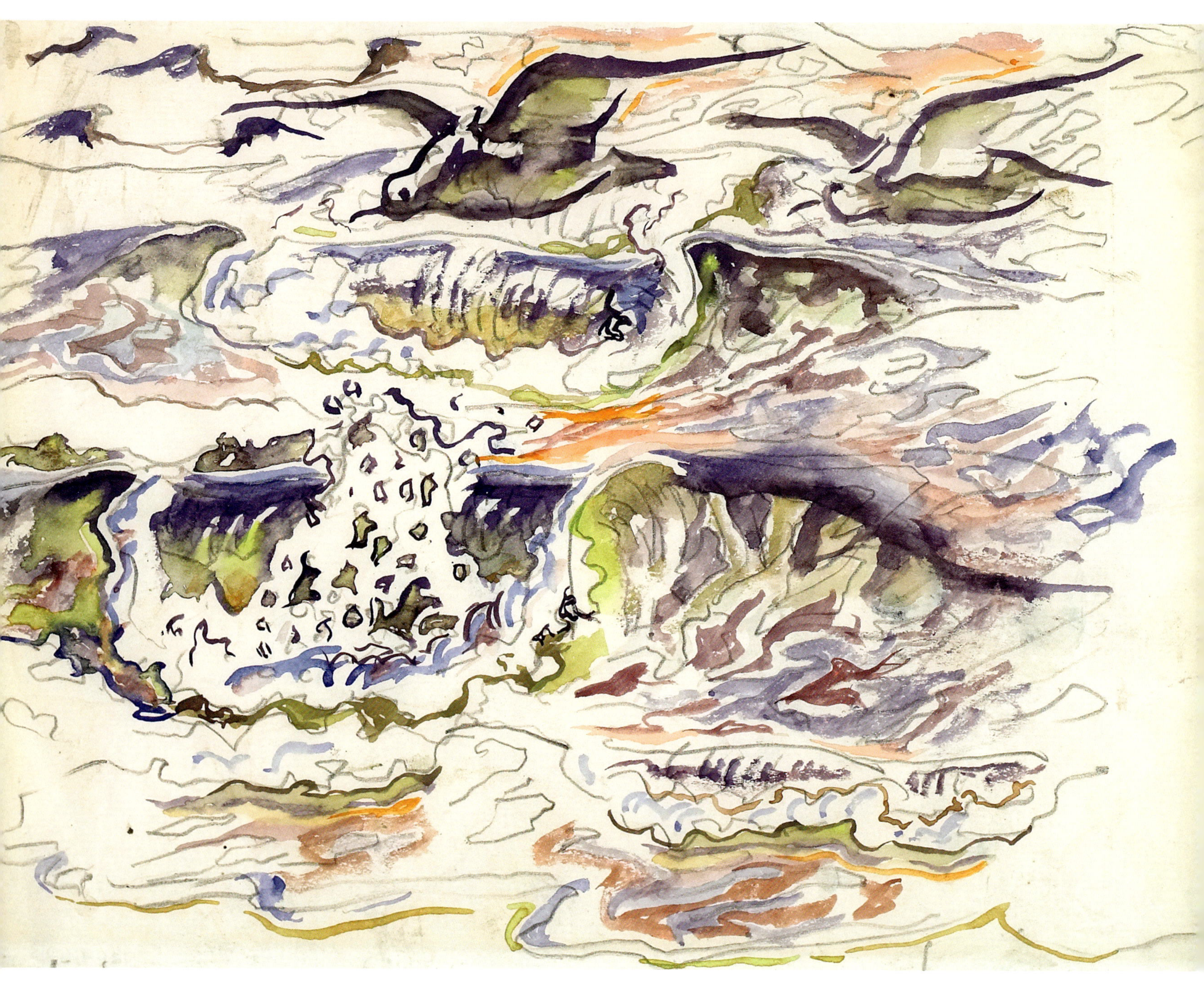

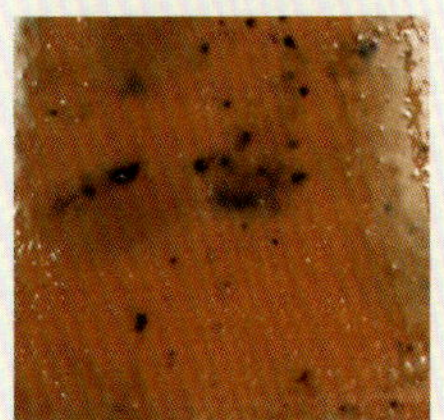

The Gulf Coast

The stretch of land fronting the Gulf of Mexico was the first area in Mississippi to be settled by Europeans. The French arrived in 1699 and after almost a hundred years of subsequent ownership by England and Spain, the Gulf Coast and Natchez District became territories of the United States. From the beginning the coast has doubled as a settlement by people with maritime backgrounds—shipbuilders, providers of naval stores, and fishermen—and as a vacation destination. New Orleanians and wealthy Mississippians before the Civil War built spacious second homes along the waterfront, from Biloxi to Pass Christian and in Bay St. Louis and Waveland. Years of hurricanes have destroyed or damaged that landscape. Beauvoir, once the antebellum home of a Delta family and later made into the Jefferson Davis Museum and Library, is one of the few antebellum homes left standing after Hurricane Katrina. The casino industry is largely leading the rebuilding effort, and the Gulf Coast is expected to return to its pre-Katrina status as one of the nation's largest casino sites. It is, however, the natural Gulf Coast that has engaged Mississippi's visual artists.

< Walter Anderson (1903-1965), *Birds and Waves*, no date. watercolor on paper, 8½ x 11. Copyright © The Family of Walter Anderson: Mary, Bill, Leif and John.

Probably no other artist has responded to elements of the natural world as intensely as Walter Anderson (1903-1965) of Ocean Springs, who created his major works on Horn Island in the Mississippi Sound. Anderson is

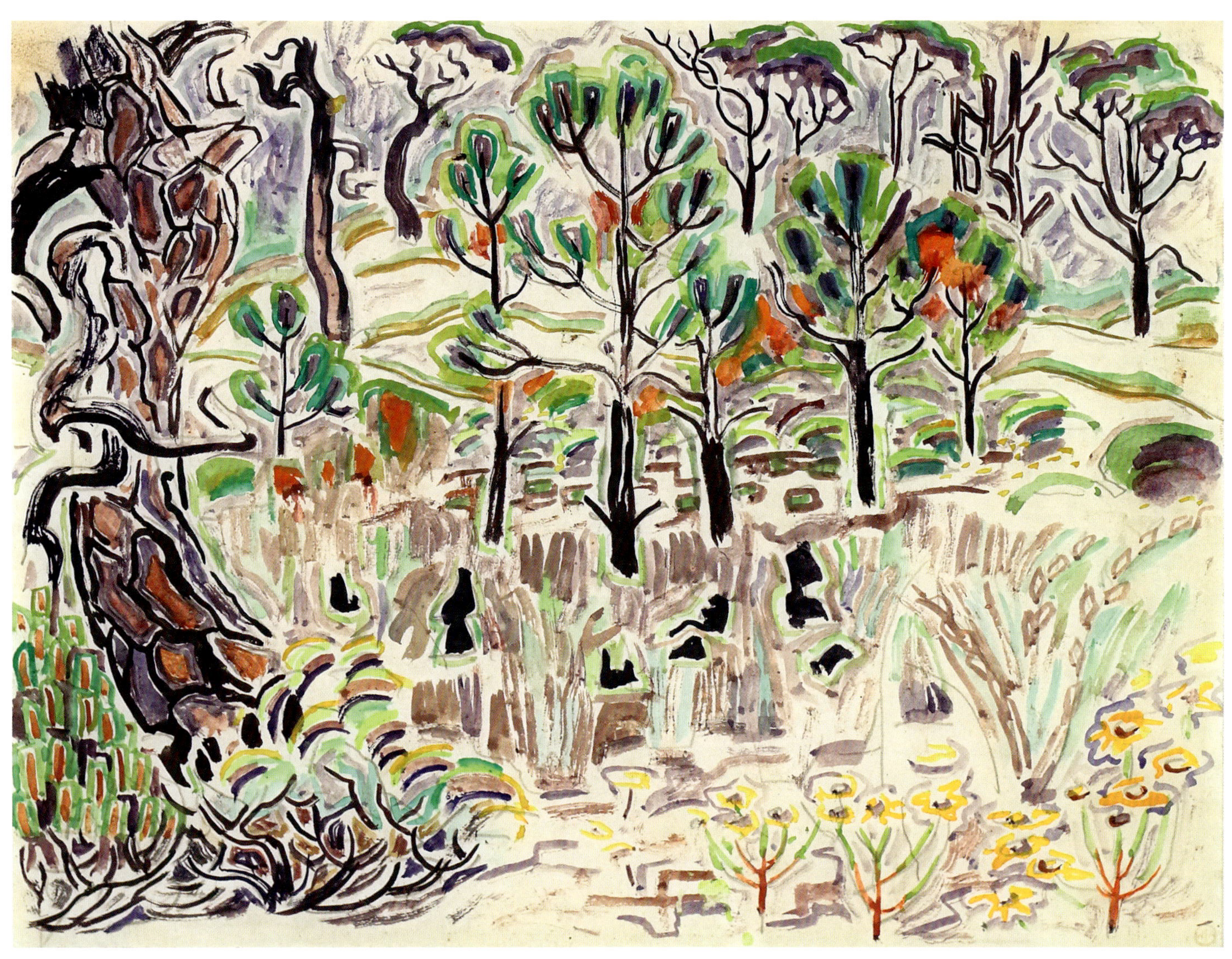

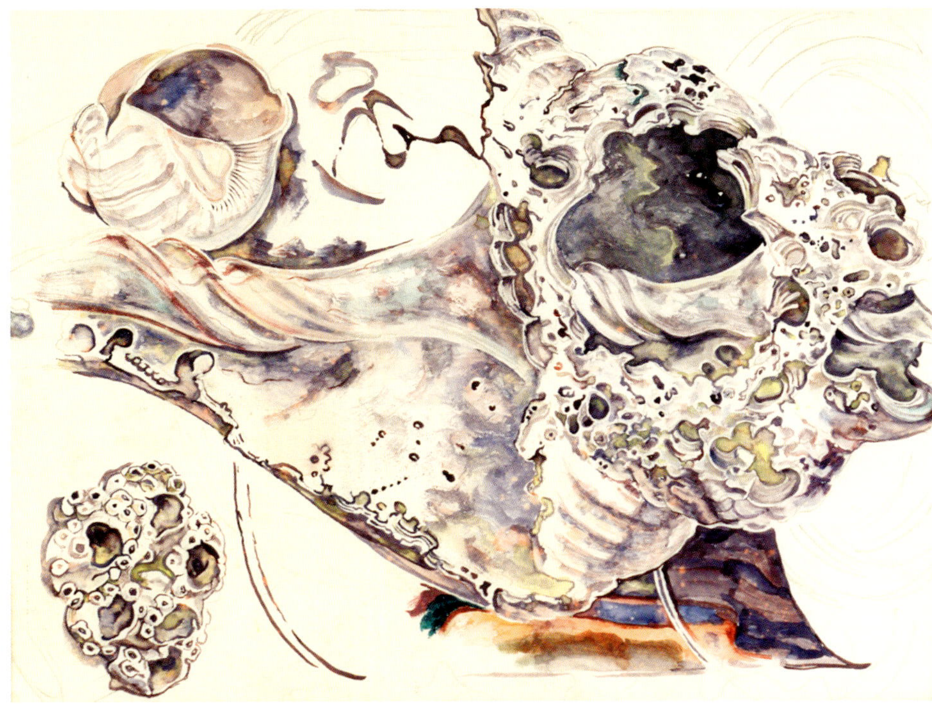

Walter Anderson (1903-1965), *Seashells*, no date. watercolor on paper, 8½ x 11. Copyright © The Family of Walter Anderson: Mary, Bill, Leif and John.

< Walter Anderson (1903-1965), *Horn Island—Fall*, no date. watercolor on paper, 8½ x 11. Copyright © The Family of Walter Anderson: Mary, Bill, Leif and John.

Mississippi's most important painter. Born in New Orleans, he was educated at a boarding school in New York and spent his summers on the Mississippi Gulf Coast. His family moved to Ocean Springs in 1922 and after graduating from the Philadelphia Academy of the Fine Arts and traveling in Europe on an art scholarship, Anderson joined his family in Ocean Springs. He is primarily known for his murals in the Ocean Springs Community Center and for his watercolors of Horn Island, a barrier island some twelve miles from shore. He spent eighteen years making regular and extended trips to the island, where he painted marine life, animal life, landscapes, and seascapes. He created a staggering quantity of other work, including oils and drawings in crayon, ink, and pencil. He carved and printed linoleum blocks of tremendous size—some seven feet long—sculpted in wood, created ceramic figures, decorated Shearwater Pottery pieces (his brother's pottery business), designed textiles, and painted murals. Exhibited are several of Anderson's watercolors of the flora and fauna on Horn Island, as well as a seascape and a landscape. All demonstrate the staggering energy of his work, his mastery of watercolor, his powers of observation, and his desire to "realize" the natural world through his art. The Walter Anderson Museum of Art opened at Ocean Springs in 1991 and has taken its place as one of the premier cultural attractions in the state.

Peter Anderson (1901-1984) of Ocean Springs, Walter Anderson's brother, established Shearwater Pottery in 1928. From the beginning the enterprise has been a family affair. Initially Peter's mother, Annette McConnell Anderson (1867-1964), and his brothers Walter and James McConnell "Mac" (1907-1998) decorated the pottery and created small figurines. Through the years, the second generation has continued these efforts. Peter's son Jim Anderson (born 1942) succeeded him as potter; his daughter Patricia Findesen (born 1933) became a lead decorator and son Michael Anderson (born 1931) took charge of the figurines. Now third- and fourth-generation Andersons are also at work: Jim's son, Peter Wade Anderson (born 1976), joined him in 1999; Christopher Stebly (born in 1967 and the son of Mary Anderson), Matthew Stebly (Mary Anderson's grandson), and Adelle Anderson Lawton (born in 1951 and the daughter of Mac Anderson) provide inventive design motifs based on the flora and fauna of the area. Jason Stebly, Mary Anderson's son and Walter Anderson's grandson, is currently reconstructing the pottery buildings, which Hurricane Katrina destroyed.

George E. Ohr (1857-1918) of Biloxi was a blazing star in the world of art pottery, beginning with his exhibition at the 1885 World's Fair in New Orleans and again at the 1904 St. Louis Exposition. He had brief stints on the staff of Newcomb Pottery, opened Biloxi Art and Novelty Pottery in 1890, and continued to work until 1909. He manipulated delicate, thin-walled pots into exotic forms by twisting, denting, ruffling, and folding the clay. His work was rediscovered in 1968, when several thousand pieces were brought out of storage and

George Ohr
(1857-1918), no title,
circa 1900. clay with
glaze, 8¼ x 4¼ x 3½.

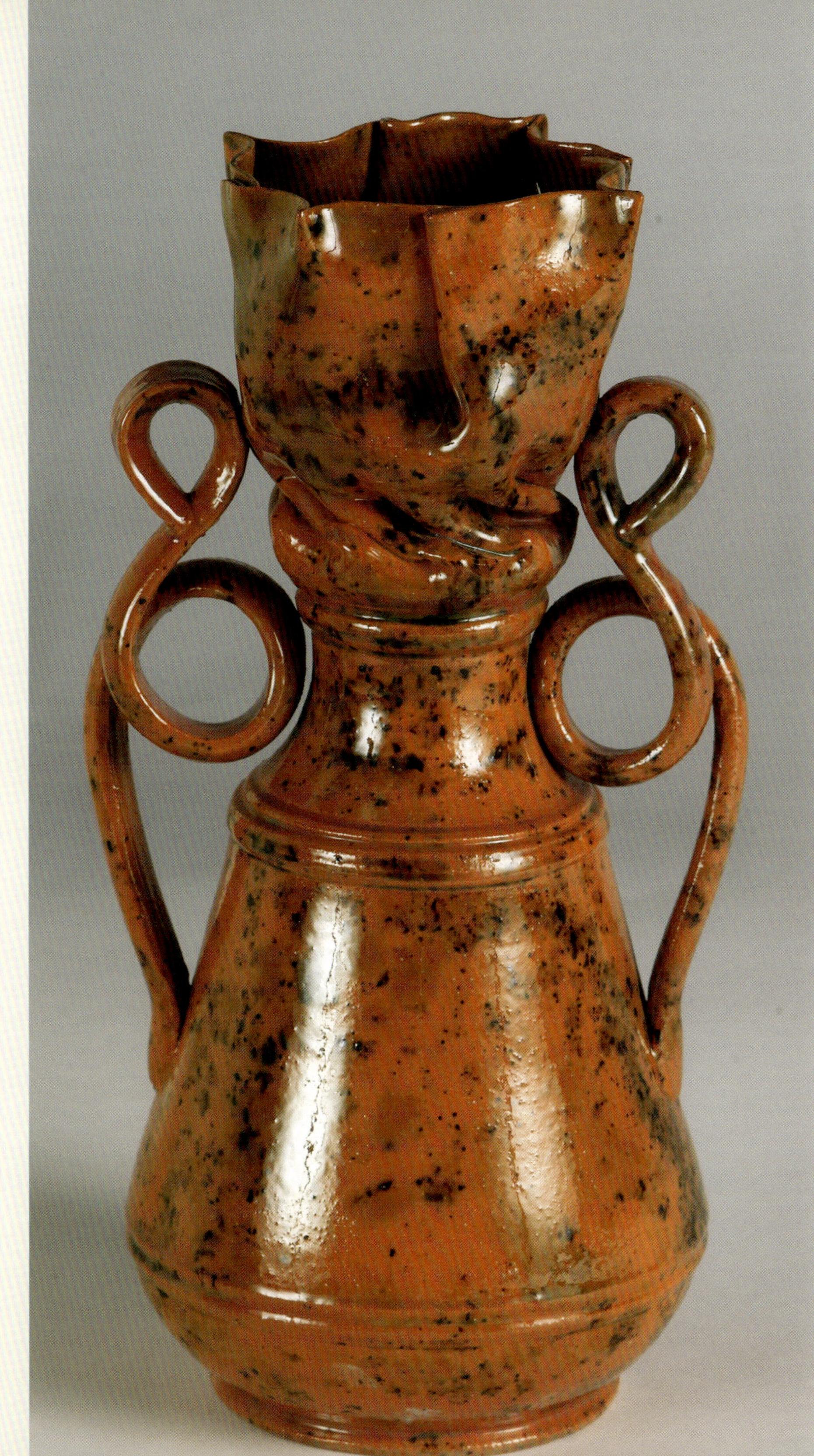

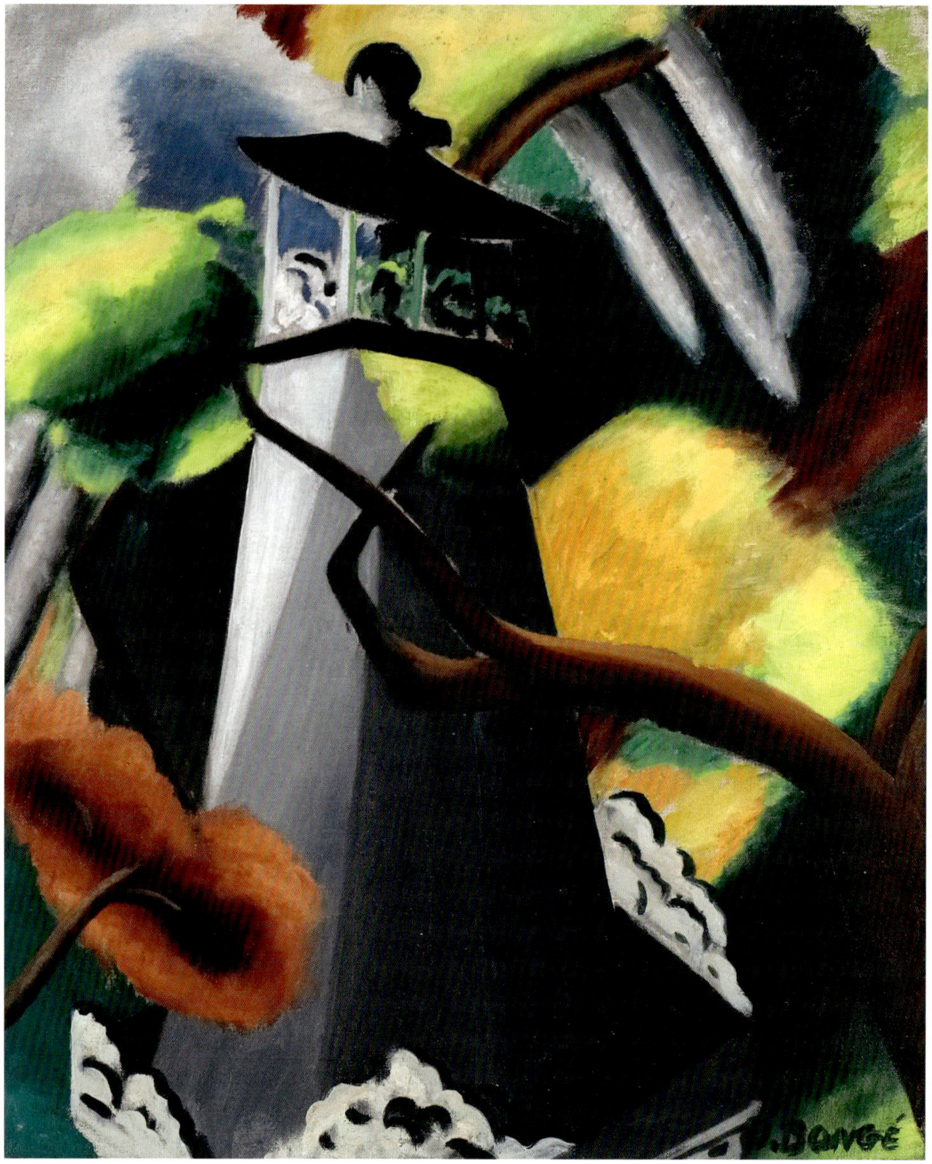

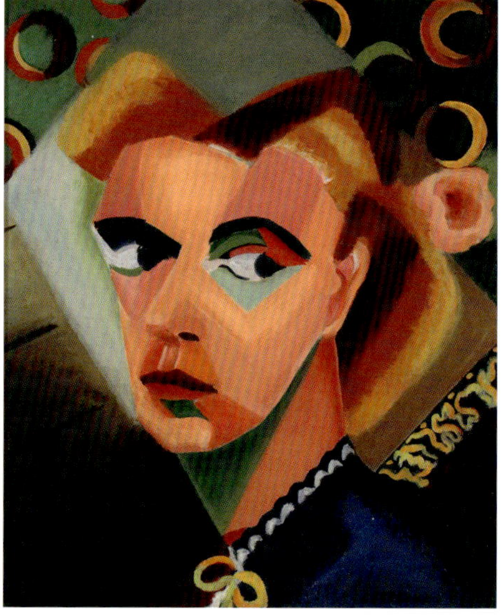

Dusti Bongé
(1903-1993), *The Balcony*, 1943. oil on canvas, 20 x 16. Courtesy of The Dusti Bongé Foundation and the city of Biloxi, Miss.

Dusti Bongé
(1903-1993), no title, 1943. oil on canvas, 20 x 16. Courtesy of The Dusti Bongé Foundation and the city of Biloxi, Miss.

Dusti Bongé >
(1903-1993), no title, 1940s. oil on canvas, 17 x 19. Courtesy of The Dusti Bongé Foundation and the city of Biloxi, Miss.

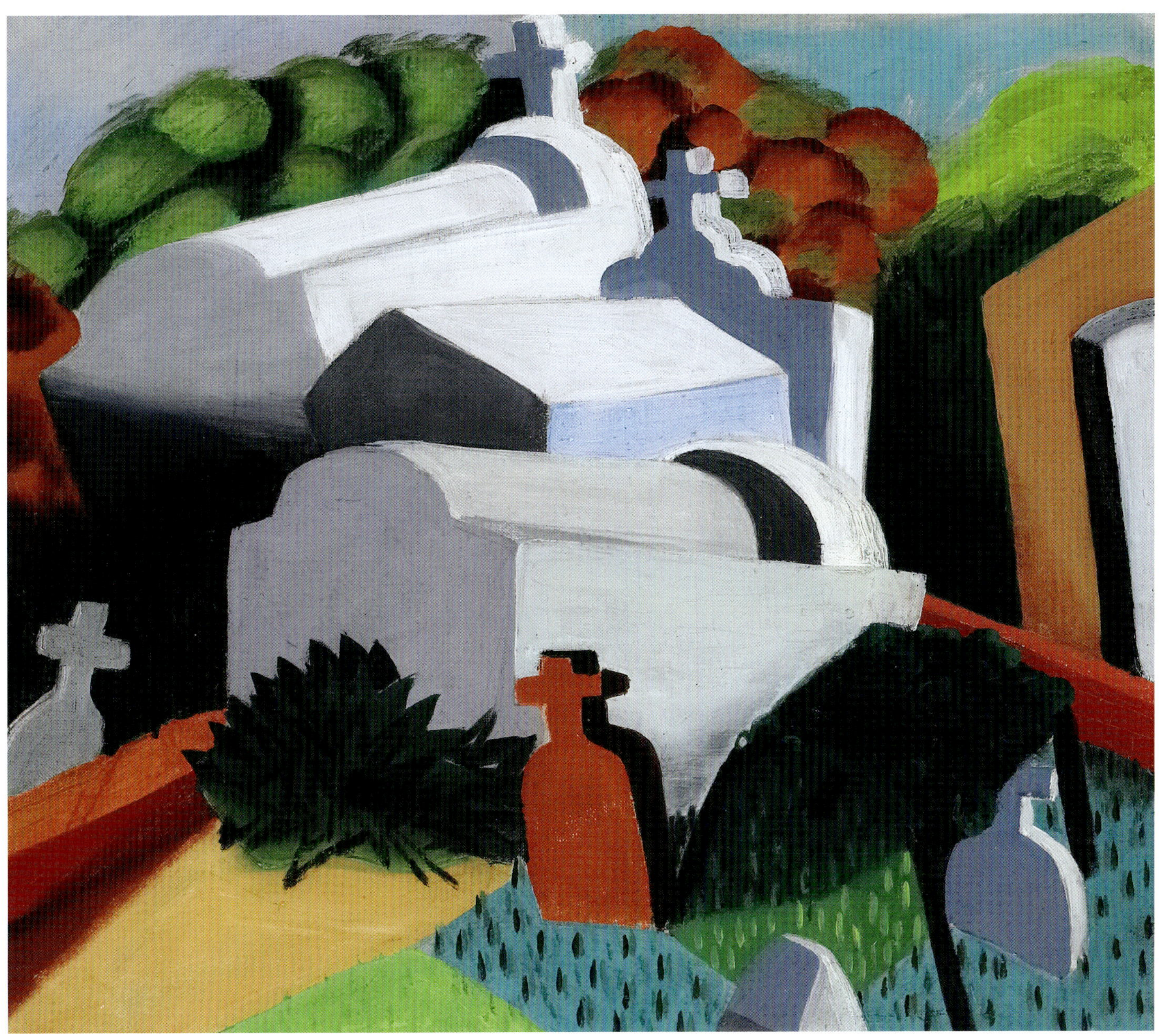

sold to collectors across the nation. Today, in tribute to his immense skill and artistry, the new Ohr-O'Keefe Museum of Art is underway in Biloxi.

Another important painter of the Gulf Coast is Biloxi's Dusti Swetman Bongé (1903-1993). A graduate of Blue Mountain College, Bongé began her career as an actress in Manhattan. She and her artist husband, Archie Bongé, returned to Biloxi in 1934 and built an art studio there. Two years later Archie Bongé died and Dusti Bongé continued to seriously pursue her own art. She had her first show in Manhattan in 1939. Her next national exposure was a show at the Betty Parsons Gallery in Manhattan in 1954. Bongé began as a representational artist but became the first Mississippi artist to firmly adopt modernism, experimenting with the style until her death at age ninety. On view are several of her canvases: a lighthouse in the land section, a self-portrait in the people section, and a Biloxi cemetery in the daily life section. All show her bold color, decisive geometric shapes, and dramatic use of chiaroscuro. Her son, Lyle Bongé, born in 1929, is a photographer of national repute. A graduate of Tulane University, his work has been made widely known through national exhibitions and with the publication of *The Photographs of Lyle Bongé* (1983) and *Sleep of Reason* (1974). Lyle Bongé is primarily concerned with form, texture, and light, rather than narrative content. He wrote, "An ordinary thing, cleaned of its context, can have strength of form, exquisiteness of texture, and hanging in space, become magical." His experimental expressionistic work in the *Cosmos* series speaks clearly of place.

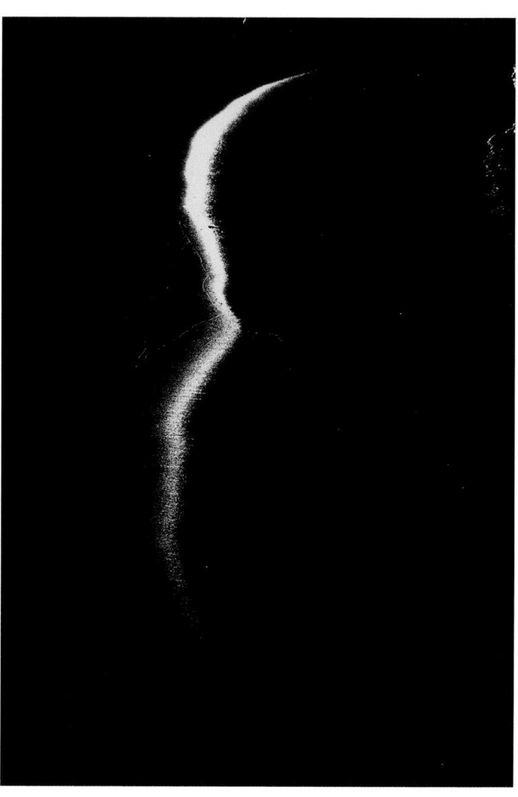

Lyle Bongé
(born 1929), *Untitled* from the *Cosmos* series, no date. gelatin silver print, 6½ x 9¾.

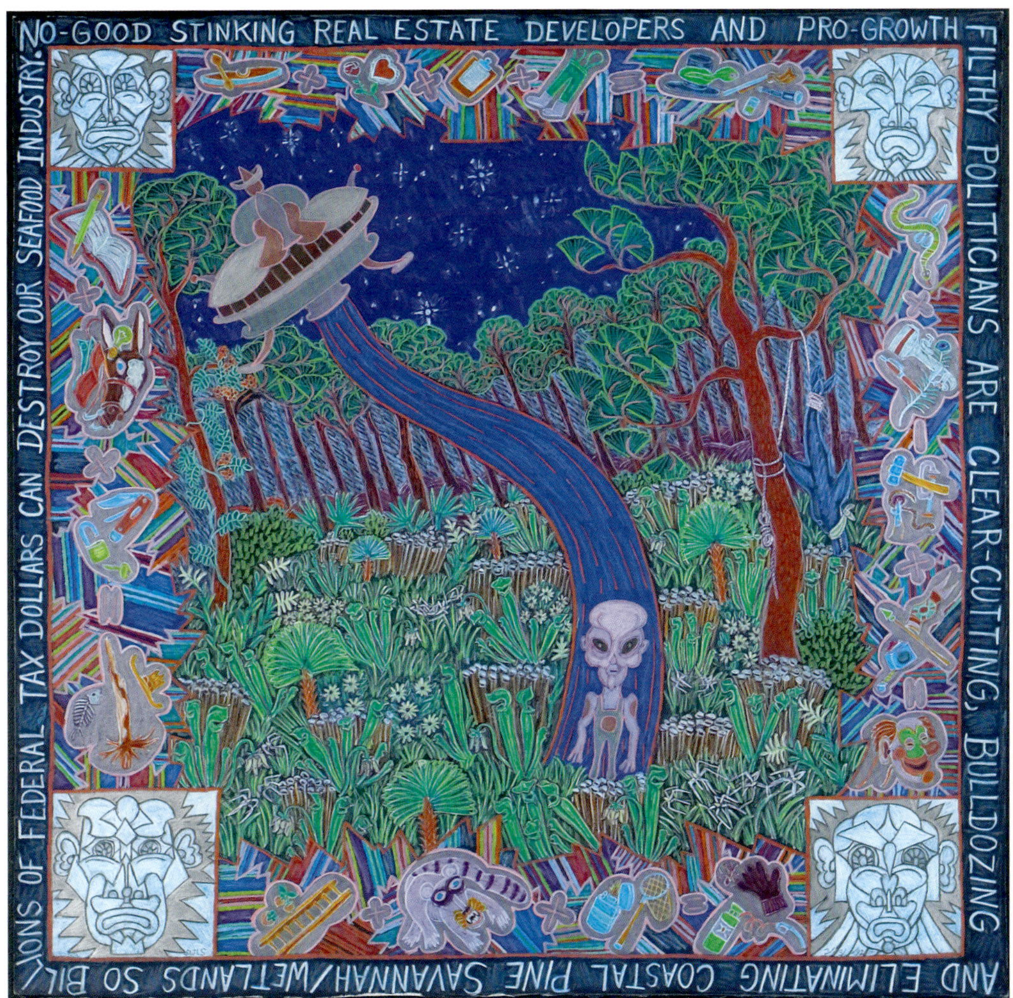

Steve Shepard
(born 1955), *No Good Stinking Real Estate Developers . . .*, 1992. colored pencil, graphite, and watercolor on paper, 24 x 24.

One of the most passionate contemporary artists working on the Gulf Coast is Steve Shepard of Gautier, whose art unabashedly argues for the ecological well being of the coastal wetlands. Shepard was born in Port Arthur, Texas, in 1955, but has spent most of his life on the Mississippi Gulf Coast. His work reflects a deep knowledge of and commitment to the natural world of the Gulf of Mexico's northern coast, from rivers and swamps to marshes and barrier islands. Shepard is the most overtly political artist working in the state today. His work not only celebrates the natural beauty of the region, its creatures and plants, Shepard uses his art to rail against developers and legislation that threaten the ecological balance of the area. He calls himself a visionary artist who favors "busy frenetic compositions with an attention to spontaneous absurdity." He uses shifts in the horizon, foregoes linear perspective, and

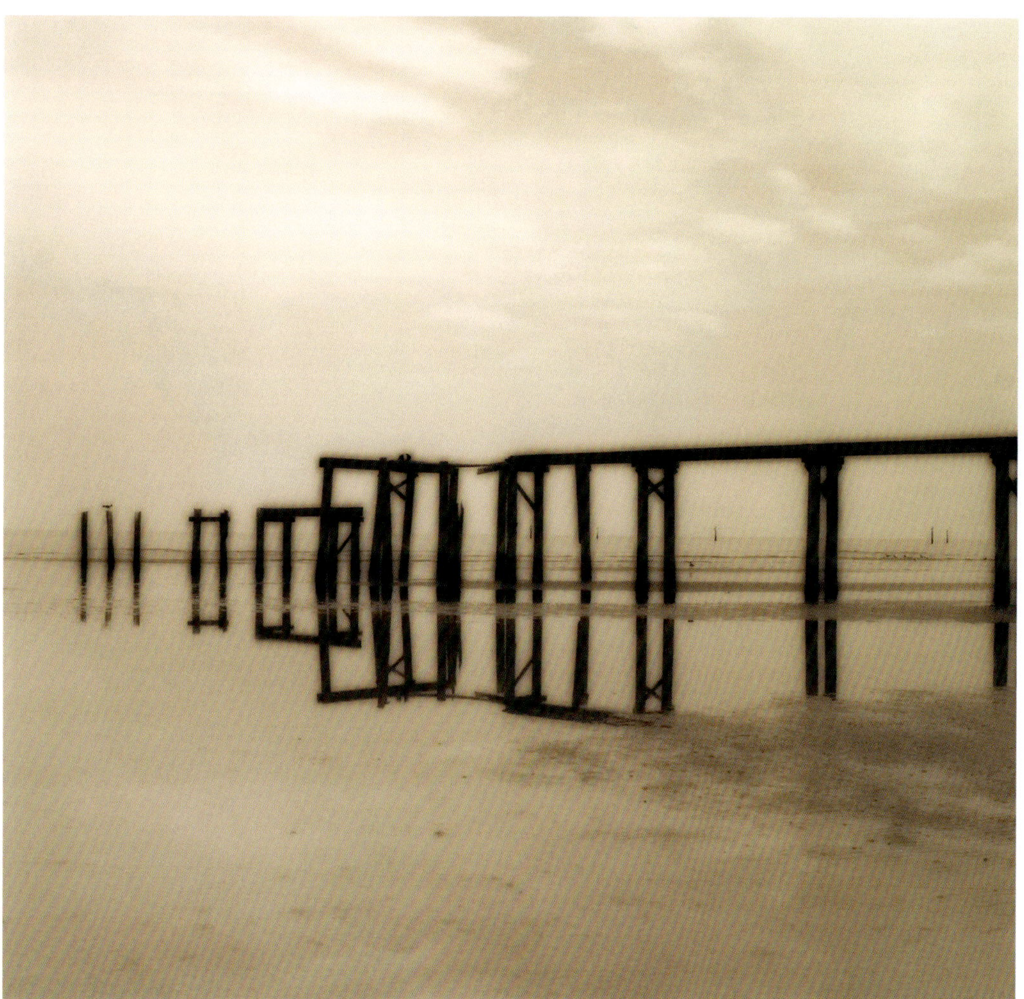

Sandra Russell Clark (born 1949), *Pier, Bay St. Louis, Mississippi,* 2001. toned gelatin silver print, 16½ x 16.

David Rae Morris > (born 1959), *Lighthouse with Piles of Debris,* 2005. pigmented inkjet print, 22¾ x 15 (sight). Copyright © David Rae Morris/ *The New York Times.*

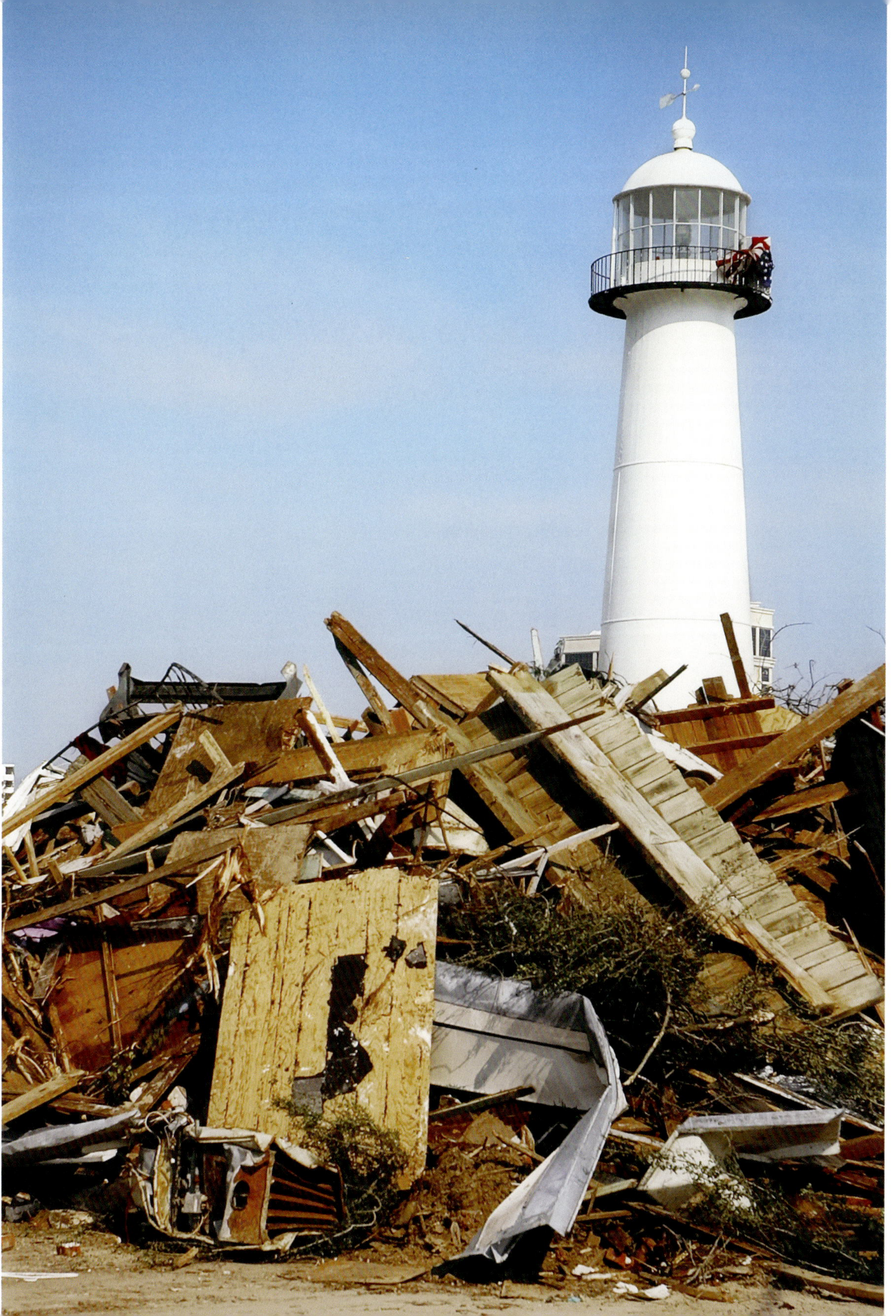

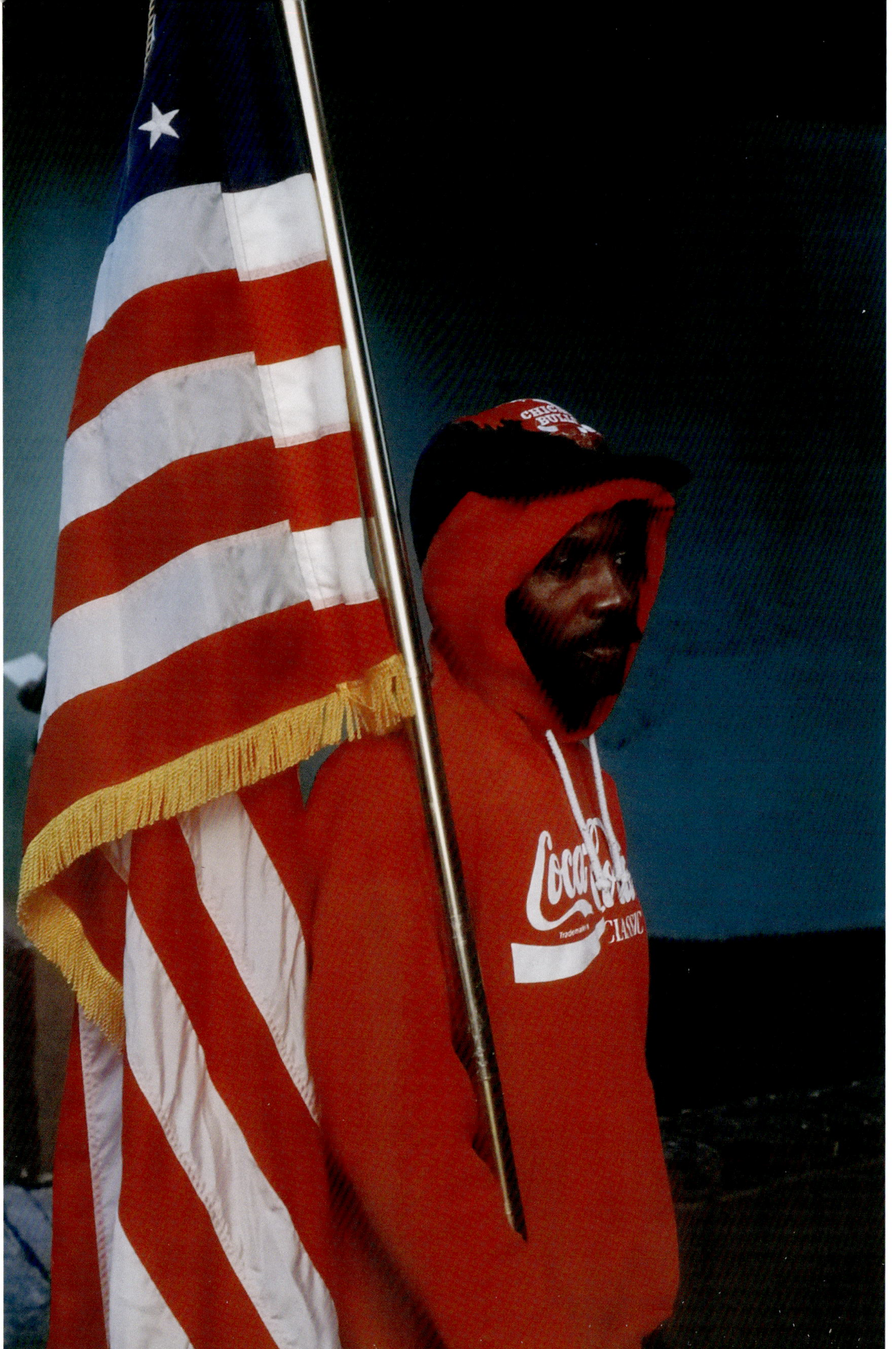

David Rae Morris (born 1959), *Leon Gray, flag bearer for the Martin Luther King Day Parade, Yazoo City, MS*, 1999. pigmented inkjet print, 20 x 16.

creates surfaces with color pencils of bright hues. Shepard's influences include outsider artists, Chicago Imagists, and ethnic artists ranging from pre-Columbian to African.

The final section about the coast deals with the destructive power of hurricanes. The earliest work is a watercolor titled *Gulf Hurricane* by Agnes Ricketts, a Jackson artist of the 1940s. It is photography, however, that brings home the devastation left by hurricanes. On exhibit is a poignantly evocative image by Sandra Russell Clark of New Orleans. Taken in 2001 of a Bay St. Louis pier, Clark's use of toning and soft edges gives the scarred structure a mystical quality. The section ends with two images of the Biloxi Lighthouse. The strong blocks of color in Dusti Bongé's 1940s modernist painting seem to forecast the endurance of the lighthouse structure. The second image shows the lighthouse after Katrina, the most powerful and destructive hurricane ever to hit the coast. David Rae Morris's timely photograph of the Biloxi Lighthouse is a testimony to its iconic role in the area.

Mississippi

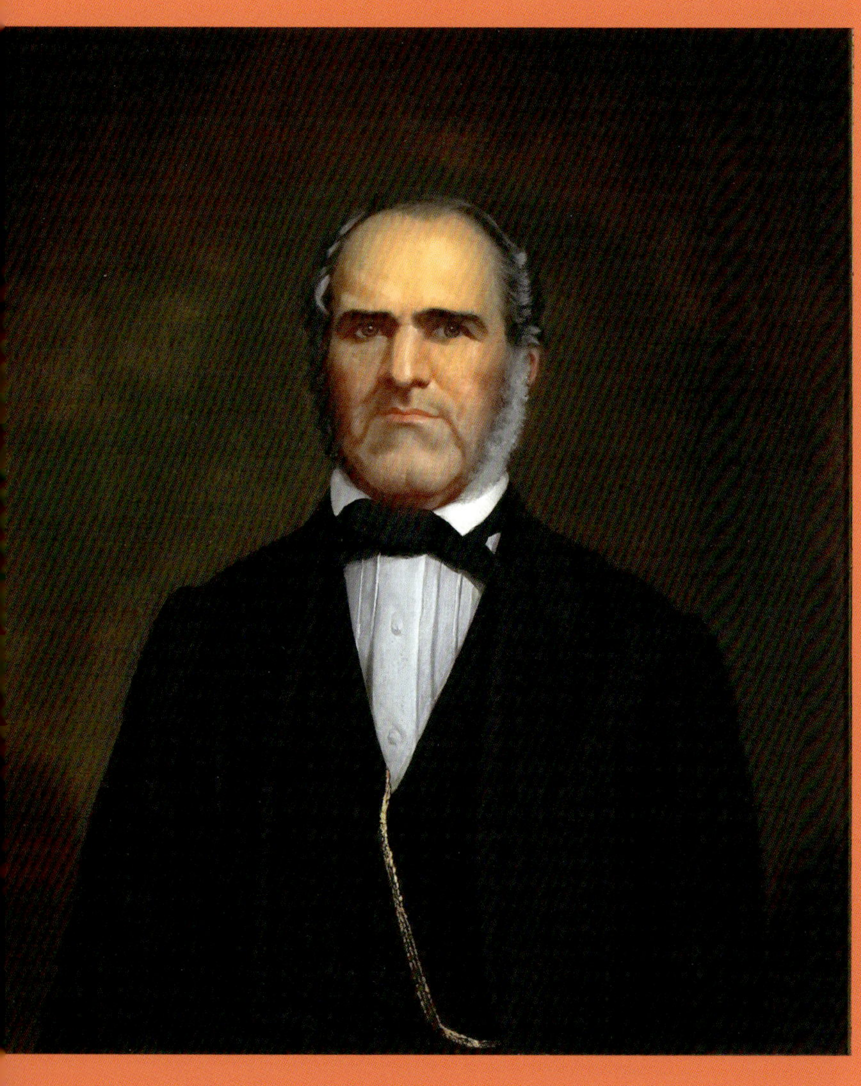

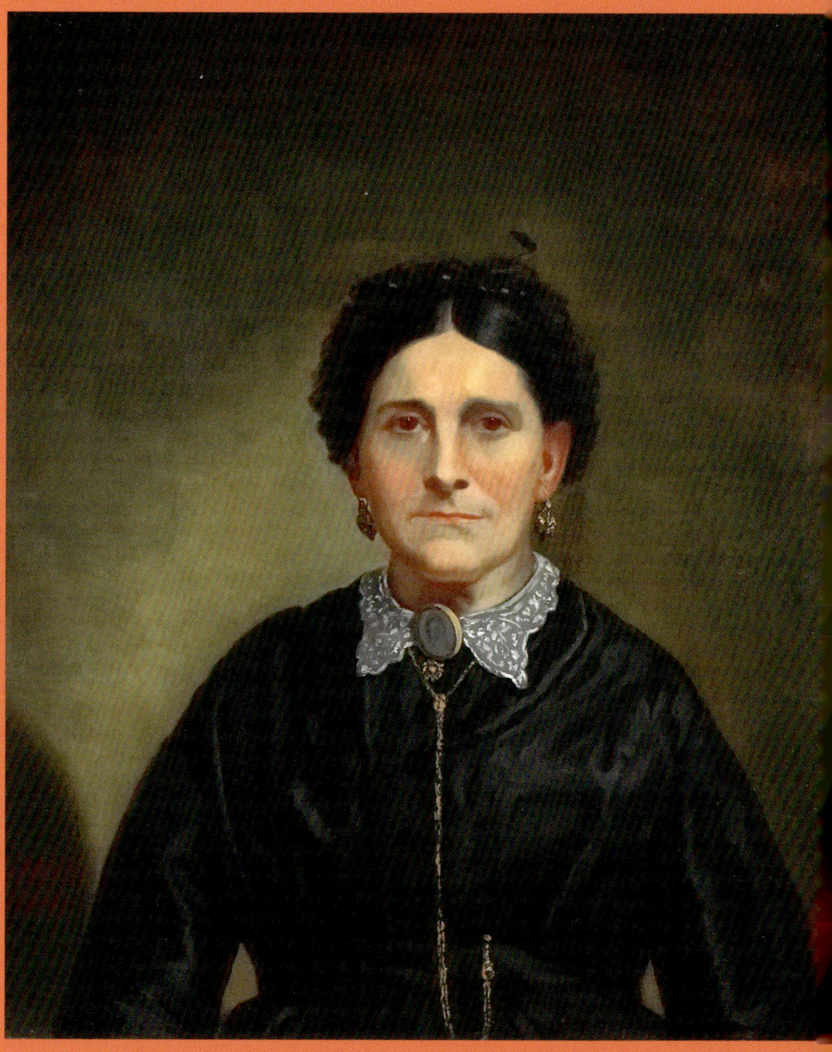

People: Portraits

Karl Wolfe (1904-1984), one of Mississippi's most successful portraitists, wrote, "People seem to imagine it might be simple to paint a portrait—just copy a person's face, his color, his suit, his tie . . . this is only the beginning. Every inch of the canvas must say something succinct about the inner life of the subject, every brush stroke and color must be orchestrated to say how his life affects the painter as one integer in a whole community. One makes a sonorous abstract whole so that it is a beautiful painting first and incidentally a portrait."

< Thomas Cantwell Healy (1820-1889), *Portrait of a Man*, 1874. oil on canvas, 30¼ x 25⅛.

< Thomas Cantwell Healy (1820-1889), *Portrait of a Woman*, 1874. oil on canvas, 30 x 25½.

Wolfe was born in Brookhaven, grew up in Columbia, and moved to Jackson with the explicit intention of making his living as an artist. After World War II his artist wife, Mildred Nungester Wolfe, joined him, and later their daughter Elizabeth also became an artist. The three of them have made the Wolfe Studio in Jackson a bastion of artistic integrity and productivity. Karl Wolfe was active in the Mississippi Art Association, served as the first director of the Allison's Wells Resort and Art Colony, and taught in the art department at Millsaps College. On exhibit is one of his early portraits painted during World War II titled *Rest and Recreation, WWII*. Wolfe later became known for

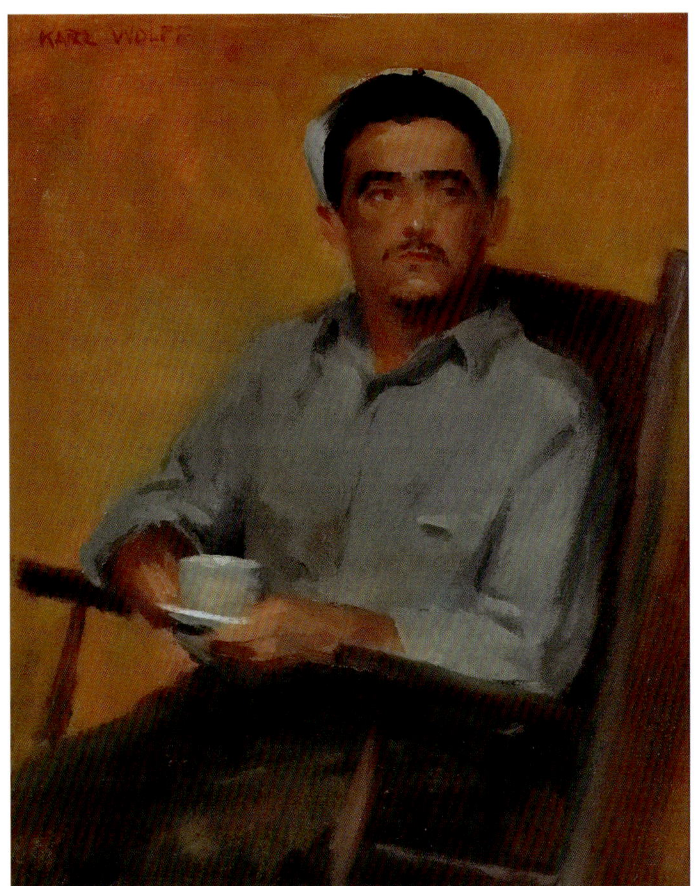

Karl Wolfe
(1904-1984), *Rest and Recreation, WWII*, 1946. oil on canvas, 14 x 11.

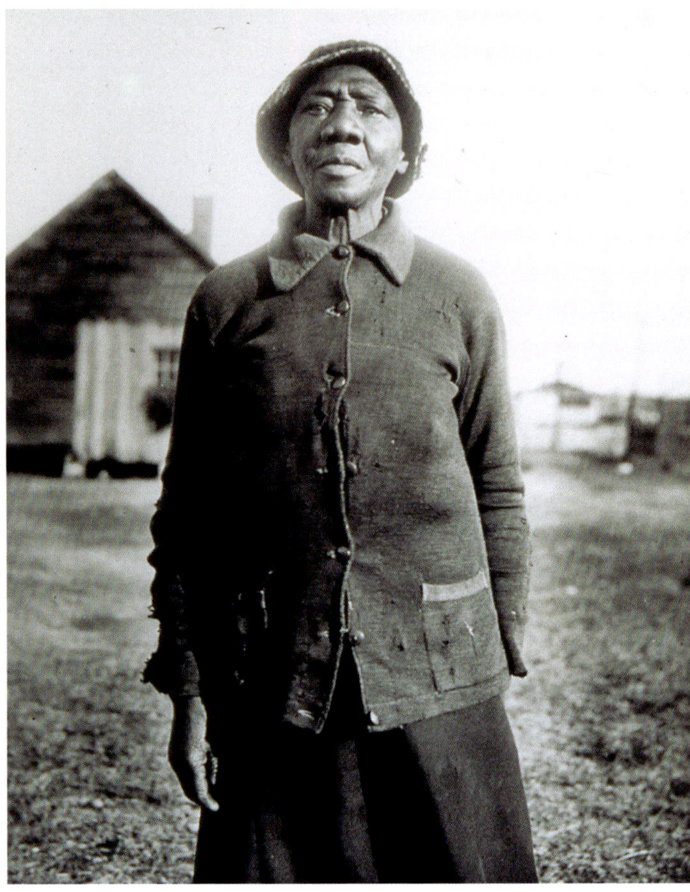

Eudora Welty
(1909-2001), *A woman of the 'thirties, Jackson*, 1935-1936. gelatin silver print, 18½ x 13¼ (sight). Copyright © Eudora Welty, LLC; Eudora Welty Collection—Mississippi Department of Archives and History.

his impressionist portraits. He wrote, "Occasionally I am accused of flattering a sitter. Never have I consciously done so. Light itself can flatter. You pose a head so that light falls on it in a beautiful, entrancing way, on cheek, on nose, hair, on cool melting into warm, pink into green, on luminosity into shadow till what you see when you begin painting is not a person at all but the miracle of light." The University Press of Mississippi published Karl Wolfe's memoirs as *Mississippi Artist: A Self-Portrait.*

Portraits are one of the few genres of art usually instigated by a patron. As such they reflect the region's culture in many ways. Patrons have sought artists to create portraits for different reasons through the years: as symbols of money and power; as expressions of grief and memory; as subjective statements on the subject depicted; as humorous pieces, paeans of respect, or commentaries of ridicule. While portrait artists may work with a wide range of impulses, we can only admire Eudora Welty's response to her famous photograph *A woman of the 'thirties, Jackson* (1935–1936):

> When a heroic face like that of the woman in the buttoned sweater . . . looks back at me from her picture, what I respond to now, just as I did the first time, is not the Depression, not the Black, not the South, not even the perennially sorry state of the whole world, but the story of her life in her face. . . . Her face to me is full of meaning more truthful and more terrible and, I think, more noble than any generalization about people could have prepared me for or could describe for me now.

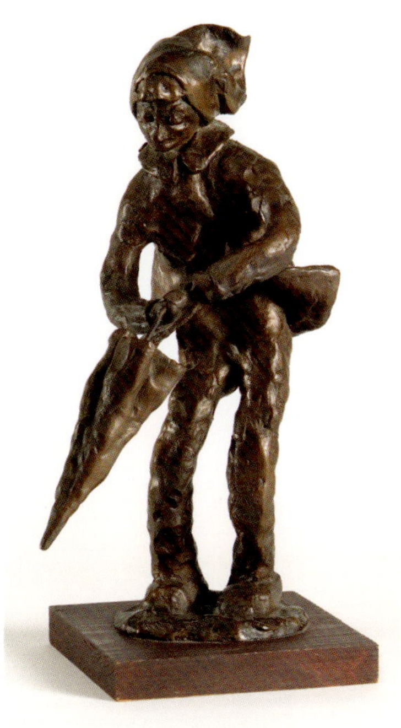

Jane Hollingsworth (1912–1986), *Showers with Winds Gusting Up to 40 M.P.H.*, 1973. bronze, 12¼ x 6¾ x 6.

The MMA collection includes a wide range of portraits, from formal oil portraits of the nineteenth century by Mississippi's first resident artist, Thomas Cantwell Healy, to the contemporary iconoclastic portraits of Lynn Green Root, from Marie Hull's oil portraits of white tenant farmers and black housekeepers to William Hollingsworth's intimate watercolor depictions of family, and from the flowing nude studies by Elizabeth Wolfe to William Steene's romantic *Tea Leaves.* Photographers have exulted in portraits: Eudora Welty, Maude Schuyler Clay, Jane Rule Burdine, Birney Imes, Eyd Kazery, Tom Rankin, Jack Kotz, Robert Hubbard, and Perry Walker. Sculptors, too, have made their cogent observations, as seen in the solid strength of Leon Koury's *The Compress Worker* and the palpable tension of Jane Hollingsworth's *Showers with Winds Gusting Up to 40 M.P.H.*

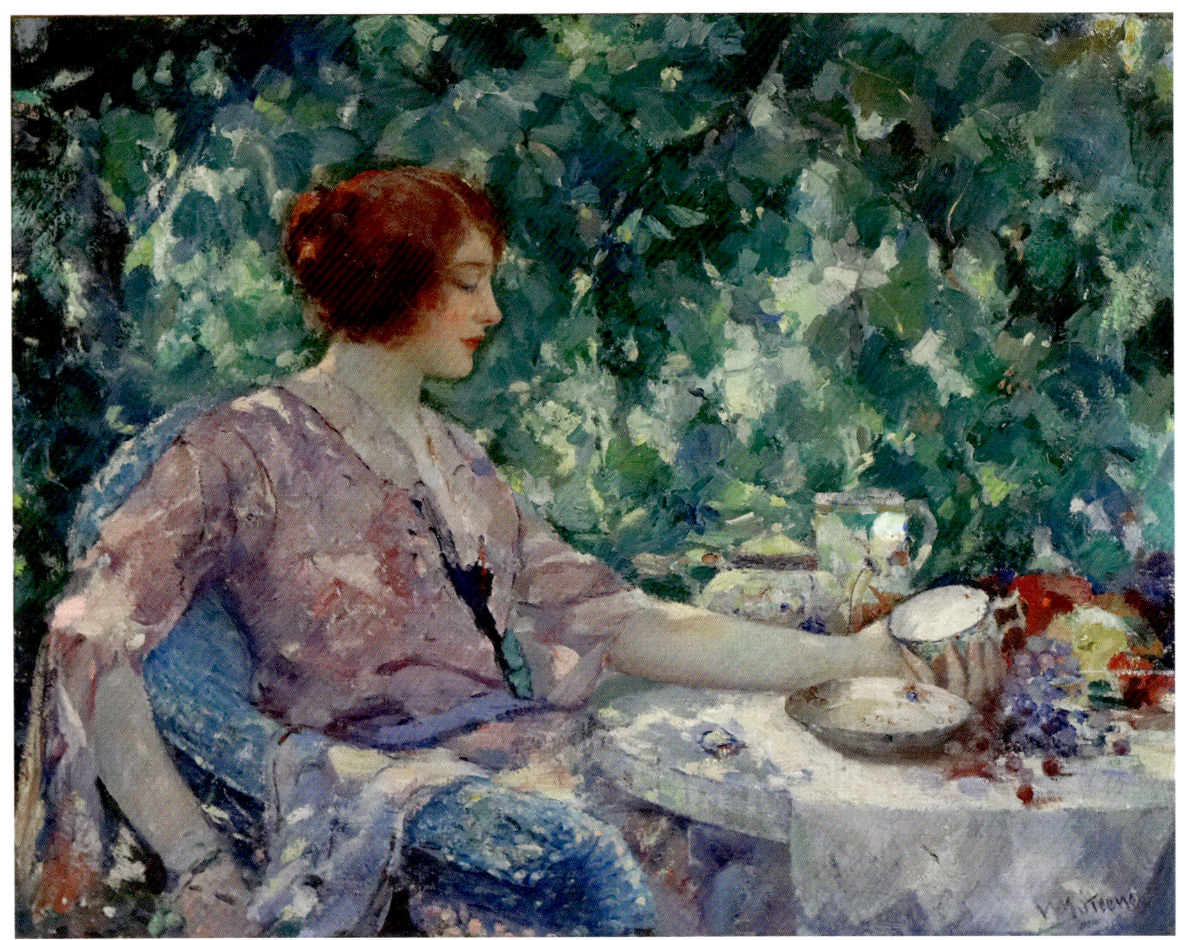

William Steene (1888-1965), *Tea Leaves*, no date. oil on canvas, 31½ x 39½ (sight).

William Steene (1888-1965), a native New Yorker, made his living as a painter in the South. He lived in New Orleans, Columbus, and for the last fourteen years of his life in Ocean Springs. He attended the National Academy of Design, the Art Students League of New York, and several Parisian art schools. *Tea Leaves*, a quintessentially southern portrait, was painted as a tribute to his study with William Merritt Chase and Kenyon Cox. The languor of the young woman, the lush dappled greenery, the wicker chair, the filmy robe, and the alfresco meal speak about climate, seasonal color, and the pace of life. Steene was a muralist as well as a portraitist. His traditional portrait work can be seen

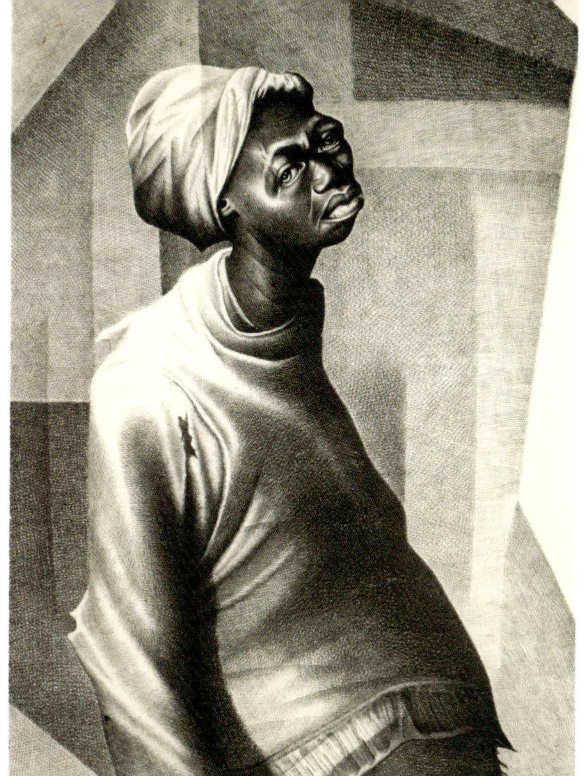

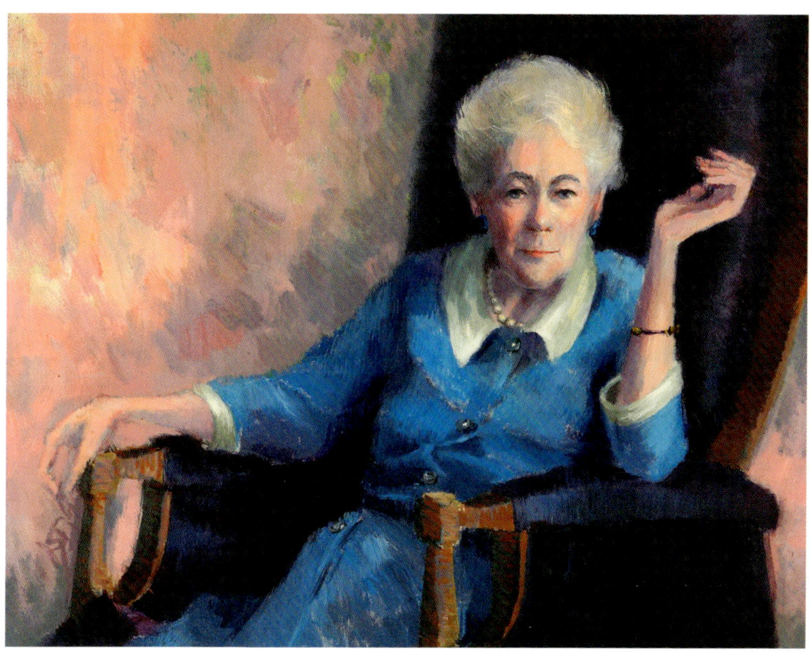

Thomas Eloby (1950–2001), no title, no date. photolithograph, 17½ x 12¾ (sight).

Myra Hamilton Green (1924-2002), *Portrait of Mrs. Joseph Blythe*, 1975. acrylic on canvas, 24 x 30¼.

at the Mississippi Hall of Fame in the Old Capitol and the Mississippi Hall of Governors in the New Capitol.

Thomas Eloby was born in Coahoma County in 1950. He studied at the Art Institute of Chicago, the University of Mississippi, and Mississippi Valley State University. The artist stated, "I feel that every black artist should say something about himself. A white artist cannot capture the black dignity to the fullest extent because he does not know the inner emotions of blacks, but those emotions are part of me. I am able, through my heritage and environment, to create a painting which depicts real life situations." His work, which is often created in large-scale ink or pencil, is powerful in its presentation and provocative in content.

Myra Hamilton Green (1924-2002) was born in Fayetteville, Tennessee, and moved to Jackson with her husband, Joshua Green, in 1949. She was educated at Virginia Intermont College, and after moving to Jackson she participated in the Allison's Wells Resort and Art Colony, the Mississippi Art Association, and the Art Students League in Woodstock. She was a pioneer in acrylics, introducing the medium to the South in 1961 through lectures sponsored by the Whitney Museum of American Art. She began giving private art lessons in Jackson in 1949, taught art to Jackson children under the auspices of the Junior League, and taught both at Belhaven and Millsaps colleges. She was primarily a portraitist but painted landscapes, horses, still lifes, and other subjects, experimenting in a variety of styles. She was the mother of artist Lynn Green Root.

Lynn Green Root (1954-2001), *Portrait of Johnny Langston*, 1981. mixed mediums on canvas, 40 x 30.

The signature elements in the work of Lynn Green Root (1954-2001) are kinetic lines and bold, assertive colors. She often squirted paint from the tube directly onto the canvas and used sparkles, neon colors, and painted frames. Many have classified her work as neo-expressionistic, while others have labeled it magic realism. Her work is, in a word, exuberant. Museum curator René Paul Barilleaux described her technique as having "this incredible quality of line. That is her strongest formal element, always strong line work." Gallery curator David Lambert noted, "She creates forms, moods, emotions, portrays action, all through continuous line . . . Sometimes it is as manic as anything could be; it takes your eye everywhere. You don't know where it stops or starts. Lynn is a standout consistently wonderful artist, based on her linear work. And, by the way, there is color!" Root's *Portrait of Johnny Langston* exemplifies her lively line work, bold color, unexpected quirkiness, and confidence. She exulted in the process itself.

Two nude figures included in the people section are by Marie Hull and Elizabeth "Bebe" Wolfe, daughter of Karl and Mildred Wolfe. Bebe Wolfe was born in 1949 in Jackson. She studied with her parents and at the Portland School of Art in Maine (now the Maine College of Art) and her work has been widely exhibited. Her untitled Conté sketch of a nude is characteristic of her economical and expressive line. Wolfe manages the Wolfe Studio and edited a

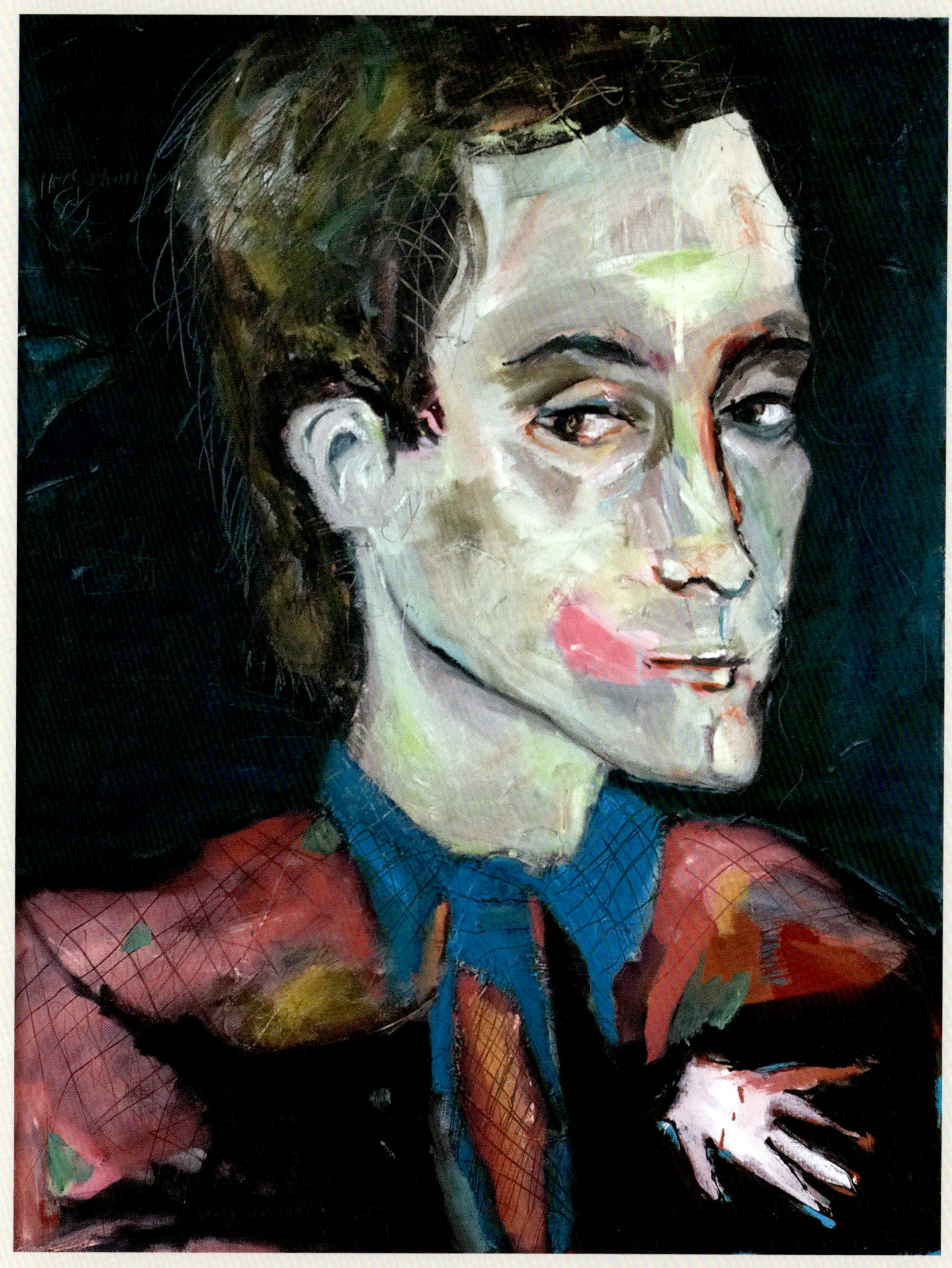

book about her mother titled *Mildred Nungester Wolfe*, published by the University Press of Mississippi in 2006.

Marshall Bouldin III of Clarksdale is the state's most distinguished portraitist working today. Born in 1923 in Dundee, Bouldin attended the Art Institute of Chicago before pursuing a career as an illustrator in Chicago, New York, and Westport, Connecticut. He returned to Clarksdale to manage his family's cotton plantation and to set up a painting studio. Upon his decision to become a professional portrait painter in 1956, he studied and mastered the techniques and philosophy of portraiture. He has created portraits for clients all over the nation, such as Richard Nixon, Jamie Whitten, General Louis Wilson, astronaut Ron McNair, and Governor William Winter. Bouldin is a member of the American Society of Portrait Artists and has exhibited by invitation with the Royal Society of British Artists. On view is his portrait of Sister Thea Bowman, a well-known and respected nun of the Mississippi Catholic Diocese who used song and dance in her ministry.

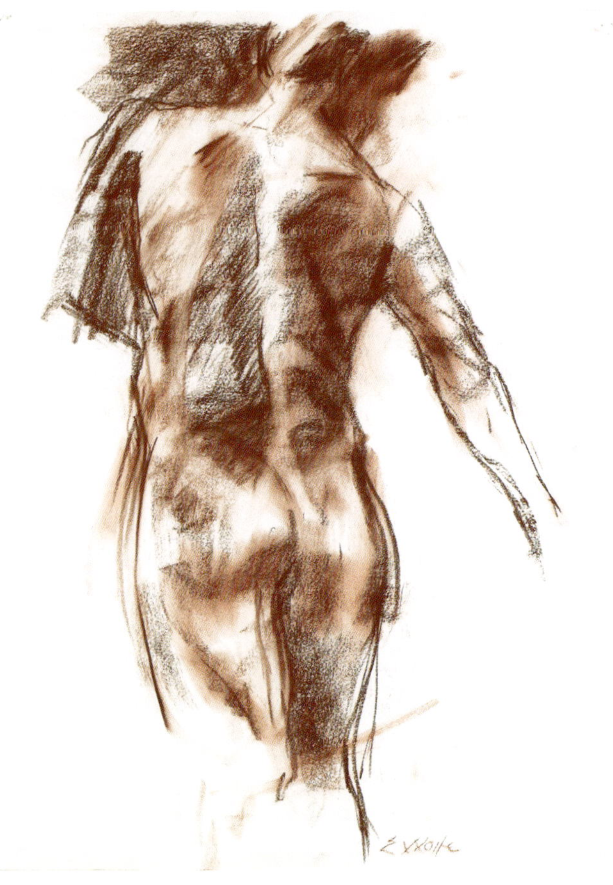

Elizabeth Wolfe (born 1949), no title, 1993. Conté crayon on paper, 20¾ x 15.

Jason Bouldin was born in Clarksdale in 1965. He attended the University of Mississippi and received his bachelor of fine arts in art history from Harvard University in 1989. After a two-year apprenticeship under his father, Marshall Bouldin III, Jason began his professional career as a portrait painter in 1991.

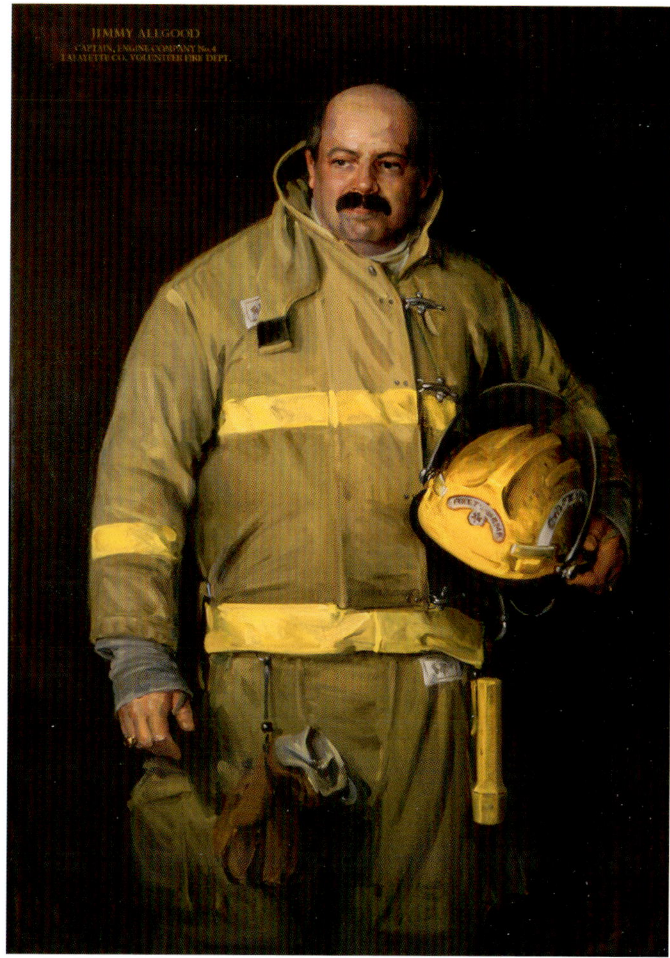

Jason Bouldin (born 1965), *Portrait of Captain Jimmy Allgood, Lafayette County Fire Department*, 2002. oil on canvas, 49½ x 33¾.

His work has been appeared in nine annual exhibitions at the prestigious Royal Society of Portrait Painters in London, England. On exhibit in *The Mississippi Story* is a portrait of Captain Jimmy Allgood, a heroic fire fighter from Oxford. The painting was awarded the Grand Prize in the Portrait Society of America's 2002 International Portrait Competition. Bouldin lives and paints in Oxford, Mississippi.

Mississippi: Depic

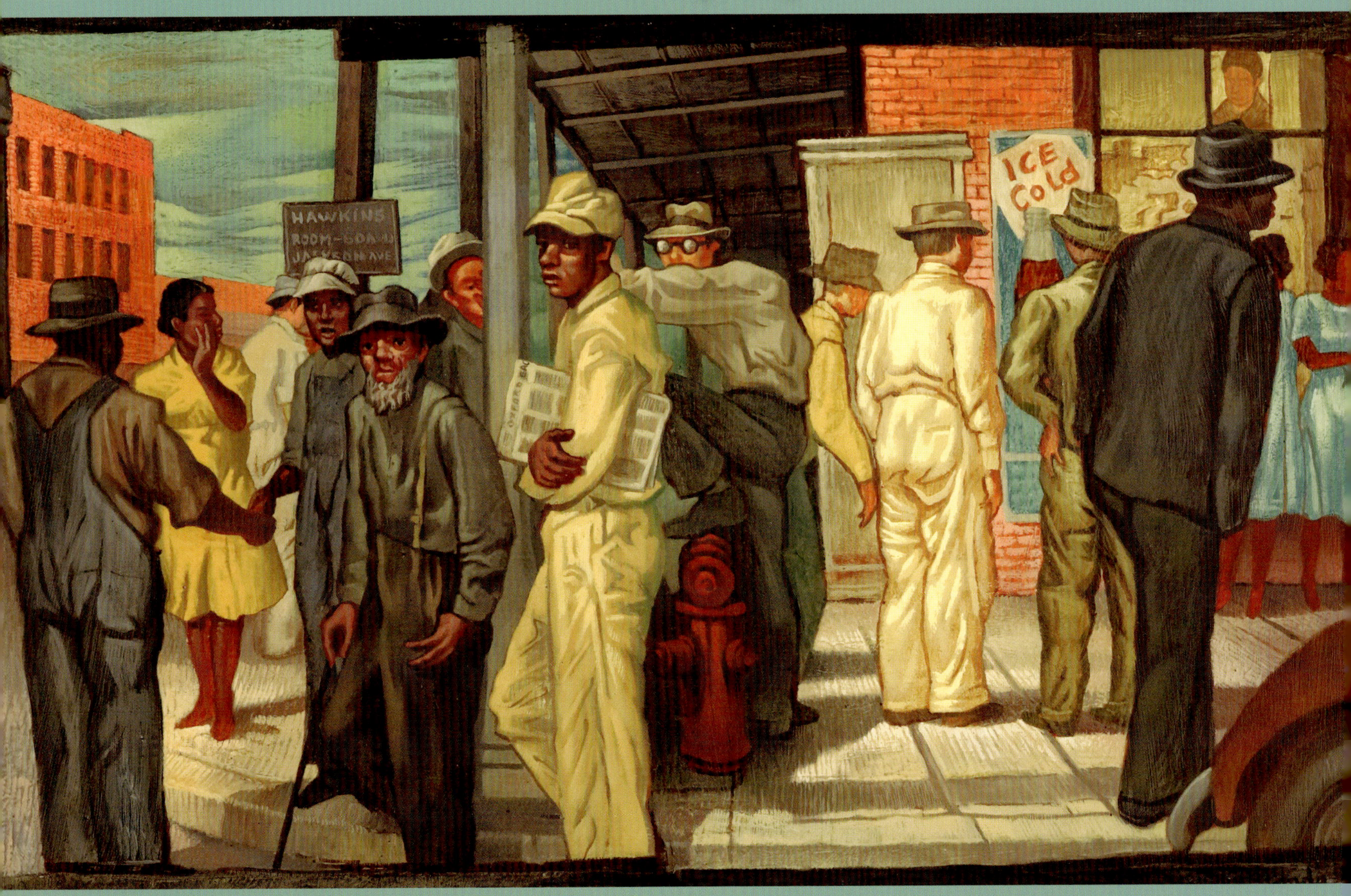

tions of Daily Life

At the heart of Mississippi's culture are the interests and activities that have engaged the people of the state. Genre painting, the traditional name given to artworks that depict scenes from everyday life, has exploded in meaning as artists through the years have adapted everyday subject matter to various styles and modes. Early genre paintings, scenes of rural and frontier life, were usually rendered in detailed realism. The concept of genre painting underwent a transformation after the French Impressionists appropriated genre and followers of the Ashcan School applied social commentary. In the development of visual arts styles and techniques, imagery from consumer culture was added to the mix. Today's genre ranges from abstraction to super realism, from impressionism to pop art.

In Mississippi, figurative artists, folk artists, and photographers have been the most evocative chroniclers of Mississippi daily life. They are also the ones most concerned with the narrative content of their art, telling Mississippi's stories of family life, small-town life, work days, sports, leisure and outdoor activities, political and racial concerns and, frequently, religious life.

< John McCrady (1911-1968), *Rural Symposium*, 1964. acrylic on board, 20 x 31.

Figurative art gives much more cultural information than portraits, since the figures are generally engaged in some sort of activity, a reflection of the American representational tradition of a Winslow Homer or Eastman Johnson. The earliest figurative work on view is Ethel Pennewill Brown Leach's watercolor *Totin' Clothes, Mississippi, Oct. 1916.* Leach (1878-1960) was a native of Delaware who visited her Mississippi relatives (the Virden, Hamilton, and Wilkinson families) of Jackson and made this painting on one of her trips. She studied with John Henry Twachtman and Howard Pyle and worked primarily in the Delaware-Philadelphia area. She was known for her figurative work, landscapes, and illustrations in well-known magazines such as *Colliers, Harper's,* and *Harper's Bazaar.* She also illustrated children's books. The Delaware History Museum held a retrospective exhibition of her work in 1999.

The 1930s were rich in genre work in Mississippi and aided by the federal government's art programs during the Depression era, which encouraged artists to use local and regional themes and styles to celebrate America, the country's history, and American ideals. Two of Mississippi's most successful figurative painters from that period were John McCrady and William Hollingsworth, whose work focused on the black and white cultures in Mississippi. Both produced memorable paintings of scenes from daily life.

John McCrady (1911-1968) was Mississippi's leading exponent of American scene painting. A Philadelphia critic wrote that McCrady "carries the local scene to its utmost possibilities. He does for the South what John Steuart Curry and Grant Wood are doing for the Middle West." The Museum collection includes *Rural Symposium,* a 1964 acrylic painting that is a masterful study of small-town Mississippi, where blacks and whites alike congregated, usually on Saturdays, to exchange news of weather, crops, and other local affairs. McCrady was born in Canton and lived in Greenwood and then Oxford after his father was named dean of philosophy at the University of Mississippi. He attended the New Orleans Art School and the Art Students League of New York. In 1937 *Time* magazine singled him out as "a star risen from the bayous whose

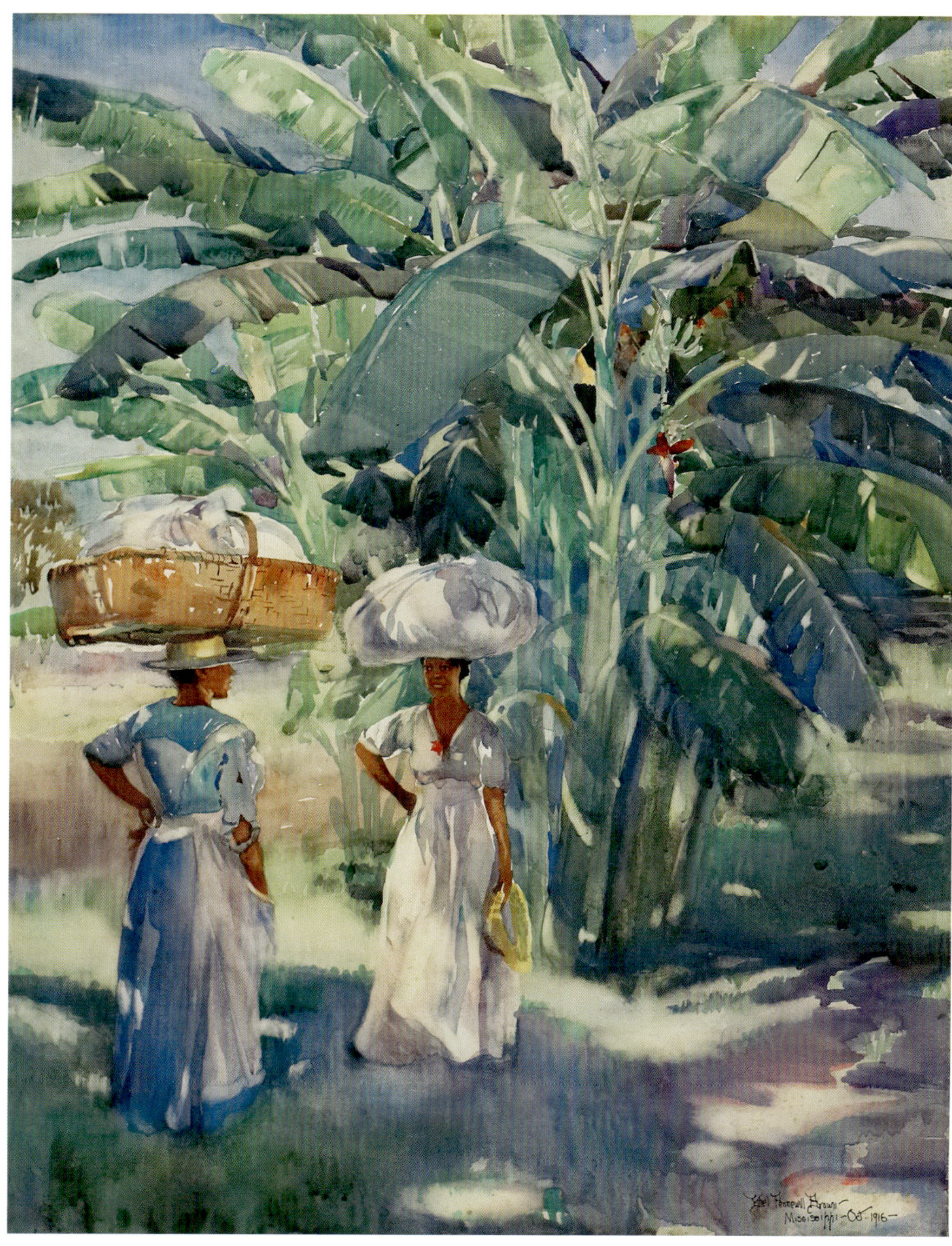

Ethel Pennewill Brown Leach (1878-1960), *Totin' Clothes, Mississippi, Oct. 1916*, 1916. watercolor on paper, 26 x 20.

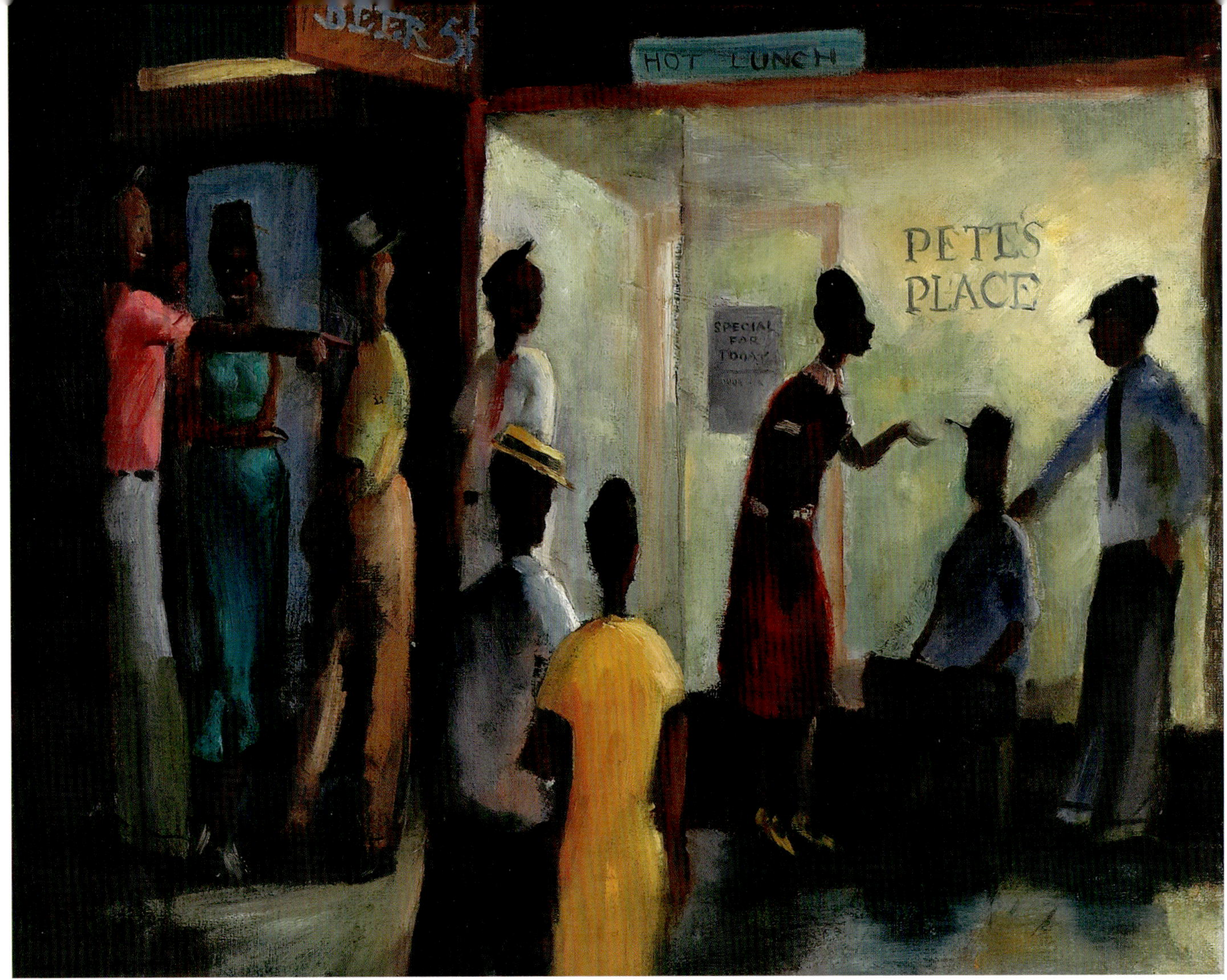

William Hollingsworth (1910-1944), *Black and White*, no date. oil on fabric, 24 x 28.

work would do for southern art what Faulkner was doing for southern literature." After World War II, however, the social and art climate of the nation shifted. Art styles raced toward abstract expressionism, and McCrady's use of black culture as subject matter became to some "racial chauvinism." McCrady pursued his art career in New Orleans and established with his wife the John McCrady School of Art, which lasted from 1942 to 1983 and was influential in the training of many southern artists.

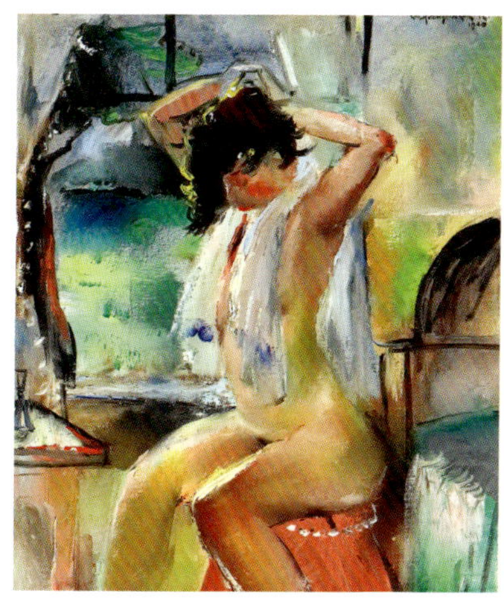

William Hollingsworth (1910-1944), *Wet Hair*, 1940. oil on canvas, 24 x 20.

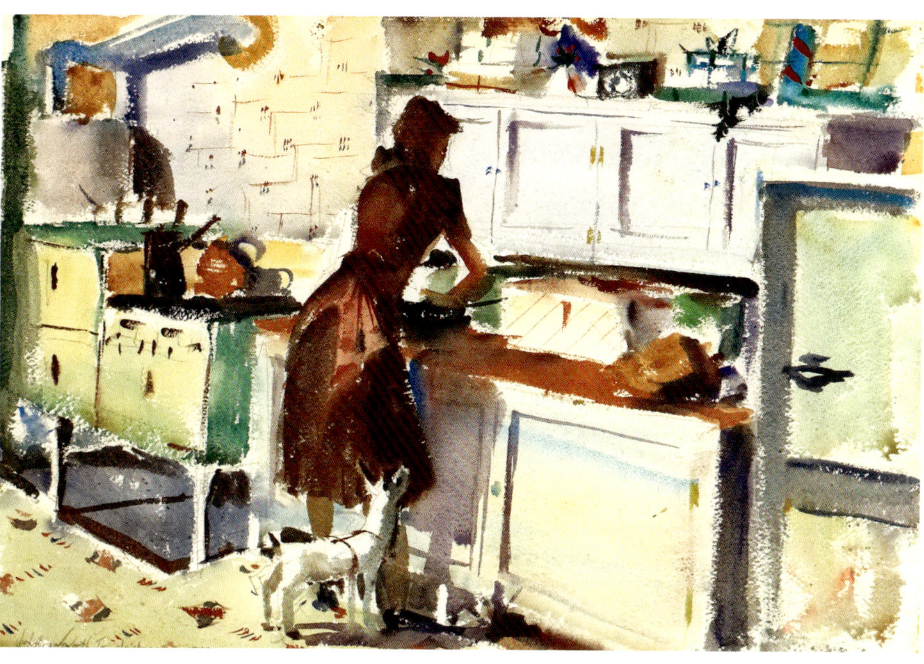

William Hollingsworth (1910-1944), *Christmas Eve*, 1942. watercolor on paper, 15⅝ x 22½.

In his brief ten-year career, William Hollingsworth produced canvas after canvas of life events in his own family, the Negro quarters of Jackson, and the larger community. Masterful in all mediums, he switched effortlessly from watercolors to oils to lithographs and pencil sketching. Outstanding among his fluid and bright genre watercolors are *Christmas Eve*, *Family at Mealtime*, *Wet Hair*, *Billy and Boy*, and *Black and White*.

Mildred Nungester Wolfe is one of Mississippi's most versatile artists. She is active in oil painting, watercolors, woodcuts, sculpture, stained glass, and ceramics. In a recent book on her life and career, Ellen Douglas wrote of Wolfe's "passionate connection with and precise evocation of the natural world." Born in 1912 in Alabama, she attended Athens College and received her bachelor of arts degree from Alabama College. Wolfe studied at the Art Institute of Chicago, Colorado Springs Fine Arts College, and the Art Students League of New York. She met Karl Wolfe at the Dixie Art Colony at Alabama

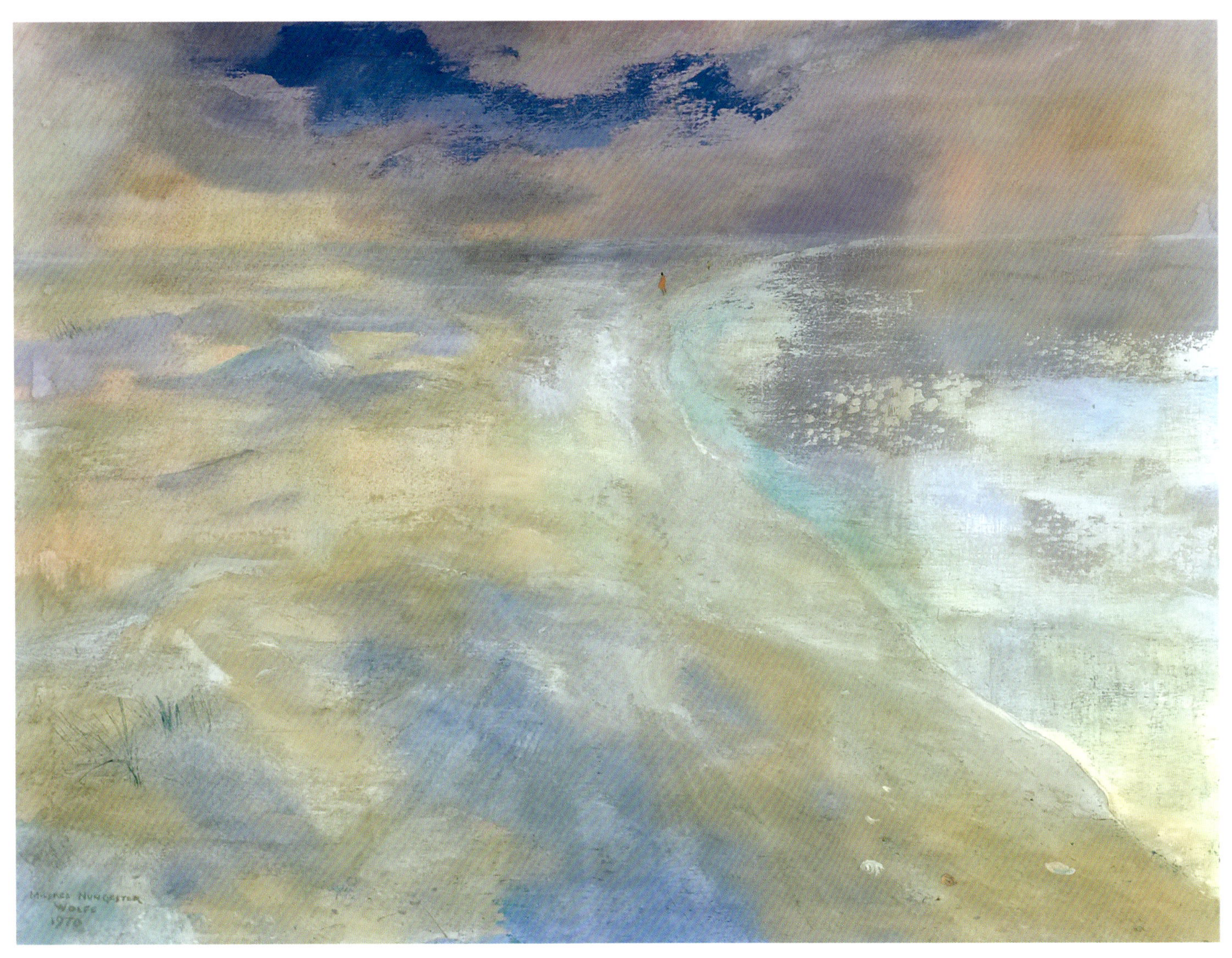

Mildred Nungester Wolfe (born 1912), *Sand, Sea and Sky*, 1970. oil on canvas, 27¼ x 35.

in 1937 and moved to Jackson after marrying in 1944. She has been an integral part of Jackson's art world since 1949, when she won first place in the National Watercolor Show. The National Portrait Gallery acquired her portrait of Eudora Welty in 1988. She has been a teacher, frequent exhibitor, and constant chronicler of her adopted state, painting or producing artworks from all over Mississippi. Many of her works capture her fascination with light and reflect a lucidity of perception and a delicate, poetic focus.

Sandy McNeal, who paints under the name of P. Sanders McNeal, is represented in the exhibition by *The Rehearsal*, a salute to Mississippi's musicians commissioned for Jackson's 2002 Jubilee!JAM. McNeal was born in Greenwood in 1949 and graduated from Mississippi University for Women. She moved to Jackson in 1962 and has become a vital member of the city's art community. She has studied art extensively in New York, France, Italy, and

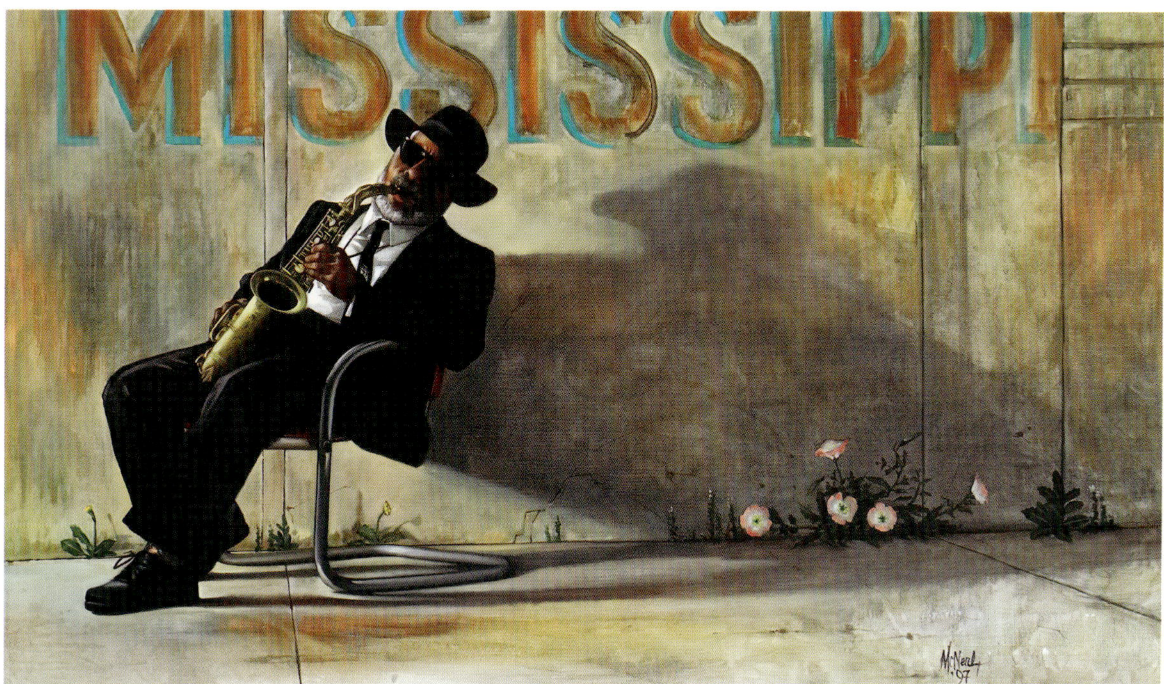

P. Sanders McNeal (born 1949), *The Rehearsal*, 1997. oil on canvas, 36 x 60.

Ireland, honing her skills in classical realism. McNeal is versatile in portraits, still life, and landscapes, which include scenes from all sections of the state. Her work has been included in numerous exhibitions throughout the United States, as well as in France and Ireland. She was commissioned to paint a mural for Union Station in Jackson in 2002, and in 2004 she accepted a commission for a painting commemorating the sixtieth anniversary of the Jackson Symphony Orchestra. McNeal was also selected as the official artist for the 2006 U.S. International Ballet Competition in Jackson. In 1999 she received the Governor's Award for Excellence in Visual Arts and the Mississippi University for Women's Alumnae Achievement Award in 2005.

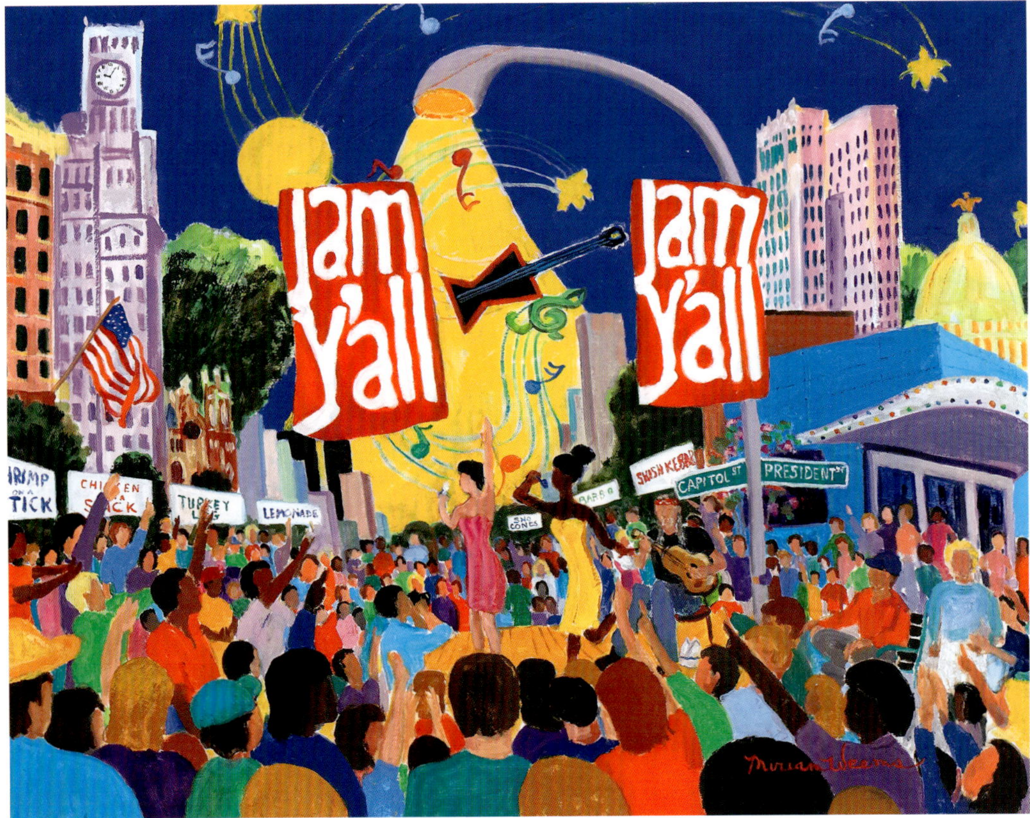

Miriam Weems (born 1941), *Stars Under the Stars*, 2001. oil on canvas, 48 x 60.

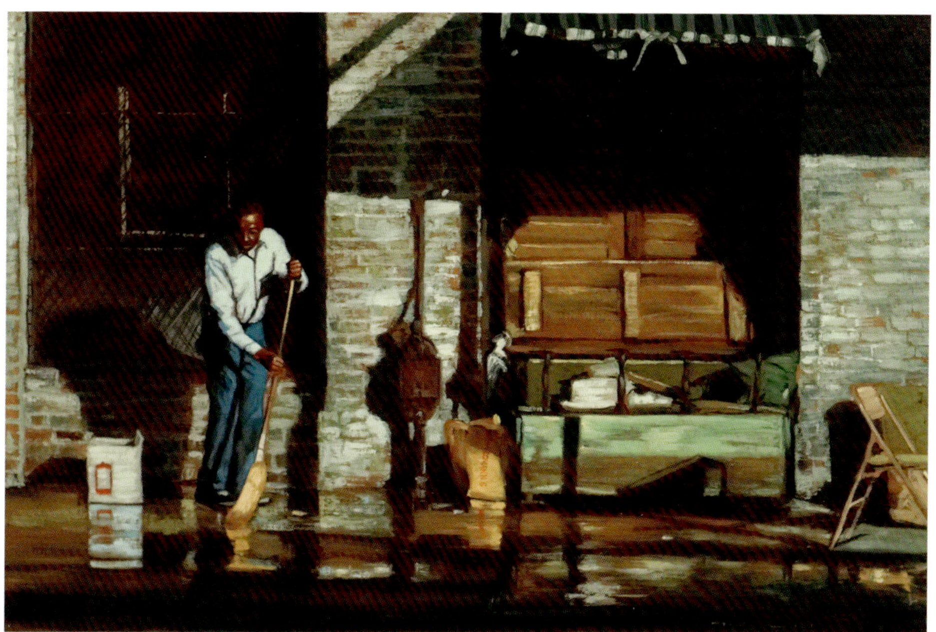

Alan Flattmann (born 1946), *Morning Light*, 1973. oil on canvas, 30 x 44.

Miriam Weems of Jackson was born in 1941 in Greenwood and grew up in Jackson. She received her B.A. and B.F.A. from the University of Mississippi, as well as a degree from the New York School of Design. Weems is noted for her generosity in making her paintings available for benefit auctions and fund raisers for the nonprofit community. She paints local scenes, both interiors and exteriors, in bright, often primary colors, using brush or palette knife to lay on her color in a bold impressionistic style. On exhibit is *Stars Under the Stars*, which was chosen for the 2001 Jubilee!JAM. Weems's intention was "to capture the jubilation part of the Jam, the excitement that it brings to downtown."

Alan Flattmann and Rolland Golden, both Louisiana artists, have created numerous canvases of Mississippi genre and landscape. Not coincidentally, both studied at the John McCrady School of Art. Flattmann, who served on the faculty there from 1967 to 1982, has lived in Laurel and Perkinston and now resides in Madisonville, Louisiana. He paints in watercolor and oil but is best

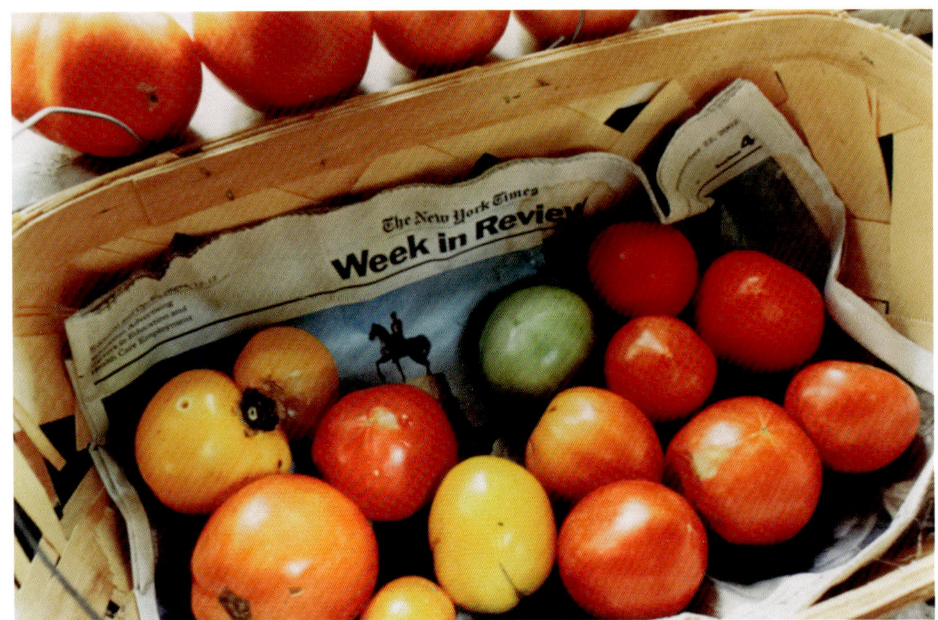

Langdon Clay
(born 1949),
tomato horse, 2002.
chromogenic color
print, 16 x 20.

known for his large-scale pastels. Seen in *The Mississippi Story* is Flattmann's genre painting *Morning Light.* He is the author of a popular book titled *The Art of Pastel* and the subject of *The Poetic Realism of Alan Flattmann* (1980). Rolland Golden, now a resident of Folsum, Louisiana, has painted extensively in Mississippi and is represented in this exhibition by *Delta Bleak.* He published examples of his work in *The Journeys of a Southern Artist.*

Still life remains one of the most popular subjects in Mississippi art and is included in the genre section. Subject matter ranges from the small objects of Glennray Tutor to some floral arrangements by Mississippi artists, who have also used fruit, vegetables, glassware, pottery, and cotton bolls. On view are the gouache on paper *Flowers and Fruit* (1986) by Emmitt Thames of Gulfport, *Still Life with Shallots* (no date) in oil by Ken Marlow of Jackson and New York, the photograph *tomato horse* (2002) by Langdon Clay of Sumner, and the oil painting *Nasturtiums* (no date) by Jessie Duncan Savage Cole of Pass Christian. Thames was born in Brookhaven in 1933 and later lived in Gulfport.

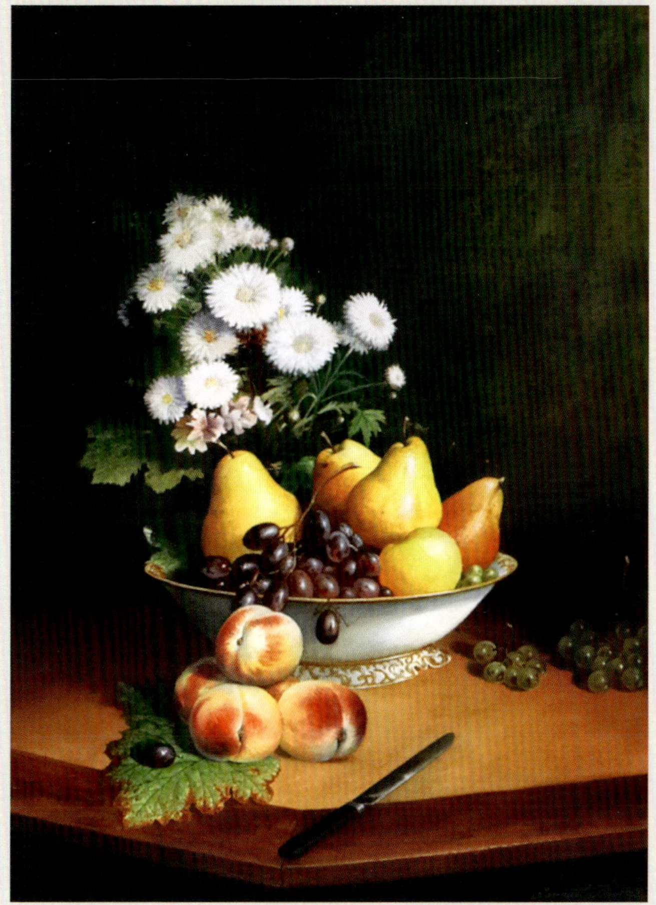

Emmitt Thames
(born 1933), *Flowers and Fruit*, 1986. gouache on paper, 20 x 14 (sight).

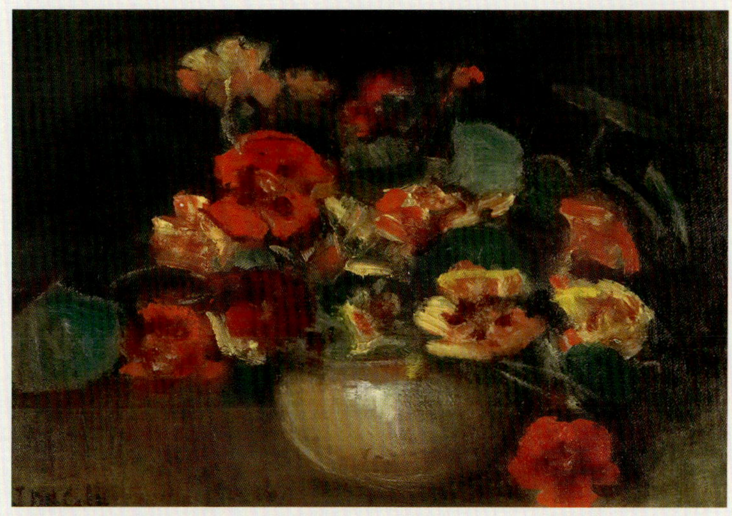

Jessie Duncan Savage Cole
(1858-1940), *Nasturtiums*, no date. oil on canvas, 10 x 14.

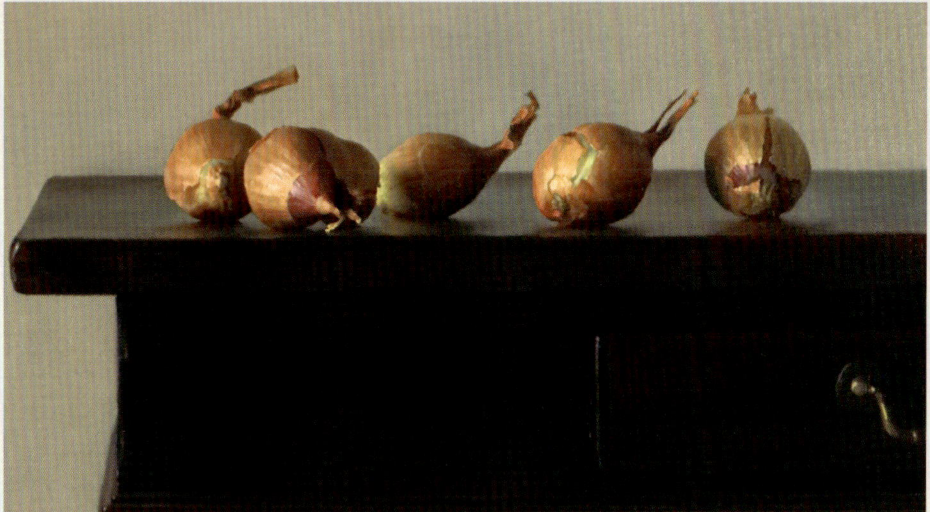

< Ken Marlow
(born 1960), *Still Life with Shallots*, no date. oil on canvas, 9 x 15¾.

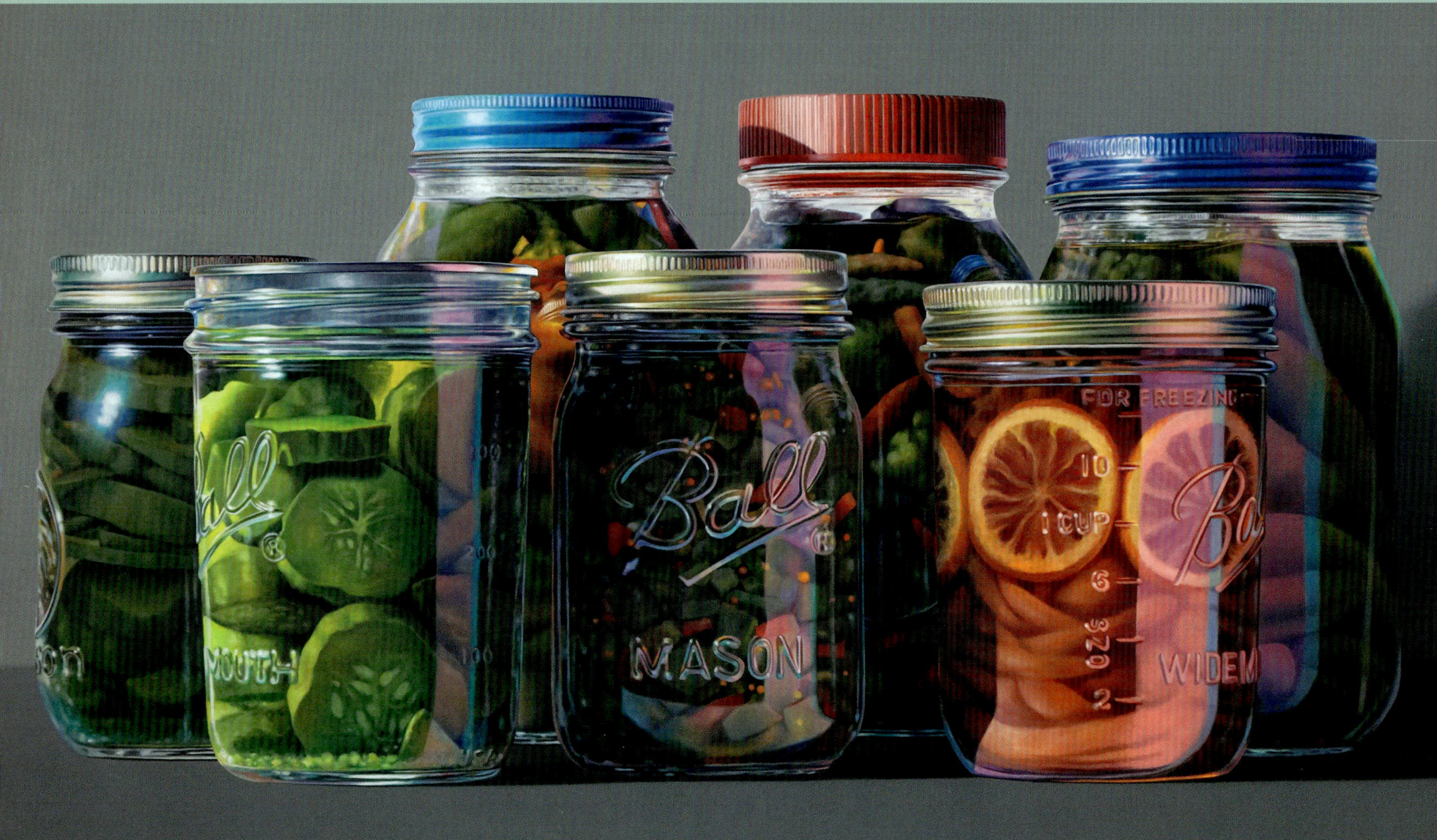

Glennray Tutor
(born 1950), *Still Life: A Season of Moment*, 2003.
oil on linen canvas,
50 x 84.

He is a self-taught artist and worked at Keesler Air Force Base as a technical illustrator. Ken Marlow, a native of Texas, won the 1986 award from the Mississippi Institute of Arts and Letters. Jessie Savage Cole (1858-1940) was born and raised in Pass Christian but spent her adult life in New York and Massachusetts.

The hyperrealism of Oxford's Glennray Tutor goes one step further than genre. His subject matter is not the events but the material objects of daily life. His paintings of canned vegetables, jars, cups, and other commonplace items are infused with light and rendered in precise detail. Barry Hannah described Tutor's paintings as "like life after a glaucoma operation. Only he [Tutor] could grab the color and the light and the spirit of life out of the stream of the usual." A native of Missouri and born in 1950, Tutor received his bachelor of arts and master of fine arts degrees from the University of Mississippi. He has lived in Oxford for the last four decades. Tutor's work can be seen as a contemporary riff on the still life tradition of seventeenth-century Dutch painters. He is represented in the collections of the Morris Museum of Art in Georgia, International Monetary Fund, University of Mississippi, and innumerable corporate collections.

The use of interior spaces in Charles Carraway's *Nina's Room* and Lynn Green Root's *Happy's Room* provides an interesting contrast. Carraway is concerned with the formal elements of line, color, depth, and light rather than narrative, but his architectural approach somehow triggers the imagination, much as Edward Hopper's lone figures do. *Nina's Room* is light-filled but as mysterious as a dark cave. Life within the door is implied but the viewer confronted with an empty space must fill in the narrative. By comparison, Lynn Green Root's *Happy's Room* vibrates with explicit life. A dog pants happily on the sofa, a book awaits its reader on the chair, art pieces cover the walls, and the room is awash with textures and colors. Carraway is a native of Terry and a 1979 graduate of Delta State University. He studied architecture and design

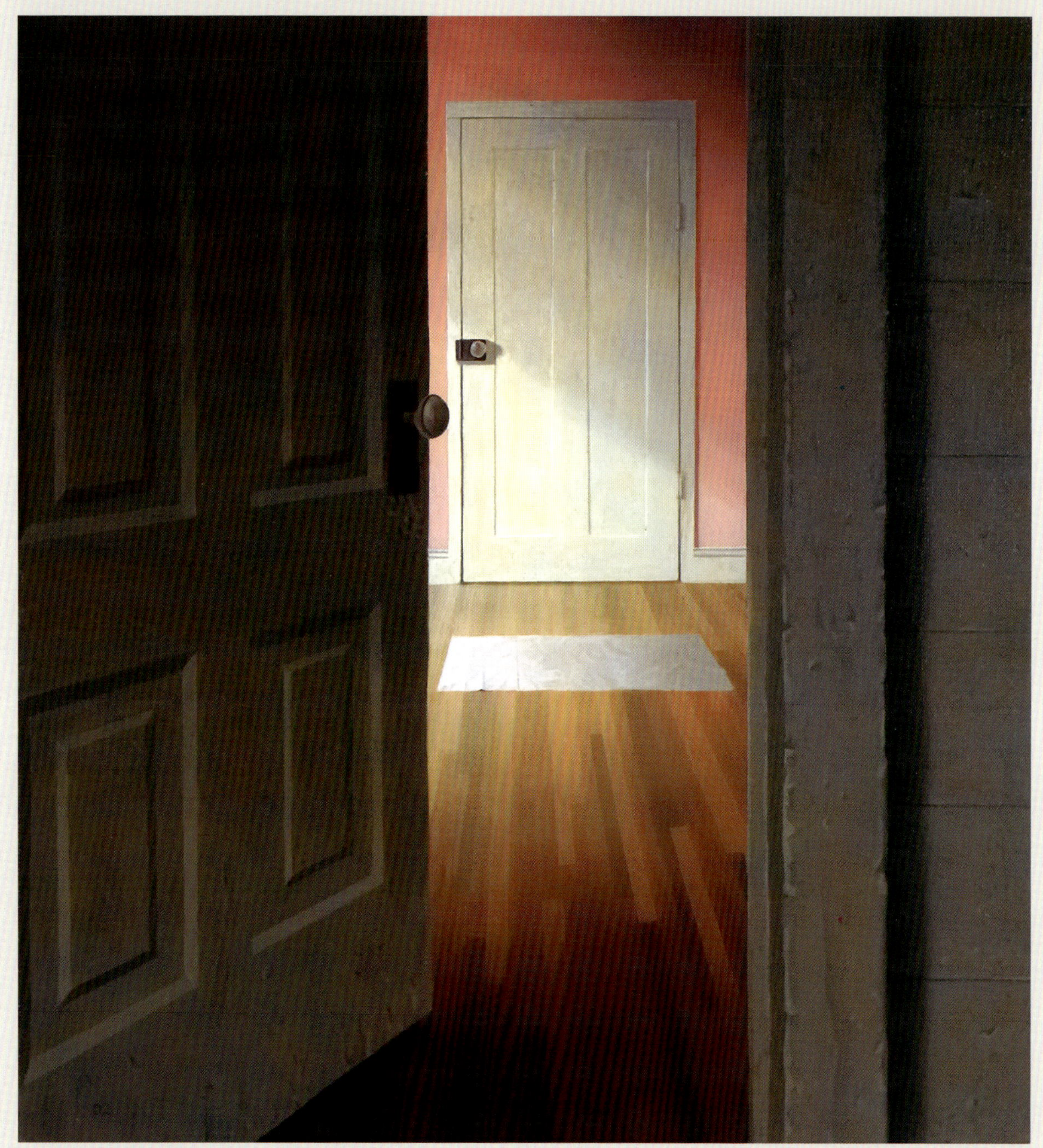

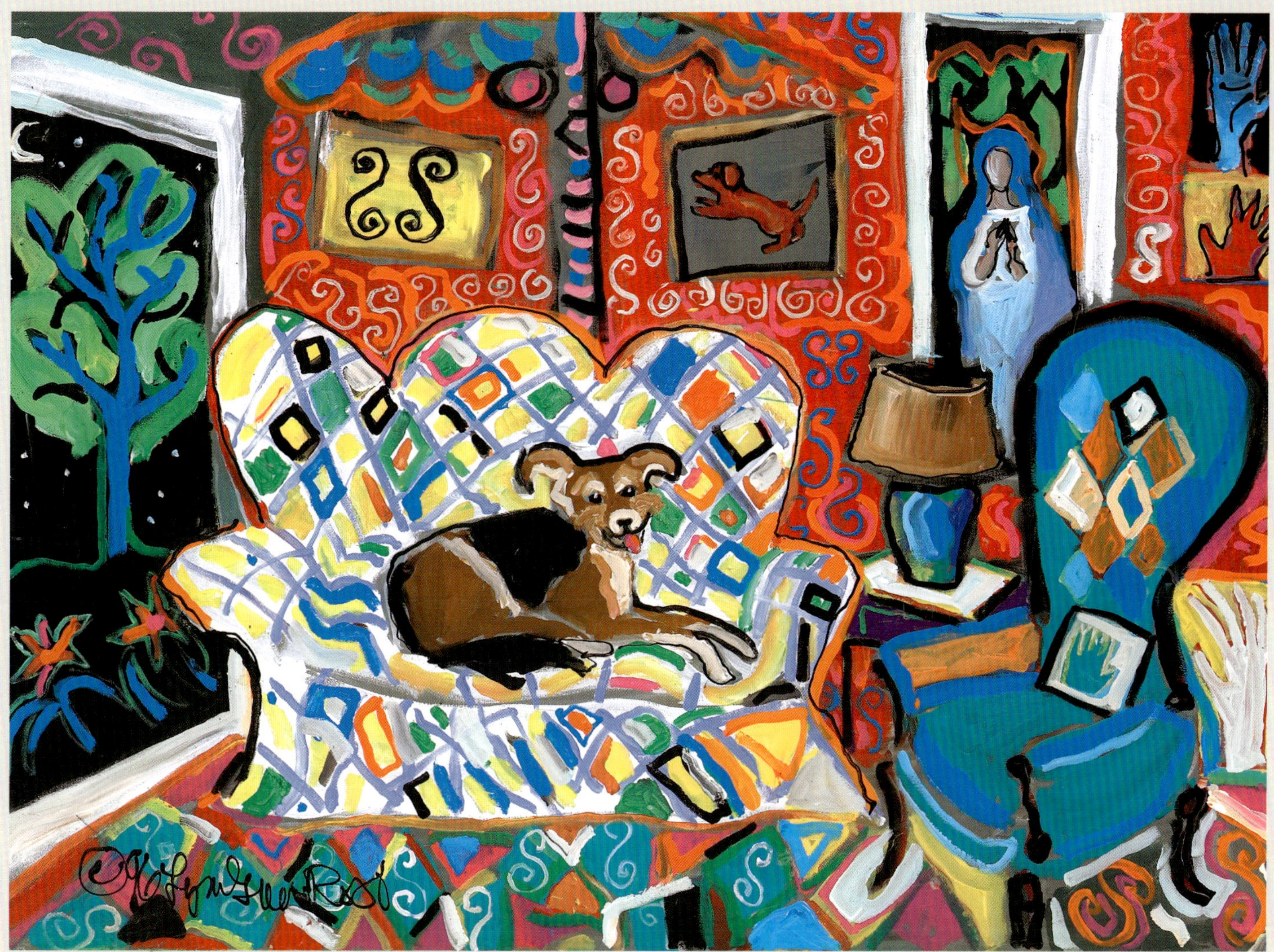

< **Charles Carraway** (born 1957), *Nina's Room*, 2002. oil on linen 27¼ x 24.

Lynn Green Root (1954-2001), *Happy's Room*, 1996. acrylic on canvas, 29⅞ x 40.

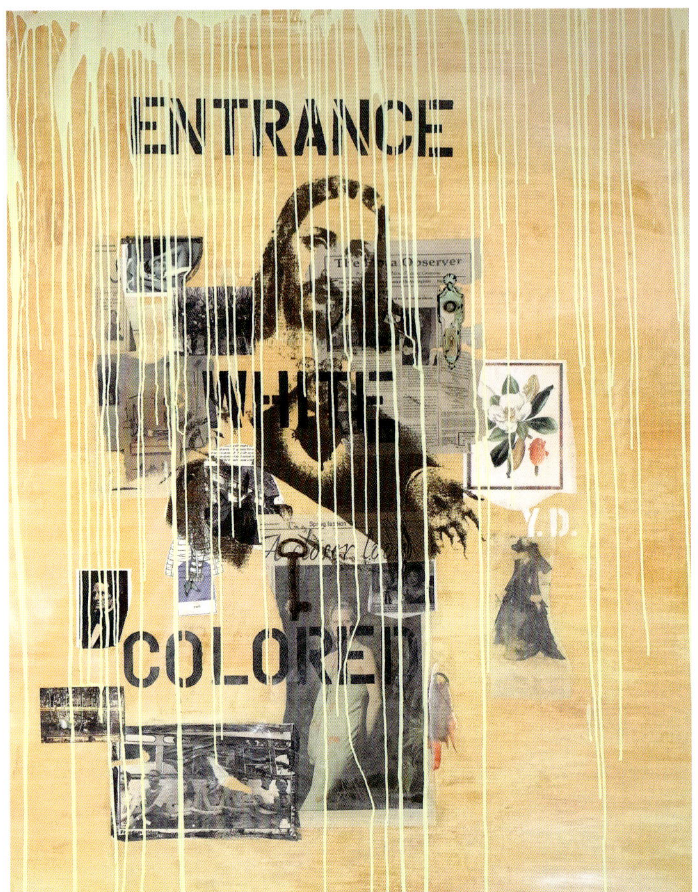

Lea Barton (born 1956), *Yellow Dog*, 1999. mixed mediums on canvas with found objects, 64 x 49.

in Rome under a program sponsored by Louisiana Tech University. In 1983 he received a master of fine arts degree in painting from the Rhode Island School of Design. Carraway currently lives and works in Jackson and teaches art at Jackson State University.

Lea Barton of Flora is one of a handful of Mississippi artists who tackles social issues in her work. Born in Yazoo City in 1956, Barton earned her bachelor of arts degree from Millsaps College and a master of fine arts degree from Pratt Institute in New York. In her painting, printmaking, and photography she is experimental and inventive, finding new ways to explore her milieu. She has called herself a "visual storyteller" and accomplishes this task on complex canvases layered with paint, photographic prints, collaged fabrics and papers, and sometimes three-dimensional objects. She has looked at religion, politics, women's history, black history, and traditions of thought and action in Mississippi culture. On exhibit is *Yellow Dog*, which incorporates many of the signature elements of her work—the multilayered surfaces and the visual allusions to cultural icons with provocative juxtapositions. Her work is in the collections of the Library of Congress, National Civil Rights Museum, National Museum of Women in the Arts, New Orleans Museum of Art, Ogden Museum of Southern Art, Portland Art Museum in Oregon, and many corporate collections.

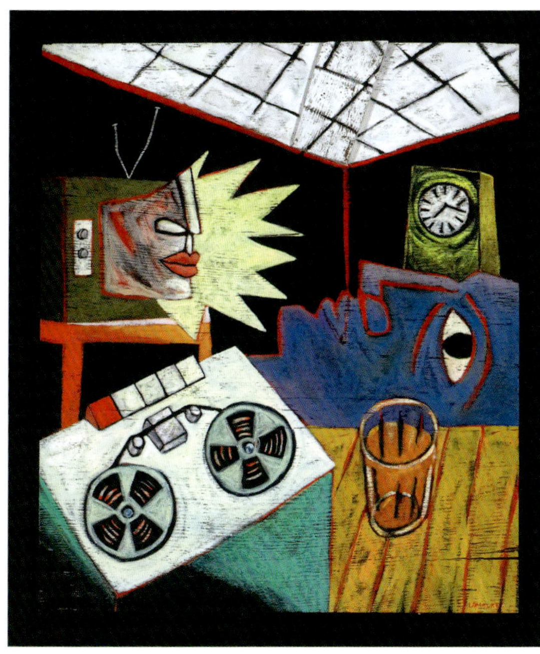

David Lambert (born 1961), *Dating Service*, 1998. acrylic on plywood, 34 x 28¾.

David Lambert's art is an excellent example of how far genre has come. His subject matter, representation, style, and techniques are resoundingly contemporary. *Dating Service* depicts a present-day social phenomenon—a man mechanically selecting an object to desire. The angularity, skewed perspective, and surprising colors of the canvas are unsettling. A blaring television, an empty glass, a wide-eyed but somber man, and a tape recorder that suggests the disembodied voice or description of his potential date add to the viewer's discomfort. It could be a stringent commentary on the malaise of contemporary life, or it could be a sardonic look at relationships. In any case, Lambert's work is always provocative and visually stimulating. Lambert was born in 1961, moved to Mississippi in 1976, and has made Jackson his home since 1986. He received his B.A. from Delta State University and an M.F.A. from the University of Mississippi. He is the manager of Bryant Galleries in Jackson.

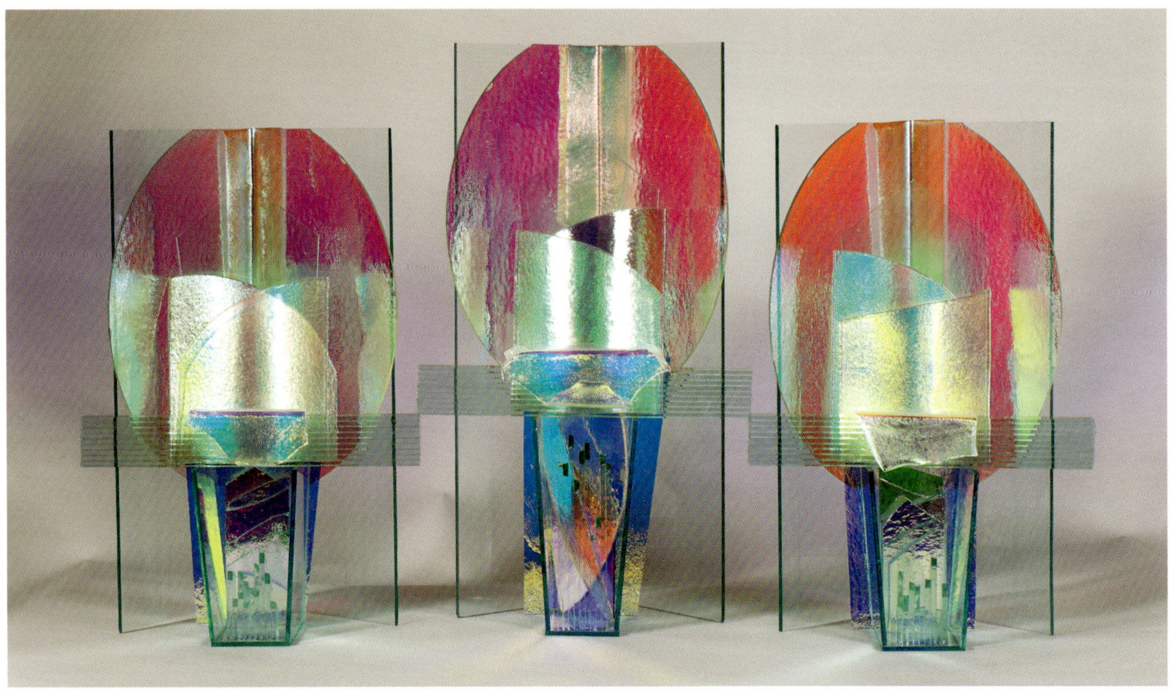

Elizabeth Robinson (born 1954), no title, 2002. glass, 28 x 44 x 12.

Several objects from the Museum's sculpture collection are on display throughout the daily life area. Glass artist Elizabeth Robinson of Jackson is represented by an untitled nonobjective piece, a virtuosic display of her sense of color interaction, balance, and control of her materials. She incorporates into her sculptures the interplay of light, whether natural or devised, making subtle change intrinsic in her pieces. Robinson was born in Louisville in 1954 and is a graduate of Mississippi University for Women. She apprenticed at Pearl River Glass Studio and worked there fifteen years before moving to her own studio. Her work is widely held in private collections.

William Norwood Beckwith (born 1952) and Obie Clark (born 1948) are part of the Taylor, Mississippi, artists community, led by the mayor and photographer Jane Rule Burdine. Originally from Greenville, Beckwith received his bachelor of fine arts and master of fine arts degrees from the University of

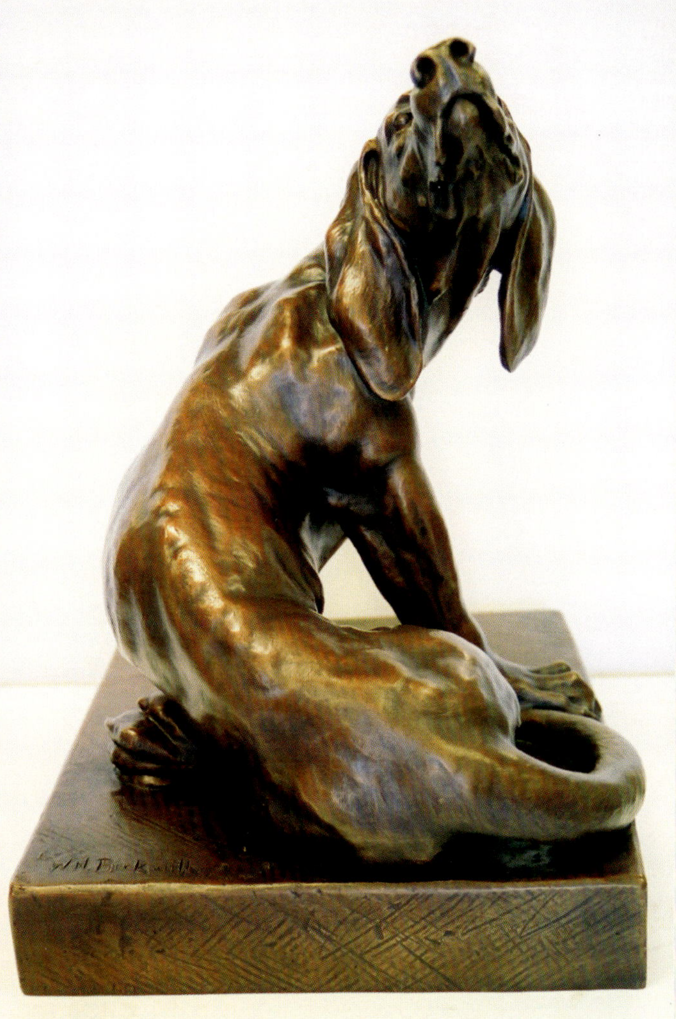

William Beckwith
(born 1952), *Houn'dog*,
2007. bronze,
20 x 17 x 13¾.
Photograph courtesy
of the artist.

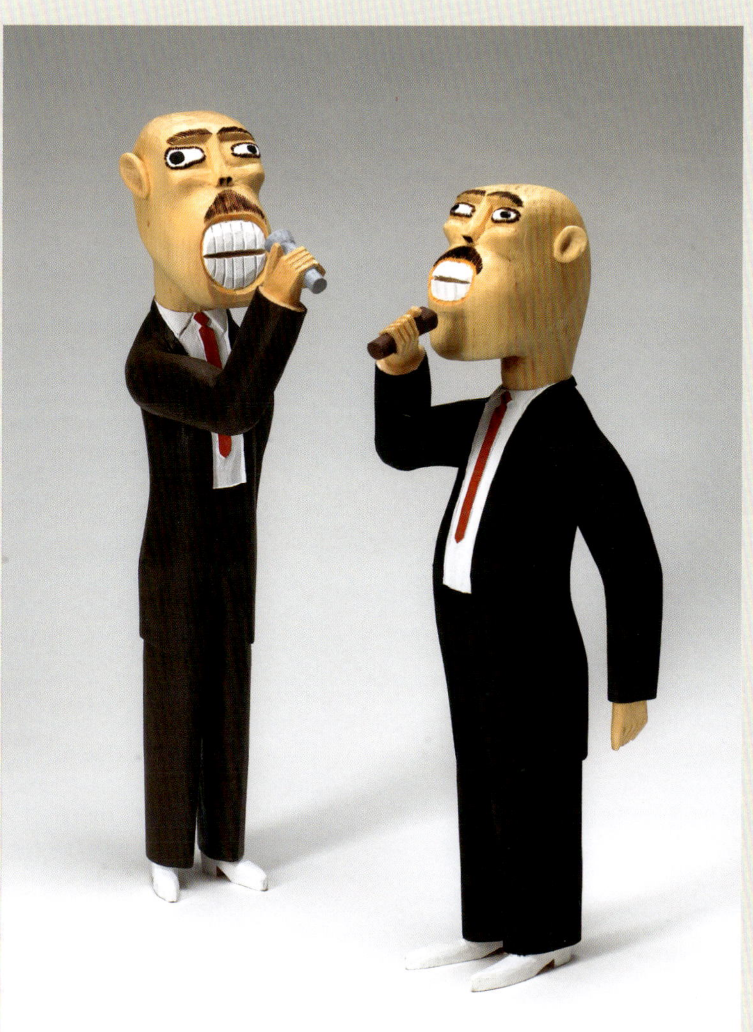

Sulton Rogers
(born 1922), Two Blues
Singers, 1989. paint on
wood. 17 x 4 x 8;
16 x 4 x 7.

Mississippi, where he is currently an adjunct professor. His works include the statue of William Faulkner on the Square in Oxford, Jefferson Davis at Beauvoir Jefferson Davis Home and Presidential Library in Biloxi, and the 11th Mississippi Infantry Monument on the Gettysburg battlefield in Pennsylvania. On display is his iconic hound dog in bronze. Artist Bill Dunlap has said that this breed is the perfect symbol for the South, "ubiquitous, obedient, intelligent, loyal, devoted, dilatory, lazy, noble, faithful, libido-driven, sly, sneaky, benign, slobbering, dangerous, mangy, flea-bitten, rabies-carrying, chicken-killing, car-chasing, egg-sucking, Southern Dog." Beckwith's *Houn'dog* is a triumph.

In Leland, musician James "Son" Thomas (1926-1993) spent years shaping local clay into familiar objects of his life. He spread putty or shoe wax over the surface to give the sculpture strength, added found materials like marbles, matches, cotton, and foil, and let his creations bake in the sun. He was best known for his skulls with corn teeth, but he also created busts of friends and neighbors, animal shapes, and other everyday objects. He usually painted his work using bright colors, after they had hardened. *Guitar Player*, which is probably a self-portrait, is on view in the exhibition.

Among the most imaginative and far-ranging dimensional imagery is that produced by woodcarver Sulton Rogers. Born in Oxford in 1922, Rogers returned there in 1986 after retiring from a carpentry career in Syracuse, New York. Rogers carves portraits of friends along with those of anonymous politicians, blues singers, vampires, voluptuous women, fanciful animals, and human bodies with dog heads. His work is witty, wry, and perspicacious, loaded with both social commentary and playfulness. On exhibit is a pair of blues singers.

The Museum's photography collection, while not all-inclusive of the state's excellent photographers, presents a remarkable evocation of the life and landscape in Mississippi—a valuable body of work that captures many moods, celebrations, people, and communities. Included in *The Mississippi Story* are

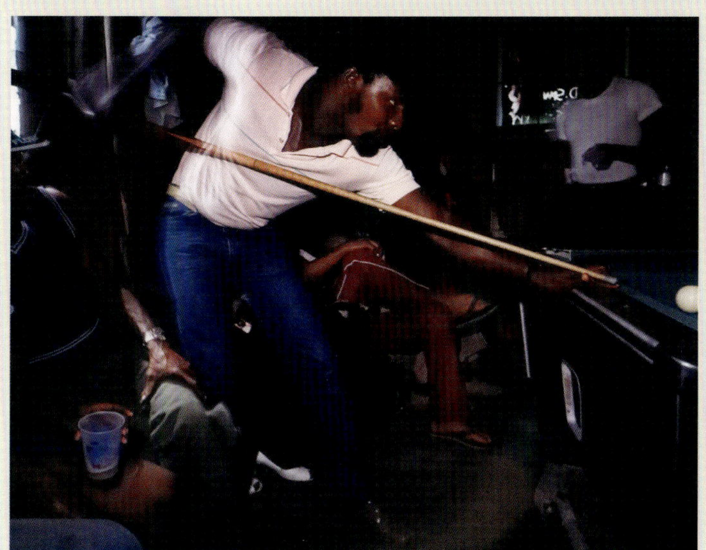

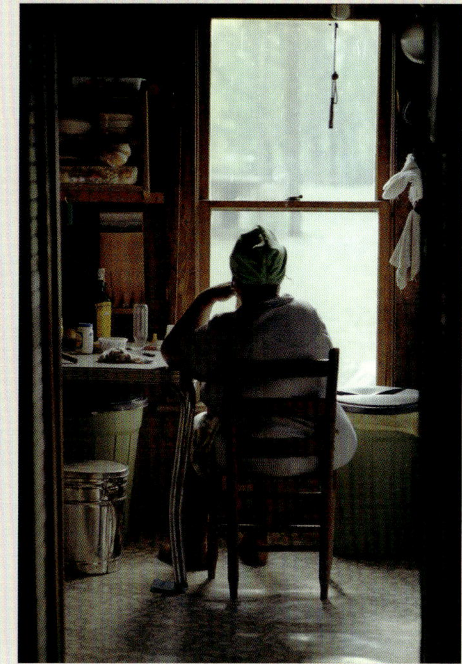

Jane Rule Burdine (born 1946), *Irene, Jackson Point Hunting Club*, 1983. giclée, 14 x 11.

Birney Imes (born 1951), *Hollandale, January 31, 1986*, 1986. chromogenic color print, 16 x 20.

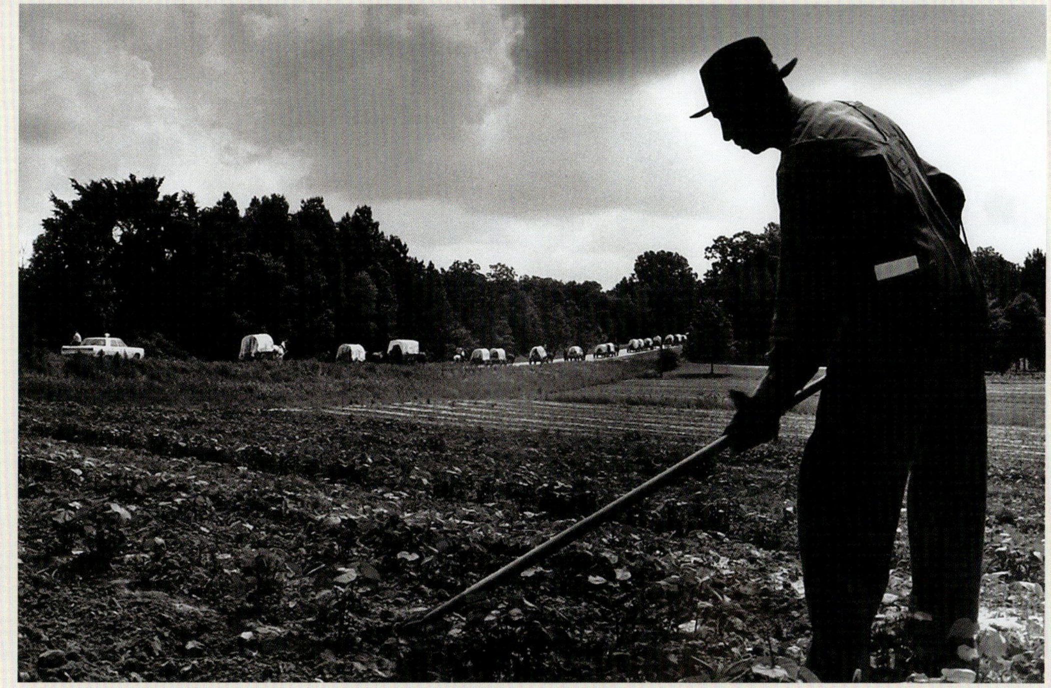

Roland Freeman (born 1936), *Mule Train leaving Marks, Mississippi for Washington, D.C., as part of the 1968 Poor People's Campaign*, 1968. gelatin silver print, 12 x 17½ (sight).

Perry Walker
(born 1945), *Rocky Moore #1, Mount Gilliam, Byhalia,* 1976. gelatin silver print, 16¾ x 16¾.

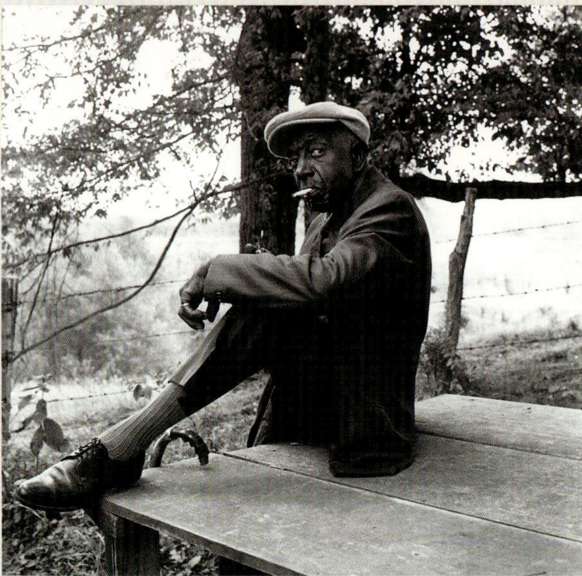

Tom Rankin
(born 1957), *Deacon Fred Davis,* 1990. gelatin silver print, 10 x 10 (sight).

Tom Rankin
(born 1957), *Moon Lake, 1990,* 1990. gelatin silver print, 16 x 20 (sight).

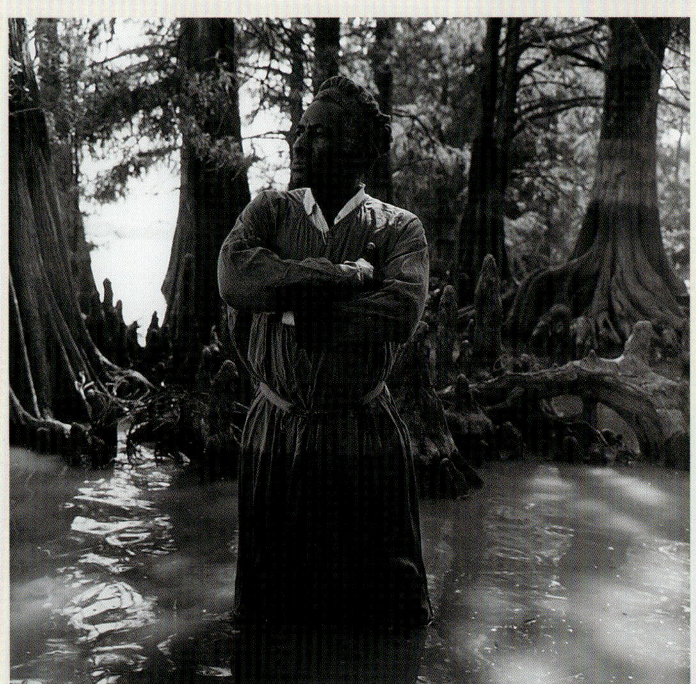

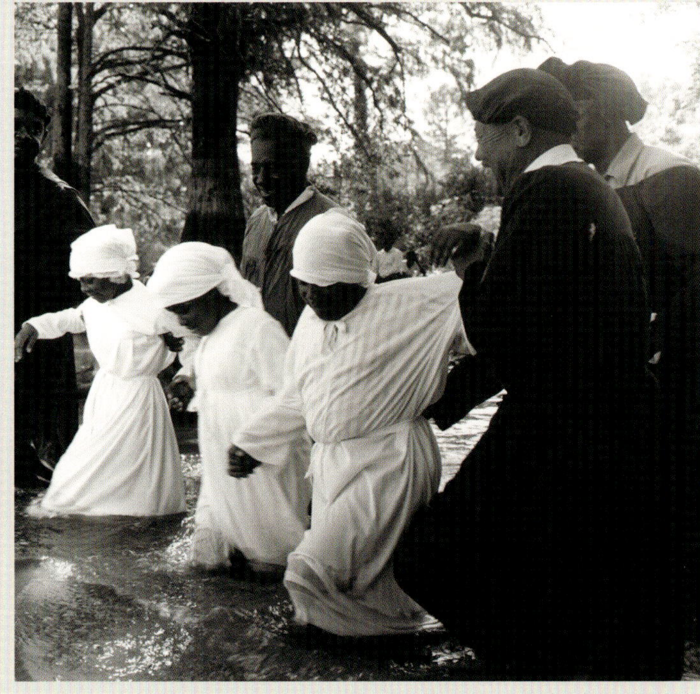

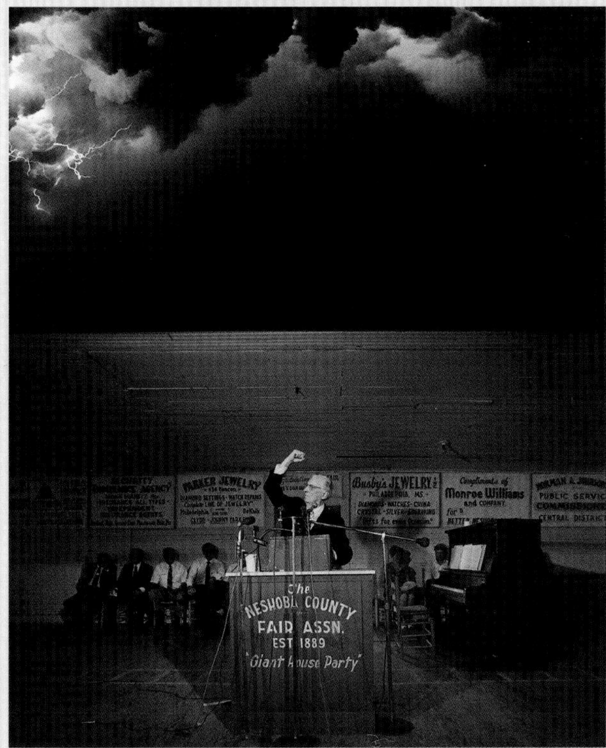

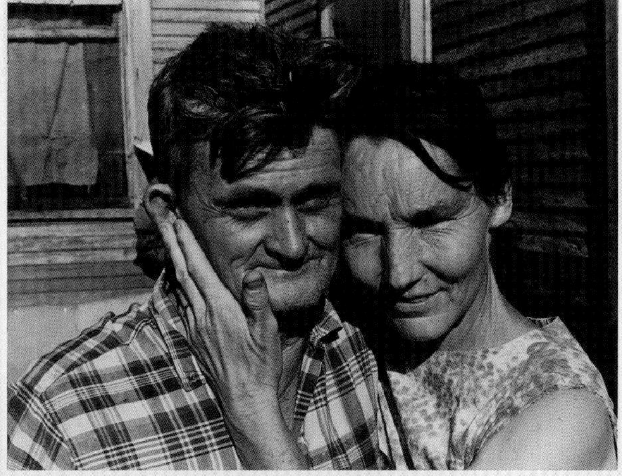

Eyd Kazery
(born 1953), *Ross Barnett, 1982 Neshoba County Fair*, 1998. gelatin silver print, 20 x 16.

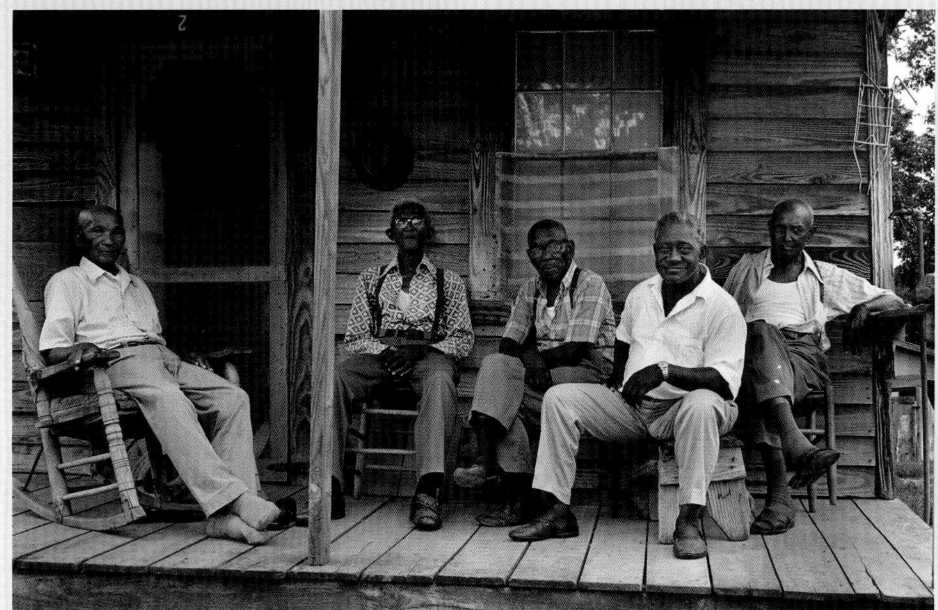

William Ferris
(born 1942), *Touch*, 1968. gelatin silver print, 10½ x 13⅜.

Roland Freeman
(born 1936), *Community Elders, Woodville, Mississippi, July 1975*, 1975. gelatin silver print, 16 x 20.

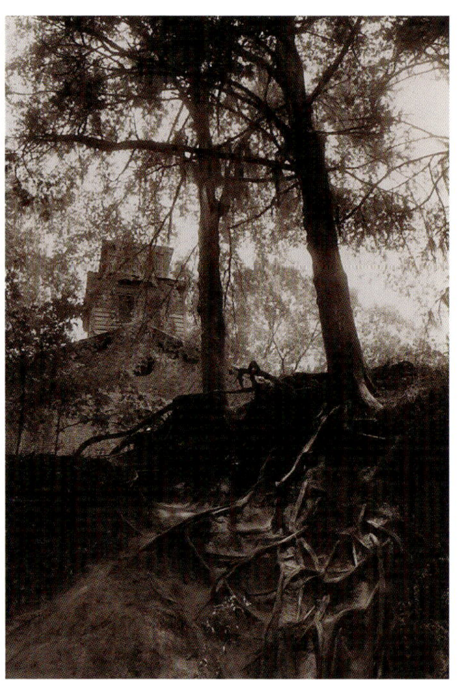

D. C. Young
(born 1948), *Rocky Springs, MS*, no date. gelatin silver print, 9¼ x 6¼ (sight).

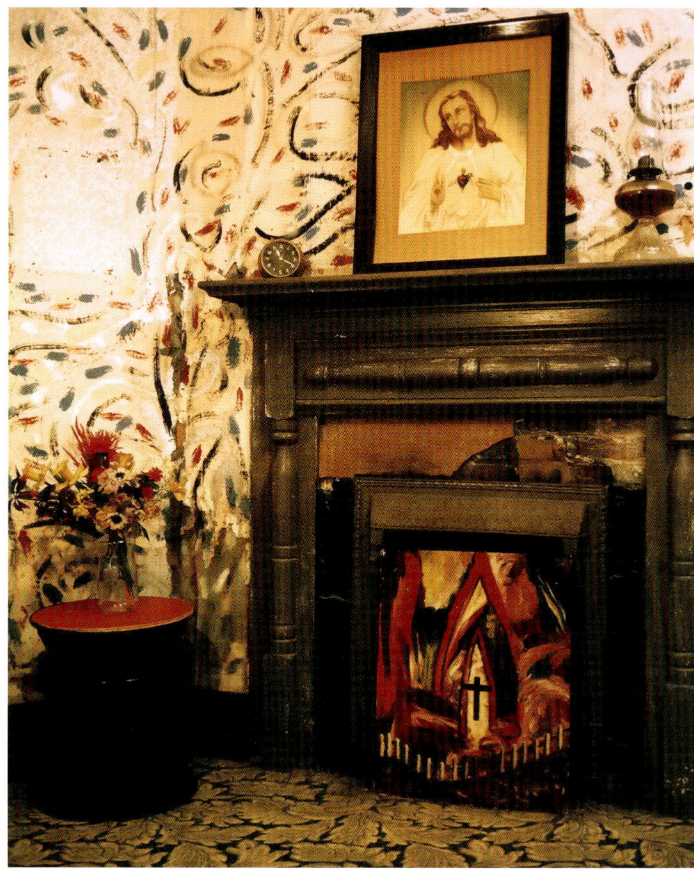

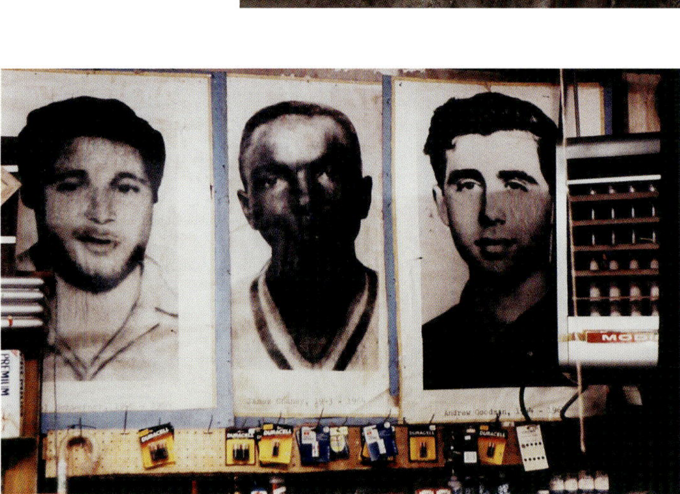

< Milly Moorhead
(now Milly Moorhead West)(born 1949), *Schwerner, Chaney & Goodman, Aaron Henry's Drug Store, Clarksdale, Mississippi*, 1983. chromogenic color print, 8 x 13.

Jack Kotz
(born 1961), *Heaven & Hell, Mathiston, Mississippi*, 1987. Cibachrome, 20 x 16.

works by Birney Imes of Columbus; Jack Spencer of Kosciusko and Nashville; Eyd Kazery of Jackson; Jane Rule Burdine of Taylor; Perry Walker of Red Banks and Memphis; Milly Moorhead of Oxford; Diana C. Young, of Hattiesburg and France; Tom Rankin, of Shaw and Chapel Hill, North Carolina; and David Rae Morris of Jackson and New Orleans.

A number of photographs throughout the exhibition are those of Roland Freeman. Freeman was born in 1936 in Baltimore and began his career as a freelance photographer in the early 1960s. When his interest turned to cultural documentation in 1967, he began to collaborate with folklorists on fieldwork projects in African American folk traditions. Working in Mississippi as a research associate for the Smithsonian Center for Folklife and Cultural Heritage, he documented the Mississippi participants in the 1974 American Folklife Festival and has continued his research in Mississippi since that time, working with the Old Capitol Museum, Jackson State University, Mississippi Cultural Crossroads, Mississippi Arts Commission, and other agencies. In addition to his work as a photo-historian, he has collected and publicly displayed Mississippi quilts, conducted interviews with folk artists, and published extensively. In 1997 he was named the Eudora Welty Visiting Professor of Southern Studies at Millsaps College. He founded the Group for Cultural Documentation and continues his work of studying black culture, using his camera to document and interpret the continuity of traditional African American folklife practices throughout the African Diaspora. His books that focus on Mississippi are *Something to Keep You Warm*, *Margaret Walker's 'For My People': a Tribute*, *Southern Roads/City Pavements*, *A Communion of the Spirits*, and *The Mule Train*.

Exporting Missis

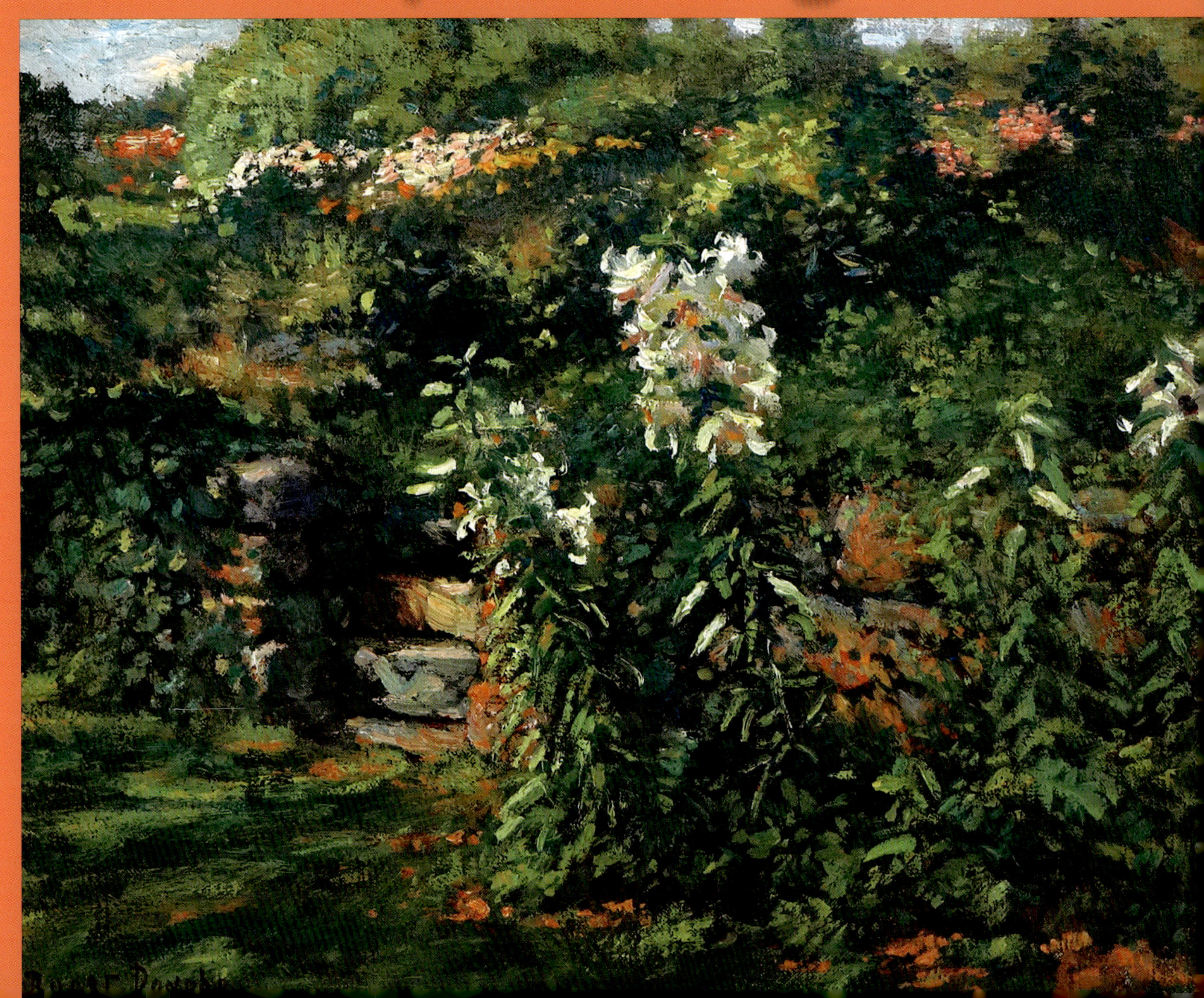

ssippi through Art

The contributions that Mississippians have made to the nation's literature and music are substantial and well known—more so than those made to America's visual arts. Some of Mississippi's most talented and eloquent artists have worked outside of the state. *The Mississippi Story* exhibition introduces a group of artists whose work has received major attention nationally and whose backgrounds were shaped in the culture of Mississippi. No attempt has been made to draw didactic conclusions about the influences of a Mississippi background on their art. However, there are many common denominators. Some have used a literary approach to their work, many reflect a love of nature, in others there is a religious impulse, and for many there is a preference for the concrete and representational.

< G. Ruger Donoho (1857-1916), *The Garden Steps*, circa 1913. oil on canvas, 16 x 20.

Most of the artists in this exhibition were educated in the state's schools, but have lived their adult life and made their reputations elsewhere. Much of the examples of art in the Museum's collection represent involvement with the adopted culture. Some lived and worked in the nineteenth century (G. Ruger Donoho of Church Hill and Kate Freeman Clark of Holly Springs, for instance). Some artists left Mississippi to escape the burden of discrimination in their native land (Richmond Barthé spent most of his life in Jamaica.) Several used the GI Bill to seek art education outside the state after World War II, because none of Mississippi's major colleges offered such training prior to 1950. Most of the expatriate artists have maintained familial and nostalgic ties to Mississippi, returning often through the years. Bill Dunlap and Randy Hayes have continued to use Mississippi images in their work, time and time again reflecting their Mississippi roots with the use of narrative and myriad details. Mary Lynn Kotz, author of *Rauschenberg, Art and Life*, characterized Dunlap's work as "reflecting the sensibility of a southern storyteller-gone-cosmopolitan." The following biographies introduce the works of some of Mississippi's expatriates.

G. Ruger Donoho (1857-1916) left the state with his mother after the end of the Civil War and settled in Washington, D.C., where he began studying art. He attended Emerson Institute there and State Normal School in Millersville, Pennsylvania. At the age of twenty-one he moved to New York and enrolled at the Art Students League. He studied in Paris at the Académie Julian and was influenced by the Barbizon School. When Donoho returned to New York in 1887, he became a well-known Impressionist, and his work was frequently exhibited. He settled in East Hampton on Long Island in 1890 and inspired a close-knit artists' colony to form there. The Metropolitan Museum of Art acquired one of his oils, *Windflowers*, in 1916. The Mississippi Museum of Art began collecting his work in 1978 and now owns nine pieces by the artist.

Kate Freeman Clark (1875-1957) was the next successful Impressionist in the eastern art scene. When she was sixteen her mother moved to New York City in order to give Clark more educational advantages. She graduated from the Gardner Institute and enrolled at the Art Students League, where she studied with John Henry Twachtman and met William Merritt Chase. She studied with Chase from 1896 to 1902. Her first show was at the National Academy of Design in 1904 under the name Freeman Clark, which she used to disguise her gender. For the next fourteen years she was widely exhibited and acclaimed. When her mother died in 1922, Clark moved back to Holly Springs and never painted again. At her death she left to the city of Holly Springs all of her paintings, which are now housed at the Kate Freeman Clark Museum.

Richmond Barthé (1901-1989), Mississippi's foremost African American sculptor, was born and raised in Bay St. Louis. With financial aid arranged by his Bay St. Louis priest, Barthé studied at the Art Institute of Chicago and briefly became part of New York's Harlem Renaissance. Like Richard Wright, his counterpart in literature, he left his native land to seek equal rights. He moved to Jamaica where he lived for almost thirty years, traveling often in Europe. Barthé's work is in the Metropolitan, Smithsonian, Pennsylvania Academy of the Fine Arts, Houston's Museum of Fine Arts, Art Institute of Chicago, Whitney Museum, and Virginia Museum of Fine Arts. On display are two bronze sculptures: *Feral Benga* (1937), the nickname of a popular dancer who worked with Josephine Baker in Paris, and *Blackberry Woman* (1932), on loan from the Smithsonian American Art Museum.

Maltby Sykes (1911-1992) of Aberdeen is one of the South's leading printmakers. He was a professor of art at Auburn University in Alabama, from 1942 to 1977. His work is in the Museum of Fine Arts, Boston; Brooklyn Museum of Art; Cincinnati Art Museum; Metropolitan Museum of Art;

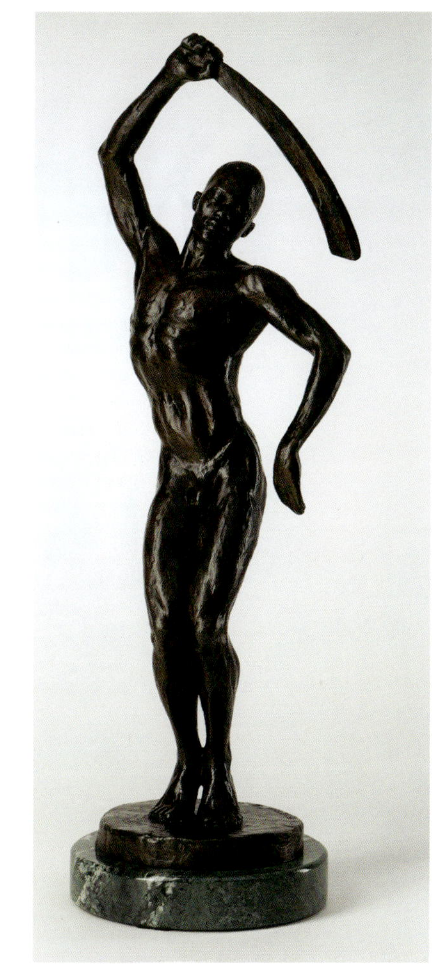

Richmond Barthé (1901-1989), *Feral Benga*, 1937. bronze, 20¼ x 7¼ x 7.

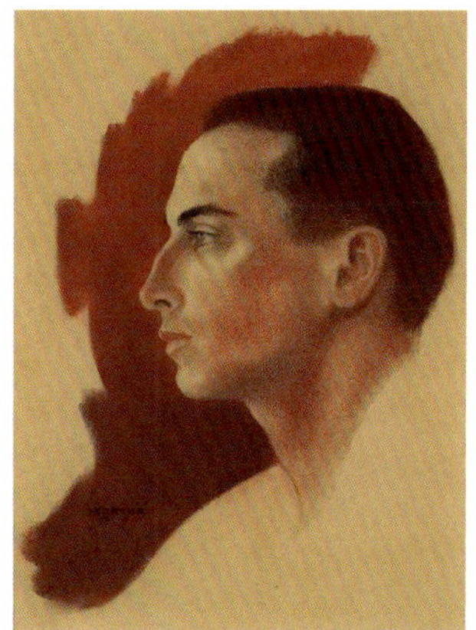

Richmond Barthé (1901-1989), *Portrait of a Young Man*, 1931. pastel on paper, 14¼ x 10½.

Maltby Sykes (1911-1992), *Pomegranate*, 1954. color lithograph, 10½ x 11½ (image).

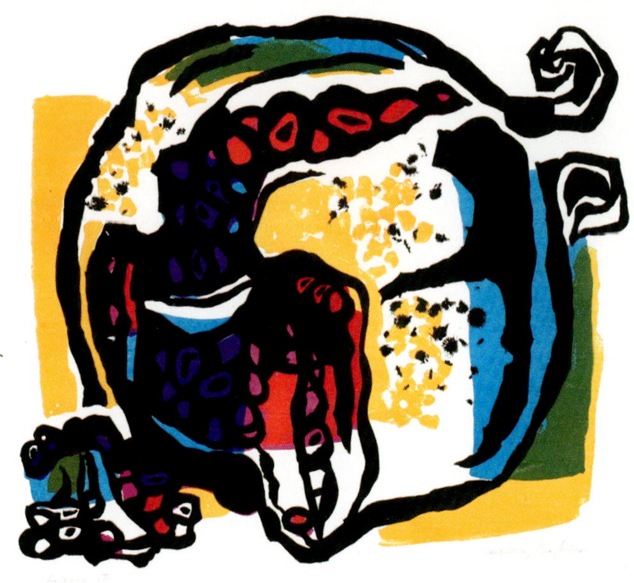

Museum of Modern Art; and Philadelphia Museum of Art. The prints in the Museum's permanent collection represent both etching and color lithography.

Byron Burford, born in 1920 in Jackson, enrolled at the University of Iowa on the GI Bill and received both his B.F.A. and M.F.A. there. He had a lifetime career on the faculty of the Iowa School of Art, retiring in 1986. A painter and printmaker of national reputation, he received many grants and honors during his career. His works are in the collections of the Municipal Art Gallery, Davenport, Iowa; Des Moines Art Center; George Eastman House, Rochester; High Museum of Art, Atlanta; Josyln Art Museum, Omaha; J. S. Guggenheim Memorial Foundation, New York City; William Rockhill Nelson Gallery of Art, Kansas City; Queens University, Kingston, Canada; San Francisco Museum of Art; Walker Art Center, Minneapolis; and Smithsonian American Art Museum.

Byron Burford > (born 1920), *Beauty Celebrates New Year*, 1987. magna (solvent-based acrylic) on canvas, 37¼ x 48¾ (sight).

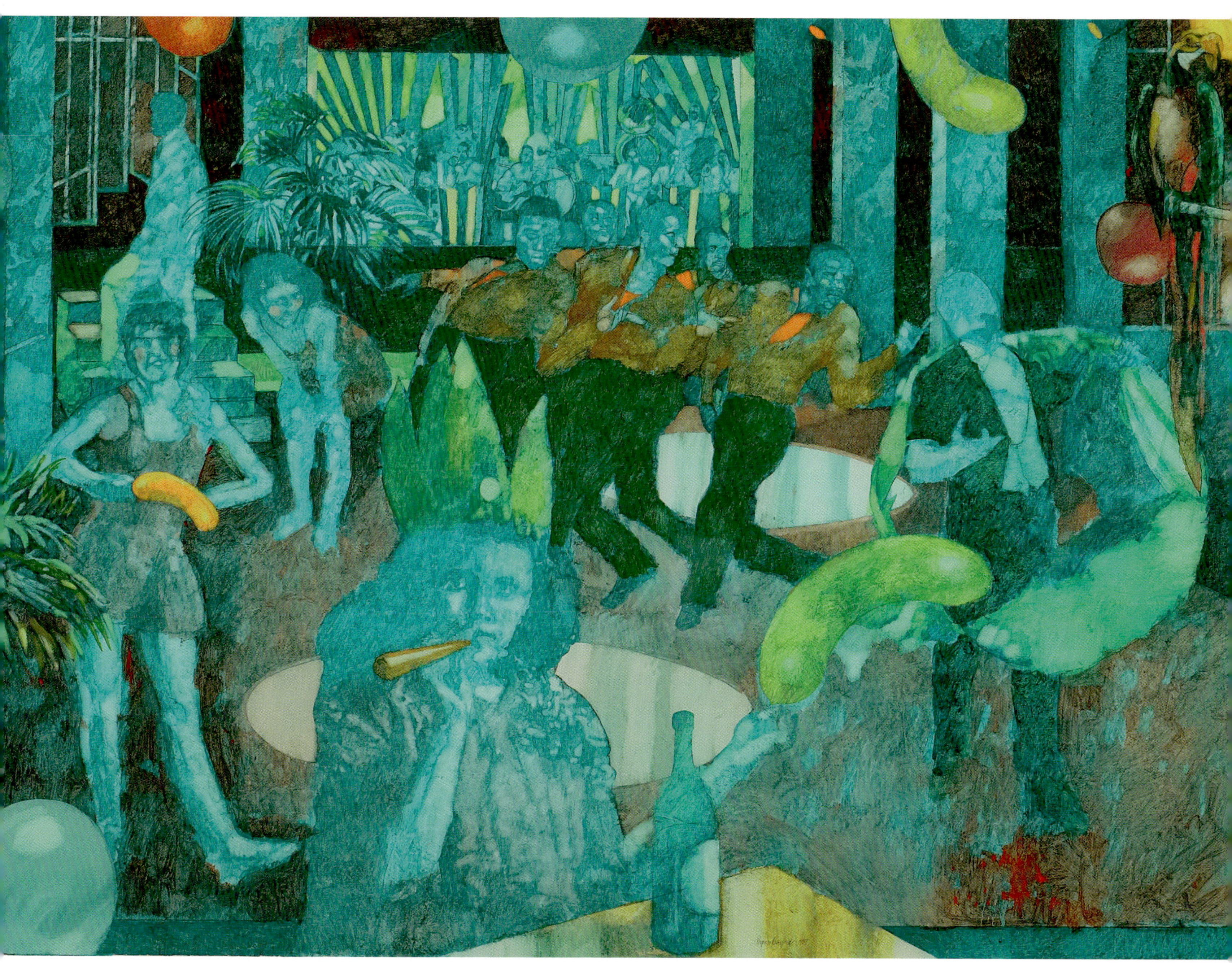

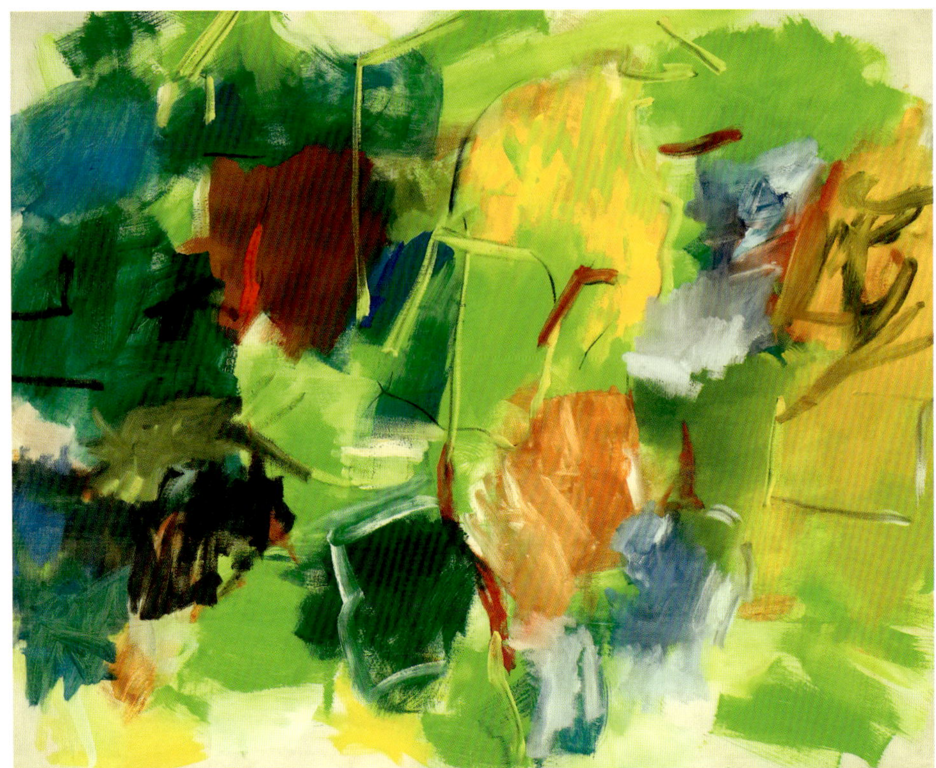

Fred Mitchell (born 1923), *Untitled*, 1961. oil on linen, 50 x 60.

Fred Mitchell was born in 1923 in Meridian and spent most of his adult life in New York City as an Abstract Expressionist, participating in a group of painters that included Ellsworth Kelly, Robert Indiana, and Agnes Martin. The Guggenheim Museum selected him as one of America's promising young painters in 1954. While the art of Fred Mitchell is very much a part of the New York School, some of his early work was inspired by his childhood in Mississippi and later visits with his artist sister, Elizabeth Pajerski of Vicksburg. He moved from realism in the 1940s to open abstractions in later life, but the desire to capture the ambiance of a particular place remained constant in his work. Before he settled in Manhattan, he studied at the Carnegie Institute, Cranbrook Academy of Art in Michigan, University of Alabama, Columbia University, and the Accademia di Belle Arti in Rome, where he lived and worked from 1948 to 1951.

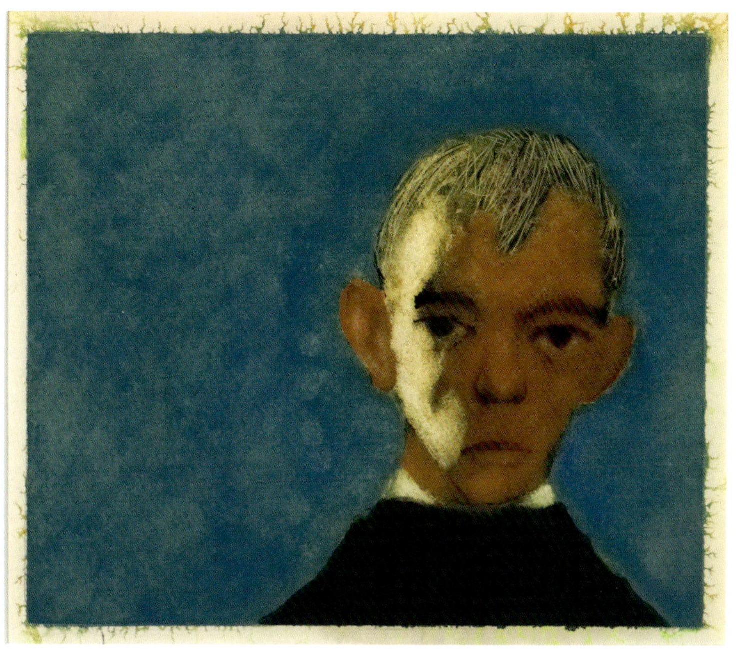

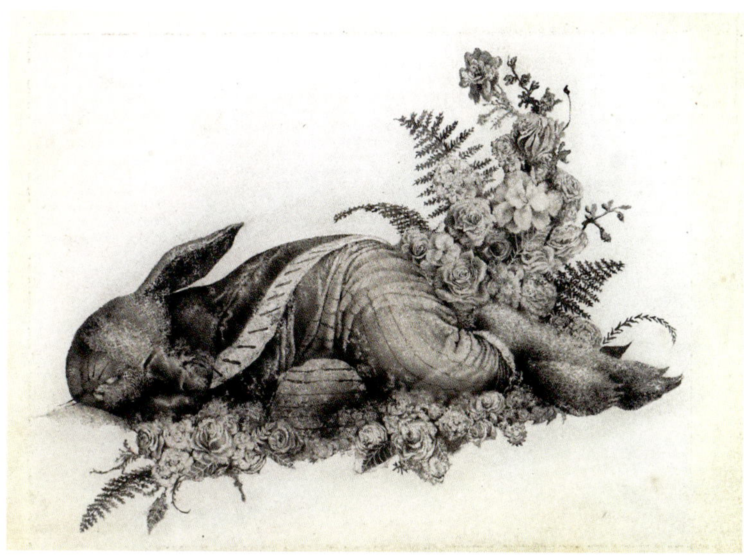

Edgar Parker
(1925-1982),
Self-Portrait, no date.
watercolor on paper,
8¾ x 9¾ (sight).

Edgar Parker
(1925-1982), *Sleeping Rabbit*, no date.
graphite on paper,
7½ x 9¾.

Meridian-born Edgar Parker (1925-1982) decided to be an artist when he was still a child. He attended Meridian Junior College and transferred to the University of Alabama to take art courses exclusively. His professor there sent him to New York, where he studied with Amédée Ozenfant and turned his attention to illustration. He became interested in children's stories and wrote and illustrated seven books from 1959 to 1969. His intricate and delicate drawings have been exhibited many times, including shows at the Brooklyn Museum of Art and the Mississippi Museum of Art. His sister, Nell Parker Downing, donated a large collection of his works to the Mississippi Museum of Art in 1982. A collection of his letters and papers is on file at the University of Minnesota.

George Wardlaw was born in 1927 in Baldwyn. After World War II he attended the Memphis Academy of Art and earned his master of fine arts degree

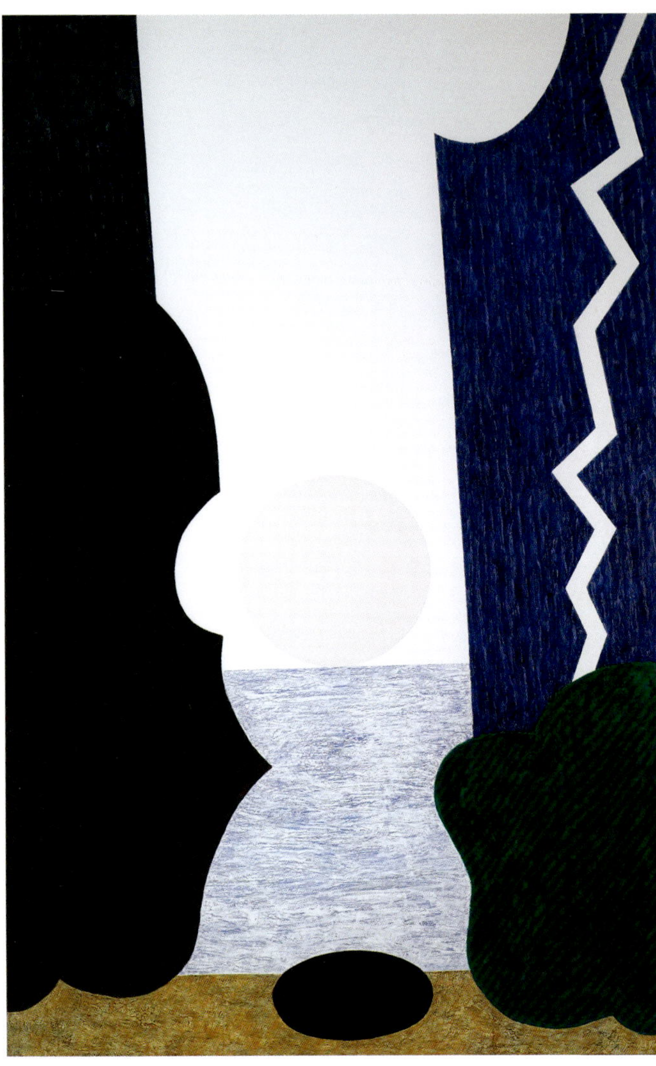

George Wardlaw (born 1927), *Guardian of the Light*, 2004. acrylic on canvas, 80 x 50.

from the University of Mississippi in 1955. He joined Yale University's art faculty in 1963 and remained there until 1968, when he became chair of the department of art at the University of Massachusetts, Amherst. He retired in 1990 and returned full time to studio work, moving from burnished and painted aluminum sculptures to his current series of paintings about the Maine coast. Wardlaw said, "Most of my work over the years has some reference to the natural world, however oblique or subtle it may sometimes appear." His current techniques involve painting, scraping, sanding, cutting, taping, erasing, painting out, and repainting, while maintaining "a constant dialogue among the working process, the work, and myself." The results in the *Maine* series are beautifully realized marine scenes of textural complexity. Abstracted shapes of clouds, waves, rocks, and elements of weather (rain, wind, lightning) evoke the essence of an ever-changing shoreline. On exhibit is *Guardian of the Light*, which depicts most of the elements that the artist is exploring in his *Shore* series: sea, clouds, weather, rocks, and shore.

Larry Edwards, born in 1931 and raised in Louisville, Mississippi, earned his B.A. from the University of Southern Mississippi and an M.F.A. from the University of Mississippi. He has been a prolific and passionate painter throughout his career as an art educator, heading up the art departments of Athens College, Appalachian State University, Pennsylvania State University, and University of Memphis. After retiring he turned to full-time studio work, where he developed a richly textured painting technique in which he combined dark humor with harsh social commentary. On view is Edwards's *Amusement Park, Fires and Fireworks*, which appears menacing in its out-of-control rides and fiery intensity. He has exhibited extensively in the South, the Midwest, and in New York City. His work is in the Southeastern Center for Contemporary Art, Arkansas Arts Center, Roane State Community College in Tennessee, and corporate and private collections.

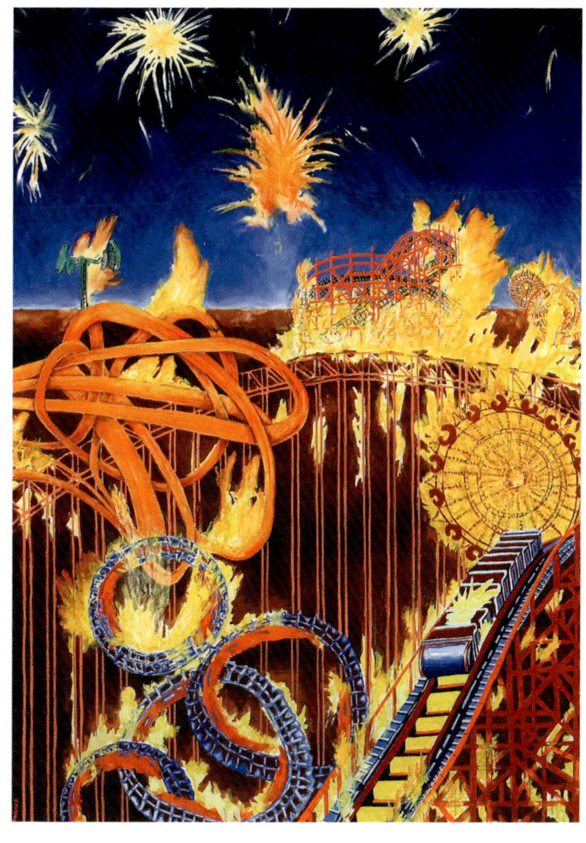

Larry Edwards (born 1931), *Amusement Park, Fires and Fireworks*, 2001. gouache and pastel on paper, 43¾ x 30¾.

Clarksdale native Warren Dennis was born in 1927. He received a bachelor of arts degree from the University of Southern Mississippi and a master of fine arts degree from the University of Mississippi. He taught art at Judson College in Illinois for a decade and spent the rest of his teaching career at Appalachian State University in North Carolina. His art is primarily figurative, using modified realism to celebrate the quotidian human life, as the canvas on display shows. *Firebuilder* connotes an ancient acknowledgment of the comfort of fire and the safety and utility of human pairing. Dennis's work is in the collections of Delta State University, Hickory Museum of Art, University of Chattanooga, Appalachian State University, and corporate collections.

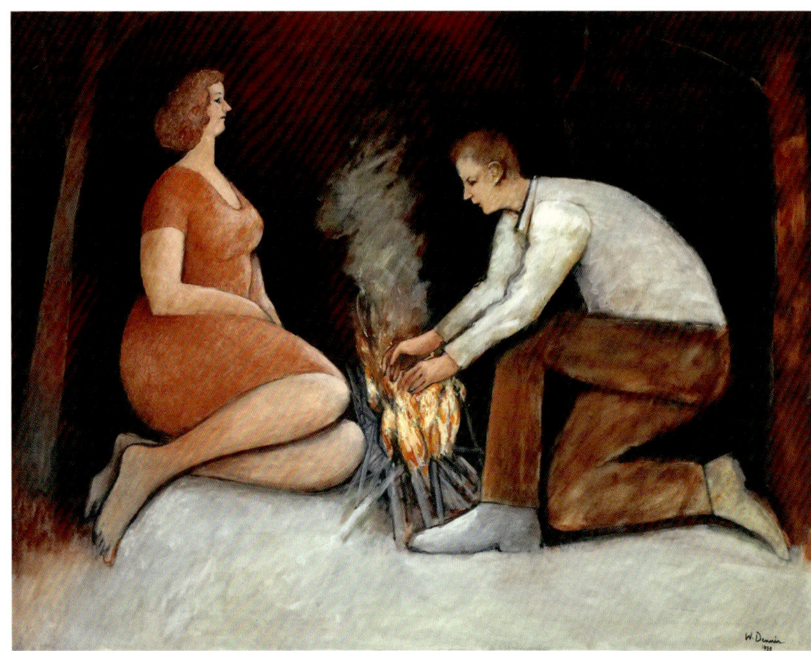

Warren Dennis (born 1927), *Firebuilder*, 1988. oil on canvas, 45⅛ x 56½.

Robert Rector was born in Pascagoula and raised in Ocean Springs, earning his bachelor of fine arts and master of fine arts degrees from Louisiana State University. A printmaker and painter, he has lived and worked in Baton Rouge for most of his career. His major influences are minimalism and expressionism and the tension between the two. For thirty years his reconciliation of the two approaches has produced complex abstractions concerned with the balance between intuition and intellect. This dynamic has produced canvases of great surface beauty, such as the one on display. Its carefully considered combination of geometric structure and spontaneity in paint is a fine example of his intuitive-intellectual approach. Rector applies and scrapes layers of color and introduces unexpected gestural elements to achieve his textures. His work is in the collections of the Old State Capitol Museum in Baton Rouge, University of Texas, Louisiana State University, and the State of Louisiana, as well as many corporate collections.

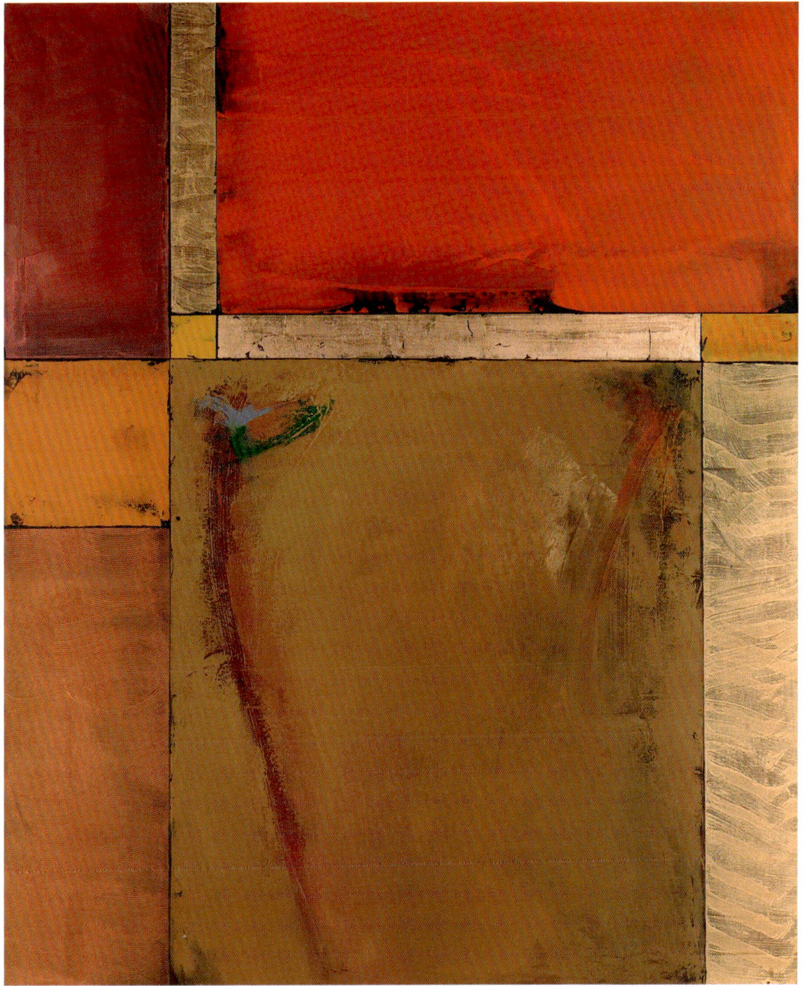

Robert Rector (born 1946), *Untitled* from the *Axis* series, 2004. acrylic on canvas, 60 x 49.

Sam Gilliam, born in 1933 in Tupelo, is America's foremost living African American painter. He received his B.A. and M.A. from the University of Louisville in Kentucky, and he currently lives and works in Washington, D.C. In 2005 the Corcoran Gallery of Art mounted a major retrospective of his work. His art is in more than fifty major institutions, including the Museum of Modern Art, Metropolitan Museum of Art, Whitney Museum, Art Institute

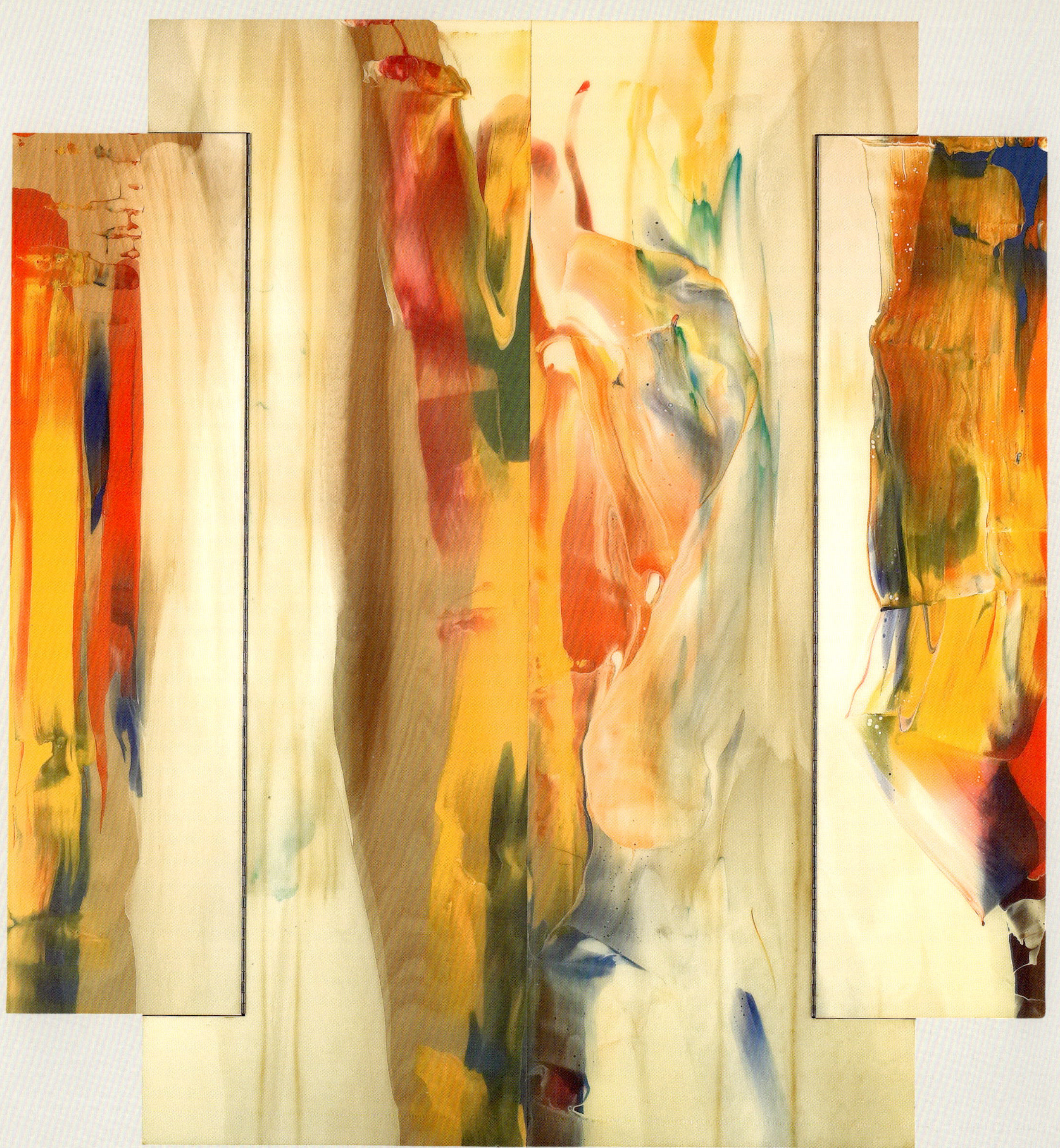

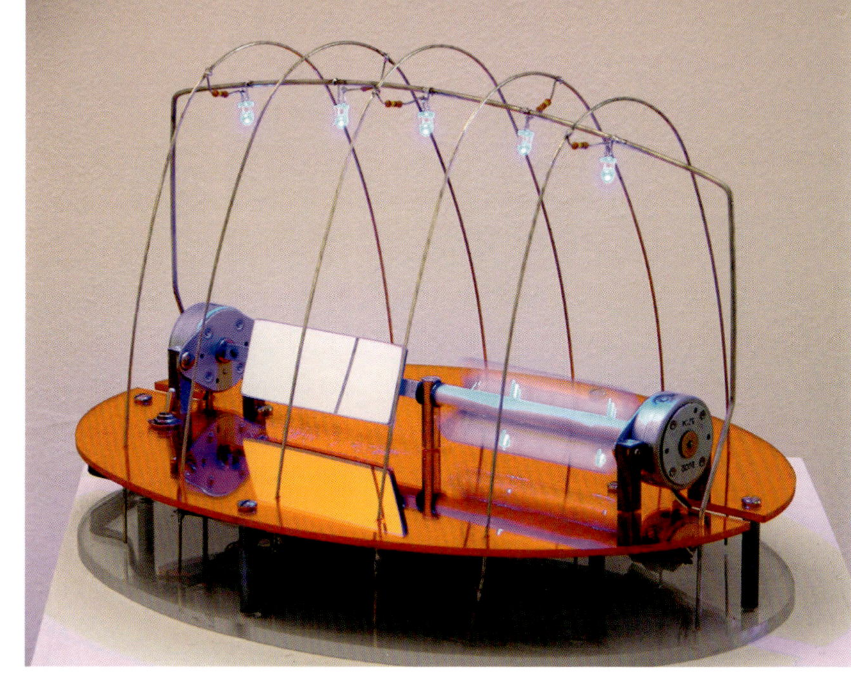

< **Sam Gilliam** (born 1933), *Birds Not Flying*, 2005. acrylic on birch with piano hinges, 53¼ x 48½ x 2¾

James Seawright (born 1936), *Carina*, 2004. mixed mediums, 9 x 12 x 9. Photograph courtesy of the artist.

of Chicago, Corcoran, Phillips Collection, four of the Smithsonian museums, J. B. Speed Art Museum, Virginia Museum of Fine Arts, Walker Art Center, High Museum, Tate Gallery in London, England, and Musée d'Art Moderne in Paris. In 2007 Gilliam received a Governor's Award for Artistic Excellence.

Born in Jackson in 1936, James Seawright is a pioneer of kinetic, electronic sculpture and America's foremost technological artist. A graduate of the University of Mississippi, he was a member of the art faculty at Princeton University beginning in 1969 and served as director of visual arts at Princeton University from 1975 to 2001. He traces his love of making objects by hand to his boyhood discovery of machine tools at a friend's house in Mississippi. Later in the U.S. Navy he had the opportunity of working with new tools and materials. He realized that he could "use modern electronics and controlled technology to apply to sculptures." He began by working with analog circuitry, and by the mid-1970s was involved with microprocessors, building specialized digital circuits to control interactive sculptures. His first art show at New York was in 1966, and since that time his work has been collected by the Museum of Modern Art, Whitney Museum, Guggenheim Museum, New Jersey State Museum, and Brandeis University. On view is *Carina*, a piece from Seawright's *Constellations* series (2001-2005). He describes these pieces as "meditations on particular constellations, their structure and their history, or rather the history of the lore that has grown up around them." The three-dimensional works are constructed of metal, plastic, and electronic parts. In discussing the future of this original genre, Seawright said, "Nowadays, embedded systems hardware is universally available, and software is the whole ball game. It seems to me that, after a few false starts along the way, digital art has a limitless future—it's no longer the language of a few isolated souls, but a language spoken everywhere." In 2003 Seawright received a lifetime achievement award from the Mississippi Institute of Arts and Letters and in 2004 was given Princeton's Behrman Award for distinguished achievement in the humanities.

After a distinguished career as a dancer and choreographer in Manhattan, Mimi Garrard expanded her art to the visual arts. Her "videodances" are wonders of light, movement, color, and form simultaneously in motion, a kaleidoscope of abstract images with the human body unmistakably primary. Garrard choreographs the dance movements, works with top electronic composers for accompaniment, lights the dance space, directs and films the dancers in motion, and then uses digital technology to integrate the dance into an abstract but thematic piece. In *The Mississippi Story* exhibition is *Time Installation*, which took the artist five years to complete. The work includes eight separate pieces that feature dancers Clare Holland and Kangi Segawa: *Synchronicity*, *Time Piece*, *Chron*, *Segawa Event Horizon*, *A Time for Barber Poles*, *Segawa Celestial Voyage*, *Wheel of Time*, and *Event Horizon with Red*.

Garrard was born in 1936 in Greenwood. She graduated from Sweet Briar College in 1958 and began her professional dance career in 1963 with the Alwin Nikolais Company. She has been artistic director of the Mimi Garrard Dance Company for over forty years. Collaborating with her husband, James

Seawright, her company was the first to combine dance with computerized lighting. Her dance repertory is one of the largest of modern dance choreographers. Garrard's videodance creations have achieved national and international attention. The pieces, now numbering seventy, are shown in galleries, auditoriums, and on broadcast television regularly. She was given the 2003 Lifetime Achievement Award from the Mississippi Institute of Arts and Letters.

Ed McGowin of Hattiesburg was born in 1938 and now lives and works in New York City and Kent, Connecticut. His highly inventive works are included in the collections at the Whitney Museum, Corcoran, Hirshhorn Museum and Sculpture Garden, Guggenheim Museum, New Orleans Museum of Art, Smithsonian Museum of American Art, and the Phillips Collection. He earned a bachelor of arts degree from the University of Southern Mississippi and his master of arts degree from the University of Alabama. He refers to himself as a "narrative sculptor" and has executed major outdoor commissions for numerous public and private organizations, including the United States General Service Administration; Veterans Administration; Dallas Rapid Transit Authority; City of Socorro, New Mexico; and Queens, New York. He has exhibited extensively in galleries and museums in the U.S. and abroad, and his work is in the permanent collections of the Whitney Museum, Guggenheim Museum, Hirshhorn Museum, and National Collection of Fine Arts. McGowin received the first award given by the Mississippi Institute of Arts and Letters in 1980, as

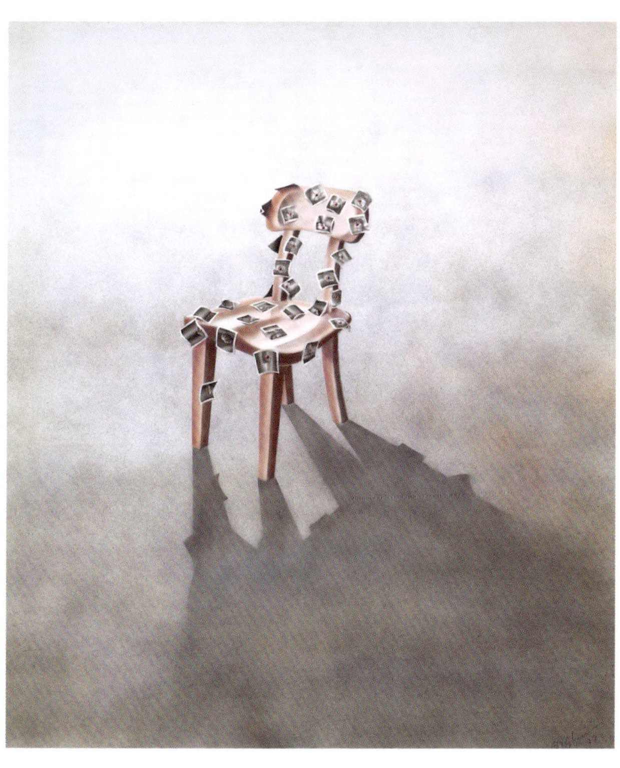

Ed McGowin
(born 1938), *Dad Knew About Wine Chair*, 1977. ink on paper, 60 x 50 (sight).

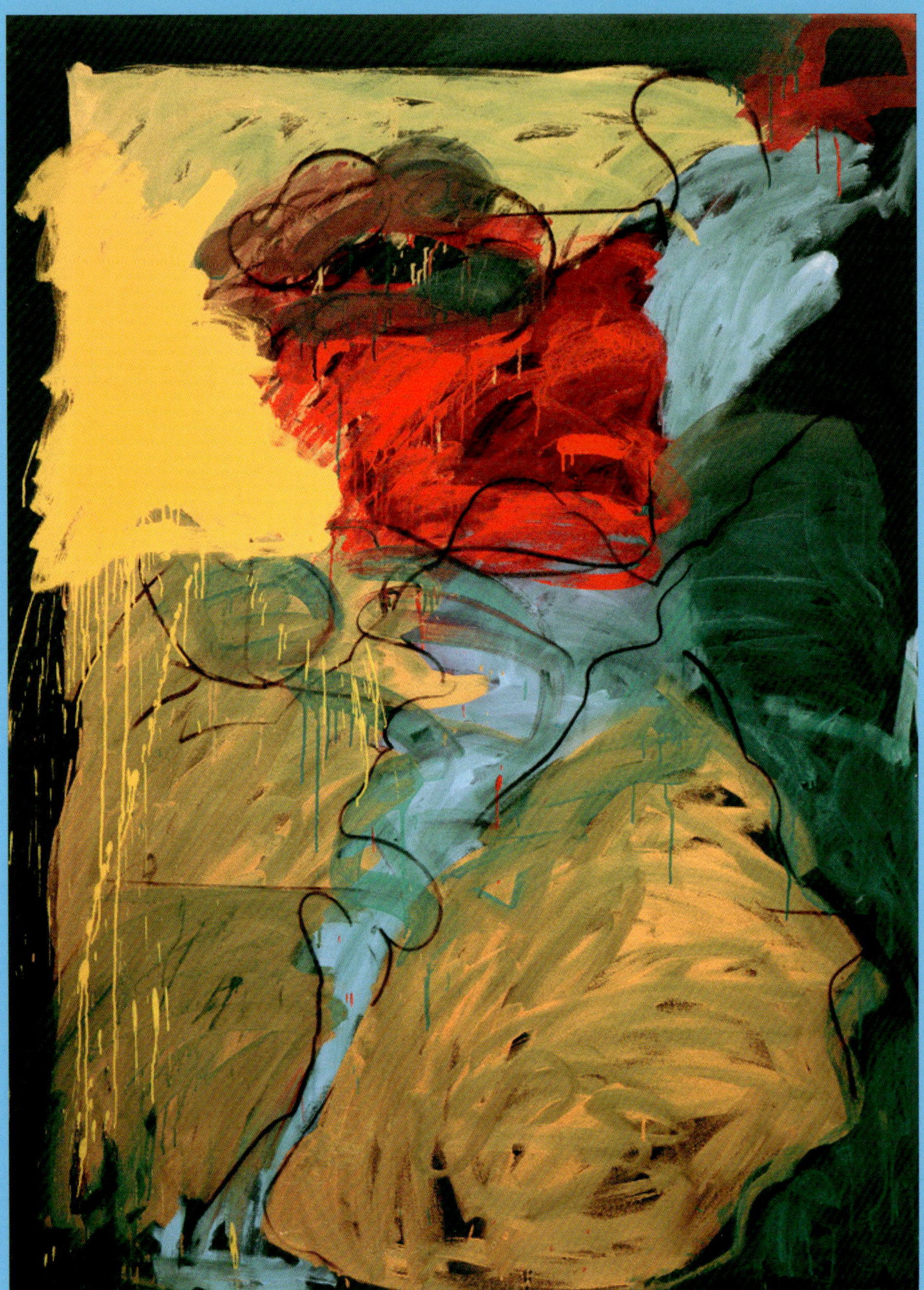

Mary Lovelace O'Neal (born 1942), *Angel of the Hood*, 1995. mixed mediums on canvas, 84 x 60. Photograph courtesy of the artist.

well as the New York City Art Commission Design Award. He teaches at the State University of New York at Old Westbury.

Mary Lovelace O'Neal was born in Jackson in 1942. She received a bachelor of fine arts degree from Howard University in 1964 and a master of fine arts degree from Columbia University in 1969. O'Neal has been a vital force in American art since the mid-1970s, and she currently teaches painting and drawing at the University of California, Berkeley. Although her dynamic compositions and vibrant colors place her work decidedly in the abstract school, her approach creates a provocative balance between narrative and pure abstraction. Her works are in the collections of the San Francisco Museum of Modern Art, Oakland Museum of California, and National Museum of Fine Arts, Santiago, Chile. She is the recipient of the Artiste en France Award from the French Government.

Randy Hayes grew up in Tupelo but was born in 1944 in Jackson. In 1968 he received his bachelor of fine arts degree from the Memphis Academy of Art after attending Rhodes College from 1962 to 1965. He spent most of his career in Seattle, Washington, where he had his first solo exhibition in 1971. Since the beginning of his career he has used photographs as source material for his paintings, but in 1991 photographs became part of his medium. Using a grid of snapshots to present a scene from all perspectives, Hayes covers the photographic images with new images rendered in semi-translucent washes of paint. This technique produces complex and layered surfaces with narrative content and provocative commentary. He frequently uses Mississippi iconography in his work and recently moved back to Mississippi, setting up his studio in Holly Springs. In 1990 he received the Mississippi Institute of Arts and Letters Visual Arts Award. His work is in the collections of the U.S. Department of State, Microsoft Corporation, McDonald's Collection, Seattle Art Museum, and Tacoma Art Museum, among others.

Valerie Jaudon, born in 1945 in Greenville, is one of the nation's leading

CLOCKWISE:

Randy Hayes
(born 1944), *The Fauna of Mississippi*, 2006. oil on photograph, pushpins, 40 x 50.

Randy Hayes
(born 1944), *Overnight Sensation*, 1987. pastel on paper, 64 x 52½.

Randy Hayes
(born 1944), *Self-Portrait with Eudora Welty and William Eggleston*, 1990. pastel on paper, 37½ x 44½ (sight).

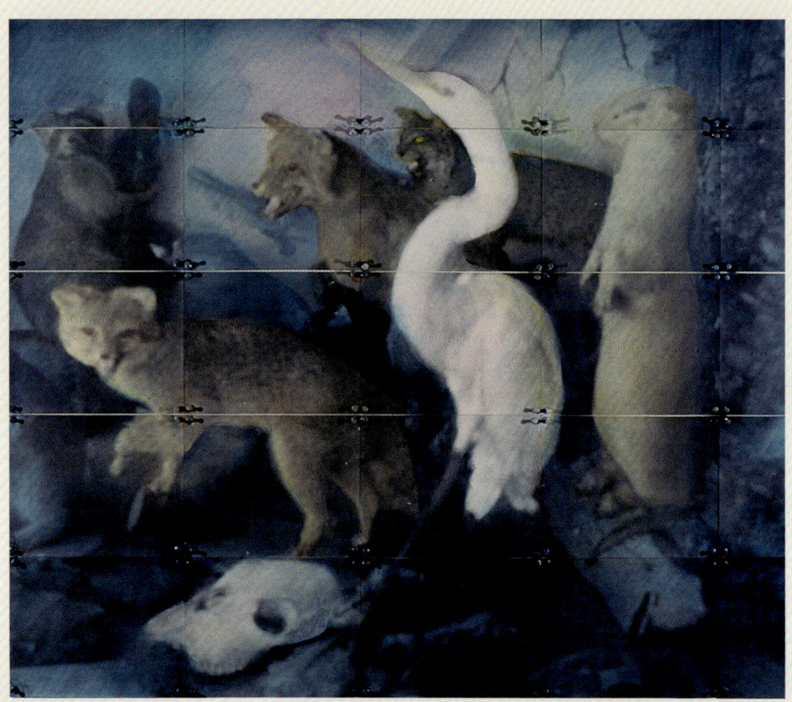

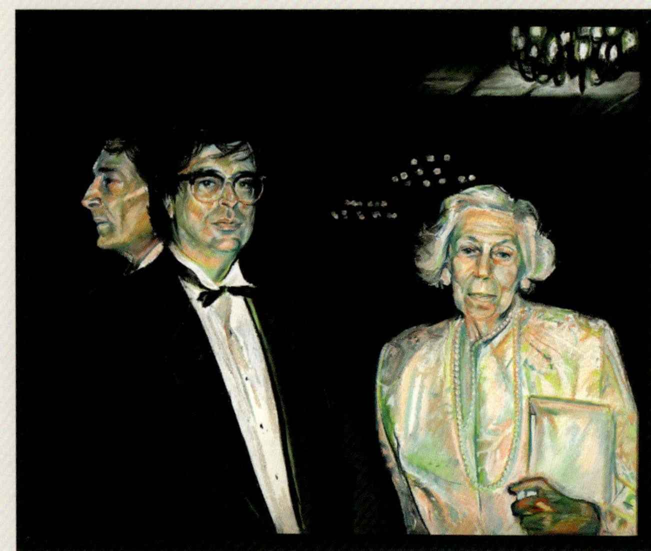

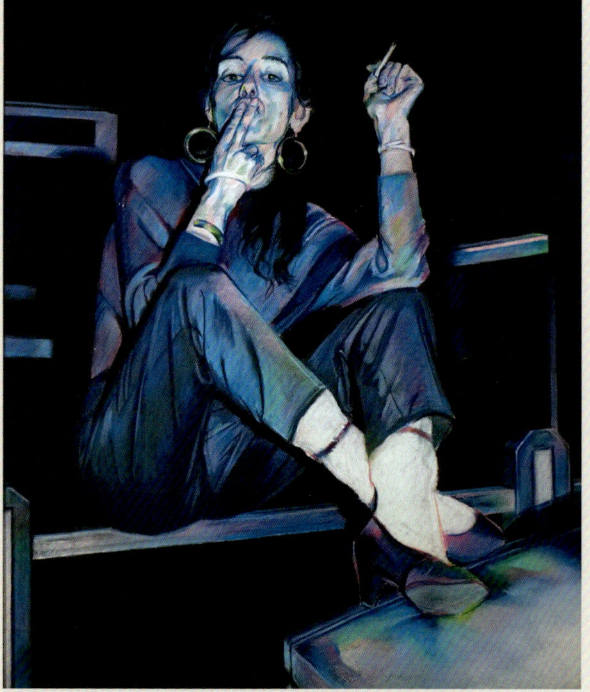

Valerie Jaudon
(born 1945), *Arcola*, 1982. oil on canvas, 81 x 120. Art © Valerie Jaudon/Licensed by VAGA, New York, NY.

painters in the pattern and decoration movement in American art. She studied at Mississippi University for Women, Memphis Academy of Art, and St. Martin's School of Art in London. Her first exhibition in New York was in 1977. Jaudon's work reflects her interest in geometric order expressed in color pattern and design. Her massive canvas titled *Arcola* dominates the central corridor of *The Mississippi Story* exhibition. Her work is in the Fogg Art Museum at Harvard, Albright-Knox Art Gallery in Buffalo, Birmingham Museum of Art, Dayton Art Institute, Hirshhorn Museum, National Museum of Women in the Arts, Museum of Modern Art, St. Louis Art Museum, and others. She has completed a number of public installation projects, including murals, mosaic

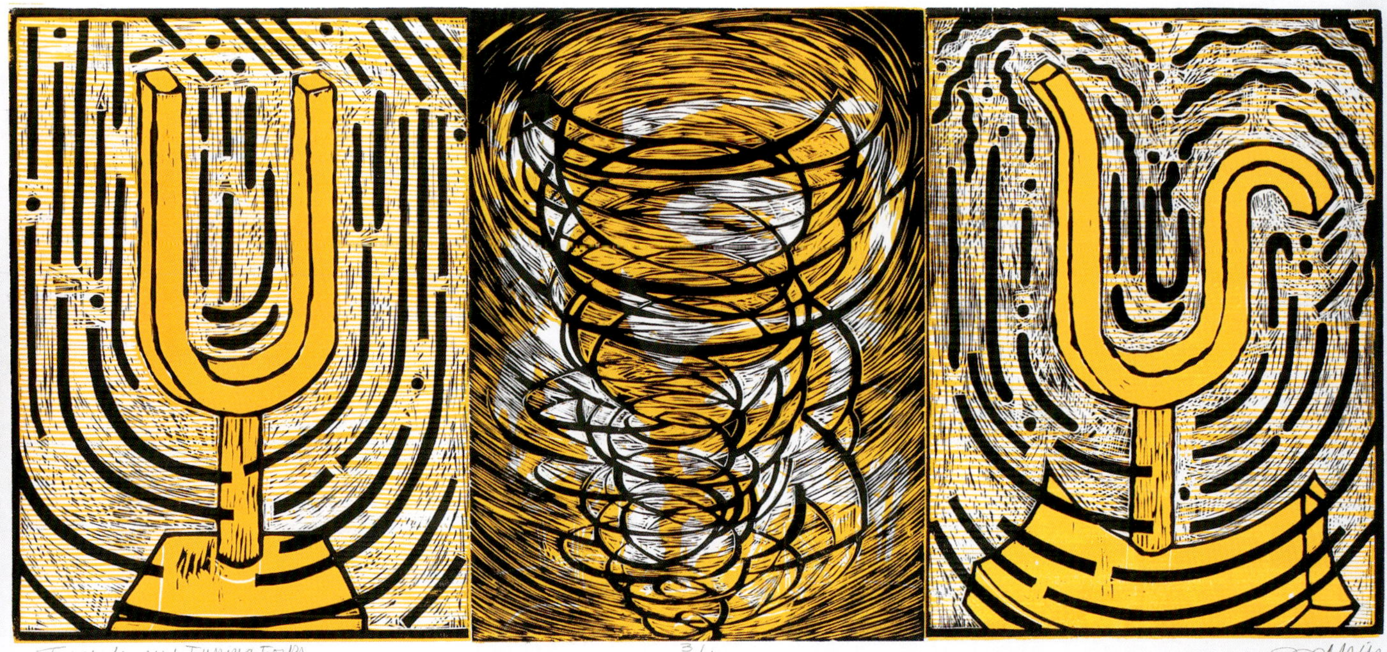

Ke Francis
(born 1945), *Tornado and Tuning Forks,* 2001. woodcut, 34 x 64.

floors, ceramic tile patterns, and a painted steel fence for the New York subway system.

Ke Francis of Tupelo was born in 1945, studied at the Memphis Academy of Art, Memphis State University, and completed his bachelor of fine arts degree at the Cleveland Institute of Art. He set up a studio in his hometown of Tupelo and worked there for more than twenty years as a printmaker, painter, sculptor, ceramist, photographer, and handmade bookmaker. He founded Hoopsnake Press through which he produces limited-edition art books. In 1996 he joined the art faculty of the University of Central Florida and gained an international reputation with his handmade books, prints, and sculpture. Francis has been dedicated to the narrative tradition from the beginning and his early work was profoundly related to his home state. On exhibit is *Tornado and Tuning Forks* (2001), a large-scale woodcut. Also on view is *Jugline Moon-*

scape, a woodblock from his 1992 handmade book (edition of 250). His work is in the collections of the Getty Museum in Los Angeles; Museum of Fine Art, Boston; National Gallery; Smithsonian American Art Museum; Library of Congress; Mint Museum in Charlotte; New Orleans Museum of Art; San Francisco Museum of Modern Art; Southeastern Center for Contemporary Art, Winston-Salem; High Museum; Memphis Brooks Museum of Art; Birmingham Museum of Art; and museums at Yale, Brandeis, and Rutgers universities and the University of Pennsylvania.

Additional Mississippians who work outside the state are also represented in the exhibition: Alex O'Neal of Greenville and Rebecca Alston of Ocean Springs, both of whom work in New York City, as well as Becky Hendrick of Jackson and Anthony, New Mexico.

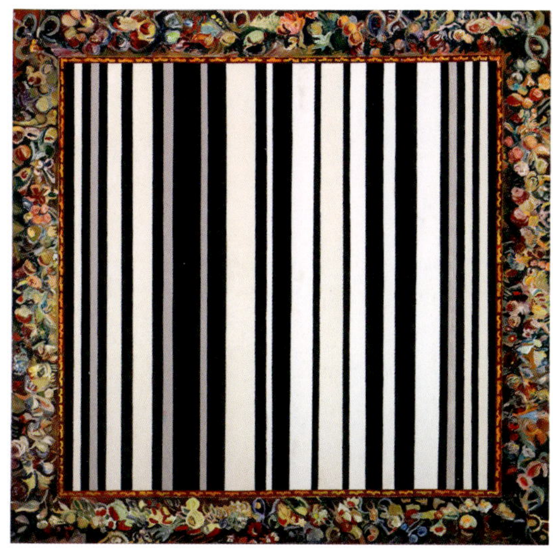

Becky Hendrick (born 1947), *Nature Morte*, late 1980s. oil and acrylic on canvas, 60 x 60.

In the last half century there has been a slowly escalating interest in southern art. A pioneering exhibition titled *American Painters of the South* opened at the Corcoran Gallery of Art in Washington, D.C. in 1960. Almost a quarter-century passed before southern art was again seriously explored, this time with a major exhibition held in 1983 at the Virginia Museum of Fine Arts called *Painting in the South, 1564-1980*. That same year Knopf published the landmark book *Art of the Old South: Paintings, Sculpture, Architecture, & the Products of Craftsmen* by Dr. Jessie Poesch of Tulane University. Since that time two museums dedicated solely to southern art have opened. Both are based on the work of private collectors. The first is the Morris Museum of Art in Augusta, Georgia, which opened in 1989 and was built around the collection of Robert Powell Coggins. The newest is the Ogden Museum of Southern Art, which opened in New Orleans in 2003 and was based on the collection of

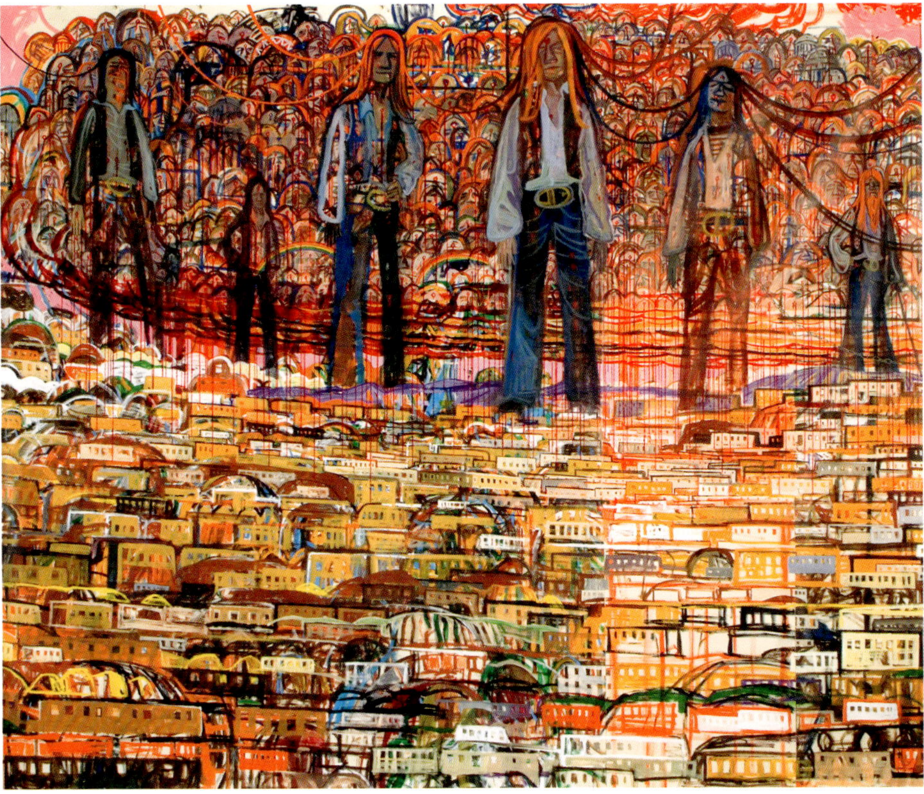

Alex O'Neal (born 1957), *Leon Koury's Backyard Messiahs*, 2000, acrylic on canvas, 95 x 112.

Roger Houston Ogden. These visionary men have challenged public museums to actively collect and exhibit the art of their regions.

It is clear that American art is an amalgamation of work from all parts of the nation. Only when every state in the union is heard from can we see the full creative panoply—the strength and diversity of America's art. The Mississippi Museum of Art will continue to add to its permanent collection of Mississippi art in order to make it the most substantive collection extant, a mission that was articulated in 1978.

The Mississippi Story Exhibition Checklist

All artwork appearing in *The Mississippi Story* is from the collection of the Mississippi Museum of Art, Jackson, unless otherwise noted.

MISSISSIPPI'S LANDSCAPE

The Delta

Bill Aron (born 1941)
Cotton Field, Mississippi Delta, 1991
giclée
14½ x 20
Purchase, with funds from Kathryn Wiener
2003.005

Marshall Bouldin III (born 1923)
Second Notice, circa 1954
oil on canvas
23½ x 42¼
Collection of the artist, Clarksdale, Mississippi

Jane Rule Burdine (born 1946)
Purnell and His Sister, 1983
Cibachrome
11 x 14
Purchase
1983.139

Maude Schuyler Clay (born 1953)
Dog in the Fog, Cassidy Bayou, Sumner, Tallahatchie County, 1997
gelatin silver print
20 x 16
Purchase, with funds from Mary Mhoon Endowment
2006.004

Maude Schuyler Clay (born 1953)
Dog on a Log, Sandy Bayou, near Glendora, Tallahatchie County, 1993
gelatin silver print
16 x 20
Purchase, with funds from Mary Mhoon Endowment
2006.001

John C. Coovert (1862-1937)
King Cotton, circa 1907
gelatin silver print
10 x 36½
Purchase, with funds from Mary Mhoon Endowment
2006.050

William Dunlap (born 1944)
Flat Out Dog Trot, 1998
mixed mediums on canvas
36 x 60
Gift of John and Melody Maxey
2005.031

Rolland Golden (born 1931)
Delta Bleak, 1979
acrylic on canvas
42 x 56
Gift of Mr. and Mrs. James Gould
1998.010

Robert Hubbard (born 1945)
Parchman Prison: View from Window, Camp 10, 1980
gelatin silver print
13½ x 9¼
Purchase
1982.030

Franke West Keating (born 1916)
High Cotton, circa 1980
chromogenic color print
13½ x 10¼ (sight)
Gift of Dr. John Geoffrey Keating
2004.152

Franke West Keating (born 1916)
Time to Go Home, circa 1963
chromogenic color print
10½ x 13⅜ (sight)
Gift of Dr. John Geoffrey Keating
2004.151

Lalla Walker Lewis (1912-2006)
Up the Levee, no date
linocut
8¾ x 11 (sight)
Bequest of Sara Virginia Jones
1991.304

Lalla Walker Lewis, attr. (1912-2006)
no title, no date
linocut
10¼ x 8½ (sight)

Joseph Rusling Meeker (1827-1889)
Day on the Yazoo, 1885
oil on canvas
24 x 14
Purchase
1991.386

Lucy Webb Millsaps (born 1936)
House with Yellow Flowers, circa 1972
gouache on illustration board
7 x 10 (sight)
Purchase
1973.011

Malcolm Norwood (born 1928)
Promise of Fulfillment, 1963
oil on canvas
50 x 40
Gift of Mississippi Power & Light
1963.004

Mildred Nungester (now Mildred Nungester Wolfe) (born 1912)
no title, 1937
oil on canvas
24 x 30
Gift of Mississippi Chemical Corporation
2003.012

James Routh (born 1918)
Mississippi Delta, 1941
lithograph
16 x 22¾
Bequest of Sara Virginia Jones
1991.037

Hill Country

Caroll Cloar (1913-1993)
Kudzu, 1976
acrylic on board
23 x 34
Gift of The Gallery Guild, Inc.
1978.002

Theora Hamblett (1893-1977)
Walking, Meditating in the Woods, 1963
oil on canvas
31 x 43
Gift of First National Bank
1966.018

James Josey (born 1945)
Off to the Factory, 1975
watercolor on illustration board
22¼ x 30
Gift of Mr. and Mrs. Harvey B. Heidelberg, Jr.
1978.053

Helen Pickle (1914-2002)
Harvesting Time, 1979
acrylic on board
16 x 18
Gift of Warren and

Sylvia Lowe
1994.058

Eugenia Summer
(born 1923)
Barricade, no date
tempera and ink on paper
35¼ x 23½ (sight)
Purchase
1968.002

Eudora Welty
(1909-2001)
Home by dark, Yalobusha County,
prior to 1935
gelatin silver print
13 x 8¼ (sight)
Gift of Mr. and Mrs. Richard L. Miller
2000.025

Jackson and Central Mississippi

Vidal Blankenstein
(born 1958)
Night Moon, 2005
mixed mediums on board
12 x 11½
Gift of the artist
2006.051

Carol Cole (born 1943)
Jackson, MS, 1979,
1979-1985
acrylic on canvas
42 x 54
Gift of the artist, in memory of Dr. Willard L. Waldron
1991.389

Stephen D. Cook
(born 1951)
Fondren Corner, 2006
oil on board
11 x 15
Collection of the artist, Jackson, Mississippi

Saul Haymond
(born 1947)
no title, 1983
oil on paper
10 x 12
Gift of Mr. and Mrs. Richard L. Miller
2000.004

William Hollingsworth
(1910-1944)
Before the Sun, 1939
watercolor on paper
17 x 22 (sight)
Gift of Mississippi Chemical Corporation
2005.017

William Hollingsworth
(1910-1944)
Crossroad, no date
oil on canvas
22 x 26
Bequest of Jane Oakley Hollingsworth
1987.064

William Hollingsworth
(1910-1944)
Low River, 1944
watercolor on paper
20 x 24
Bequest of Jane Oakley Hollingsworth
1987.081

Frank Neal (born 1955)
A Place for Everyone,
no date
oil on Masonite
14 x 12
Gift of Marcie Ferris
2004.021

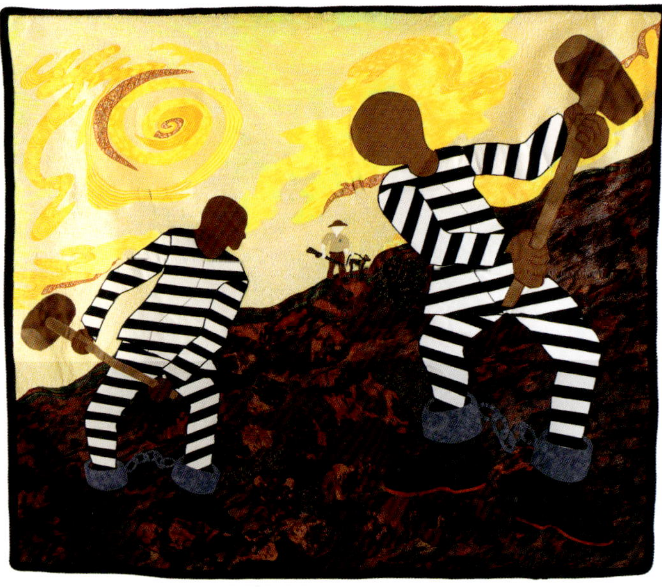

Gwendolyn A. Magee (born 1943), *Five Years Hard Labor*, 2007. textile, 58 x 67.

Mary Evelyn Stringer
(1921-1995)
Gullies at Allison's Wells,
circa 1950
watercolor on paper
10 x 15
Gift of the artist
2003.072

Wyatt Waters
(born 1955)
High Notes, 1999
watercolor on paper
29 x 29 (sight)
Gift of John and Melody Maxey
2005.032

River Country

Bill Aron (born 1941)
Mississippi River at Natchez, 1991
silver halide print
20 x 16
Purchase, with funds from Kathryn Wiener
2003.003

Robert Havell (1793-1878) after John James Audubon (1785-1851)
Finches and Tanager
from John James Audubon's *The Birds of America*, 1837
hand-colored aquatint and engraving on Whatman paper
38 x 25½
Bequest of Sara Virginia Jones
1991.114

Andrew Bucci
(born 1922)
Red Swamp, no date
oil on canvas
30 x 42
Gift of Marie Hull
1977.010

Andrew Bucci
(born 1922)
Summer Snow, 1980
oil on canvas
48 x 36
Gift of the artist, in memory of Marie Hull
1980.123

Caroline Compton
(1907-1987)
The River at Vicksburg,
no date
oil on board
18 x 24
Gift of First National Bank
1963.006

William Constable
(1783-1861)
View Down the Mississippi from Ellis's Cliffs 28 Feby. 1807, 1807
watercolor and graphite on paper

6¾ x 9½ (sight)
Purchase
2000.003

Alfred Eisenstaedt
(1898-1995)
Sternwheeler near Natchez, no date
gelatin silver print
10¼ x 13 (sight)
Purchase
1997.098

Eudora Welty
(1909-2001)
Ruins of Windsor, near Port Gibson, post 1936
gelatin silver print
10¾ x 13½ (sight)
Gift of Mr. and Mrs. Richard L. Miller
2000.021

D. C. Young (born 1948)
Rocky Springs, MS, no date
gelatin silver print
9¼ x 6¼ (sight)
Gift of the artist
1988.001

Piney Woods

Ruth Atkinson Holmes
(1909-1981)
For the Space Age, 1965
oil on canvas with found objects
48 x 54
Purchase
1965.059

Ethel Ketcham
(1913-1965)
Tall Timber, no date
watercolor on paper
16 x 10¾ (sight)
Bequest of the artist
1965.012

Mary Katherine Loyacono McCravey
(born 1910)
Birds in Winter, no date
oil on canvas
18 x 24
Gift of the artist
2003.038

Mary Katherine Loyacono McCravey
(born 1910)
Landscape, no date
oil on board
22 x 28
Gift of First National Bank
1964.007

Eudora Welty
(1909-2001)
A house with bottle trees, Simpson County, 1936
gelatin silver print
10½ x 10½ (sight)
Gift of Mr. and Mrs. Richard L. Miller
2000.020

The Coast

Walter Anderson
(1903-1965)
Birds and Waves, no date
watercolor on paper
8½ x 11
Purchase
1967.023

Walter Anderson
(1903-1965)
Blue Crab, no date
watercolor on paper
11 x 8½
Purchase
1967.024

Walter Anderson
(1903–1965)
Grasshoppers, no date
watercolor on paper
8½ x 11
Purchase
1967.032

Walter Anderson
(1903-1965)
Green Heron, no date
watercolor on paper
11 x 8½
Purchase
1967.011

Walter Anderson
(1903-1965)
Horn Island—Fall, no date
watercolor on paper
8½ x 11
Purchase
1967.034

Walter Anderson
(1903-1965)
Seashells, no date
watercolor on paper
8½ x 11
Purchase
1967.004

Walter Anderson
(1903-1965)
Thistles, no date
watercolor on paper
11 x 8½
Purchase
1967.010

Walter Anderson
(1903-1965)
Red Oak, no date
watercolor on paper
11 x 8½
Purchase
1967.040

Walter Anderson
(1903-1965)
Two Frogs, no date
watercolor on paper
11 x 8½
Purchase
1967.015

Dusti Bongé
(1903-1993)
no title, 1943
oil on canvas
20 x 16
Gift of The Dusti Bongé Foundation, Inc.
1999.011

Sandra Russell Clark
(born 1949)
Pier, Bay St. Louis, Mississippi, 2001
toned gelatin silver print
16½ x 16
Purchase
2001.032

David Rae Morris
(born 1959)
Lighthouse with Piles of Debris, 2005
pigmented inkjet print
22¾ x 15 (sight)
Gift of the artist
2006.087

George Ohr (1857-1918)
no title, circa 1900
clay with glaze
8¼ x 4¼ x 3½
Purchase
1978.004

George Ohr (1857-1918)
no title, circa 1900
clay with glaze
4 x 5 x 5
Purchase
1978.007

George Ohr (1857-1918)
no title, circa 1900
clay with glaze
4¼ x 3½ x 3½
1991.382

Agnes Fairlie Ricketts
(died 1964)
Gulf Hurricane, no date
watercolor on paper
14¼ x 21½ (sight)
Gift of the artist
1953.003

Shearwater Pottery, decorated by Walter Anderson (1903-1965)
Shearwater Art Pottery Plate with Rooster Motif, circa 1940
earthenware with glaze
9¼ x 9¼
Gift of the family of Richard Paul and Mary Jean McMichael
2007.037

Shearwater Pottery, Christopher Inglis Stebly (born 1967)
Shearwater Art Pottery Vase, no date
earthenware with glaze
5½ x 5½
Gift of Jack Lyons
2007.038

Steve Shepard
(born 1955)
No Good Stinking Real Estate Developers . . ., 1992
colored pencil, graphite, and watercolor on paper
24 x 24

Ella Miriam Wood
(1888-1976)
Boats, 1913
oil on canvas
12⅞ x 12
Purchase
1913.001

MISSISSIPPI'S PEOPLE

Richmond Barthé
(1901-1989)
Blackberry Woman, 1932
bronze
33¾ x 11 x 14
Collection of Smithsonian American Art Museum, Washington, D.C.
Purchase, through the Luisita L. and Franz H. Denghausen Endowment

Richmond Barthé
(1901-1989)
Portrait of a Young Man, 1931
pastel on paper
14¼ x 10½
Purchase
2004.019

Dusti Bongé
(1903-1993)
The Balcony, 1943
oil on canvas
20 x 16
Gift of The Dusti Bongé Foundation, Inc.
1999.015

Jason Bouldin
(born 1965)
Portrait of Captain Jimmy Allgood, Lafayette County Fire Department, 2002
oil on canvas
49½ x 33¾

Frank Neal
(born 1955), *The Existential Roofer: A Tribute to Giotto*, 1981.
oil and wax on canvas,
44 x 52

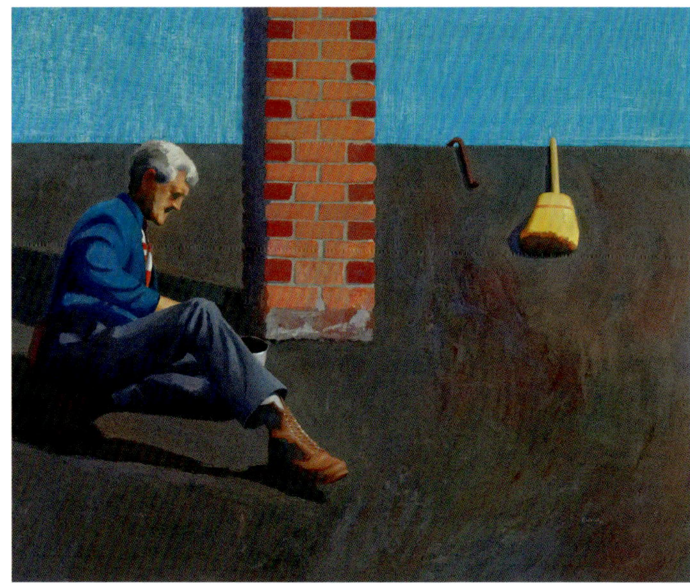

Gift of Dr. Alicia Bouldin
2007.041

Marshall Bouldin III
(born 1923)
Portrait of Sister Thea Bowman, 1988
oil on canvas
43⅛ x 34
Collection of Roman Catholic Diocese of Jackson, Mississippi

Douglas Bourgeois
(born 1951)
Blue Christmas, 1981
oil on canvas
14 x 14
Gift of George Febres
The Jules Laforgue Collection of Louisiana Art
1994.003

Jane Rule Burdine
(born 1946)
Irene, Jackson Point Hunting Club, 1983
giclée
14 x 11
Gift of the artist
2007.036

Henri Cartier-Bresson
(1908-2004)
William Faulkner, 1947
gelatin silver print
20 x 16
Purchase
1997.090

Obie Clark (born 1948)
no title, no date
ceramic
15⅛ x 10⅜ x 5¾
Gift of Howard and Susan Shands Jones
2006.085.a-b

William Dunlap
(born 1944)
Wm Faulkner Commemorative Print, 1970
color etching and engraving
28 x 24
Gift of Norma Latimer Watkins, in memory of her mother Norma Latimer Watkins and her aunt Hosford Latimer Fontaine
1987.149

William Eggleston
(born 1939)
Eudora Welty, no date
UltraStable print
18½ x 12½ (sight)
Purchase
1997.094

Thomas Eloby
(1950–2001)
no title, no date
photolithograph
17½ x 12¾ (sight)
Gift of Harvey B. Heidelberg
1986.141

Thomas Eloby
(1950–2001)
no title, no date
photolithograph
10½ x 12 (sight)
Gift of Harvey B. Heidelberg
1986.140

William Ferris
(born 1942)
Touch, 1968
gelatin silver print
10½ x 13⅜
Purchase
1971.008

Roland Freeman
(born 1936)
Community Elders, Woodville, Mississippi, July 1975, 1975
gelatin silver print
16 x 20
Purchase
1995.007

John Gaddis
(1929-1993)
no title, no date
watercolor and graphite on paper
18½ x 17½ (sight)
Gift of Robert Burns, Jr., in memory of his parents, Robert and Hortense Burns
2004.054

Myra Hamilton Green
(1924-2002)
Portrait of Mrs. Joseph Blythe, 1975
acrylic on canvas
24 x 30¼
Collection of Joshua Green, Jackson, Mississippi

Randy Hayes
(born 1944)
Self-Portrait with Eudora Welty and William Eggleston, 1990
pastel on paper
37½ x 44½ (sight)
Gift of the artist, in memory of his brother Charles
1994.063

Thomas Cantwell Healy
(1820-1889)
Portrait of a Man, 1874
oil on canvas
30¼ x 25⅛
Gift of Mrs. Phyllis Herman
1986.075

Thomas Cantwell Healy
(1820-1889)
Portrait of a Woman, 1874
oil on canvas
30 x 25½
Gift of Mrs. Phyllis Herman
1986.076

William Hollingsworth
(1910-1944)
Mr. H, 1943
graphite on paper
9¾ x 7¼ (sight)
Bequest of Jane Oakley Hollingsworth
1987.039

William Hollingsworth
(1910-1944)
Woman with Child,
no date
paint on wood
9½ x 1⅝ x 1⅝
Bequest of Jane Oakley
Hollingsworth
1987.072

Marie Hull (1890-1980)
Melissa, 1930
oil on canvas
30 x 25
Purchase
1972.006

Marie Hull (1890-1980)
One Standing Black Nude, no date
charcoal on paper
25 x 18½
Gift of the artist
1978.019

Marie Hull (1890-1980)
Sharecroppers, 1938
oil on canvas
40 x 40¼
Gift of the artist
1978.146

Marie Hull (1890-1980)
no title, no date
color woodcut
14 x 11 (sight)
Gift of Andrew Bucci
1990.009

Jack Kotz (born 1961)
Kelly on the Porch, Webster County, Mississippi, 1989
chromogenic color print
16 x 20
Gift of William Dunlap
1999.007

Leon Koury (1909-1993)
The Compress Worker, 1941
bronze
44 x 23 x 12
Private Collection

Helen Jay Lotterhos
(1905-1981)
Rubbin, 1935
charcoal on paper
18¾ x 12½
Gift of the family of
Helen Jay Lotterhos
2002.017

Elizabeth Robinson
(born 1954)
no title, 2002
glass
28 x 44 x 12
Gift of Mississippi
Museum of Art
Auxiliary
2003.001

Lynn Green Root
(1954-2001)
Portrait of Johnny Langston, 1981
mixed mediums on canvas
40 x 30
Gift of William Ferris
2004.028

Jack Spencer
(born 1951)
Razorblade, 1998
gelatin silver print
17½ x 17½ (sight)
Purchase, with funds
from Mary Mhoon
Endowment
2004.141

William Steene
(1888-1965)
Tea Leaves, no date
oil on canvas
31½ x 39½ (sight)
Gift of Bette Painter
1968.017

Merle Tennyson (now
Merle Tennyson
Montjoy) (born 1920)
Mary Alice, The Journalist, 1971
acrylic on canvas
24 x 24
Gift of Virginia Alice
Bookhart Patterson, in
memory of Mary Alice
Bookhart
2004.146

Perry Walker
(born 1945)
Rocky Moore #1, Mount Gilliam, Byhalia, 1976.
gelatin silver print
16¾ x 16¾
Purchase, with funds
from Mary Mhoon
Endowment
1979.103

James Winston
Washington, Jr.
(1911-2000)
Young Queen of Ethiopia, 1956
limestone on wood base
16½ x 6⅝ x 9¾
Collection of
Smithsonian American
Art Museum,
Washington, D.C.
Gift of the artist
1984.115

Wyatt Waters
(born 1955)
no title, no date
watercolor on paper
11 x 15
Gift of Ferrell Tadlock
2002.009

Eudora Welty
(1909-2001)
Child on the porch, 1935-1936
gelatin silver print
13¾ x 10¾ (sight)
Gift of Mr. and Mrs.
Richard L. Miller
2000.010

Eudora Welty
(1909-2001)
A woman of the 'thirties, Jackson, 1935-1936
gelatin silver print
18½ x 13¼ (sight)
Gift of AmSouth Bank
2001.038

Bruce West (born 1953)
Three Girls, Tchula, Mississippi, 2000
chromogenic color print
16 x 20
Gift of the artist
2006.020

Elizabeth Wolfe
(born 1949)
no title, 1993
Conté crayon on paper
20¾ x 15
Gift of the artist
1997.029

Karl Wolfe (1904-1984)
Portrait of Bessie Cary Lemly, circa 1947
oil on canvas
30 x 24
Gift of the Art Study
Club
1948.002

Karl Wolfe (1904-1984)
Rest and Recreation, WWII, 1946
oil on canvas
14 x 11
Gift of Mr. and Mrs.
Harvey B. Heidelberg,
Jr.
1978.047

Terry Wood (born 1929)
no title, circa 1956
gelatin silver print
8 x 10
Gift of Ken and Lea
Barton
2006.029

LIFE IN MISSISSIPPI

Bill Aron (born 1941)
Jewish Cemetery. Woodville, Mississippi, 1989
silver halide print
16 x 20
Purchase, with funds
from Kathryn Wiener
2003.004

Lea Barton (born 1956)
Yellow Dog, 1999
mixed mediums on
canvas with found
objects
64 x 49
Purchase, with funds
from McCravey Fund
2001.034

William Beckwith
(born 1952)
Houn'dog, 2007
bronze
20 x 17 x 13¾
Purchase
2007.019

Dusti Bongé
(1903-1993)
no title, 1940s
oil on canvas
17 x 19
Gift of The Dusti Bongé
Foundation, Inc.
1999.016

Dusti Bongé
(1903-1993)
Where the Shrimp Pickers Live, 1940
oil on canvas
16 x 20
Gift of The Dusti Bongé
Foundation, Inc.
1999.012

Charles Carraway
(born 1957)
Nina's Room, 2002
oil on linen
27¼ x 24
Purchase
2005.095

Langdon Clay
(born 1949)
tomato horse, 2002
chromogenic color print
16 x 20
Purchase, with funds
from Mary Mhoon
Endowment
2005.101

Jessie Duncan Savage
Cole (1858-1940)
Nasturtiums, no date
oil on canvas
10 x 14
Gift of Paul and Celia
Mabry
2004.010

William Dunlap
(born 1944)
Landscape and Variable—Self Portrait with Fighting Cock, 1973
watercolor and graphite
on paper
39½ x 28

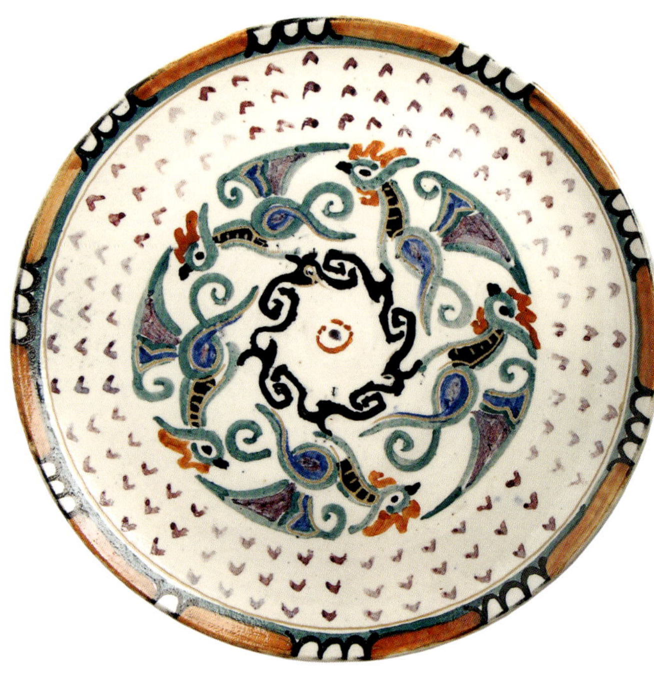

Shearwater Pottery
decorated by Walter Anderson (1903-1965), Shearwater Art Pottery
Plate with Rooster Motif, circa 1940.
earthenware with glaze,
9¼ x 9¼.

Gift of Norma Latimer Watkins, in memory of her mother Norma Latimer Watkins and her aunt Hosford Latimer Fontaine
1987.137

William Eggleston
(born 1939)
no title, circa 1978
chromogenic color print
14¾ x 9¾ (sight)
Purchase
1985.020

Alfred Eisenstaedt
(1898-1995)
Melon Salesman and Fiddler, Scott, Mississippi, 1936, 1936
gelatin silver print
11¾ x 17¼ (sight)
Purchase
1997.096

Alan Flattmann
(born 1946)
Morning Light, 1973
oil on canvas
30 x 44
Gift of Mr. and Mrs. Harvey B. Heidelberg, Jr.
1978.076

Susan Ford (born 1951)
Cobalt Blue Vase, 2002
blown glass
8 x 6 x 6
Purchase
2002.027

Susan Ford (born 1951)
Ruby Pop Bottle, 2002
blown glass
12⅛ x 3⅛ x 3⅛
Purchase
2002.028

Ke Francis (born 1945)
Jugline Moonscape, 1992
woodcut
10 x 14¼ (sight)
2004.068

Roland Freeman
(born 1936)
Mule Train leaving Marks, Mississippi for Washington, D.C., as part of the 1968 Poor People's Campaign, 1968
gelatin silver print
12 x 17½ (sight)
Gift of Kathryn Wiener
1993.002

Roland Freeman
(born 1936)
Sunday Baseball Game, near Buffalo, Mississippi, September 1976, 1976
gelatin silver print
16 x 20
Purchase
1995.010

Jane Hollingsworth
(1912-1986)
Showers with Winds Gusting Up to 40 M.P.H., 1973
bronze
12¼ x 6¾ x 6
Gift of Joe Bennett
2005.020

William Hollingsworth
(1910-1944)
Billy and Boy, 1942
oil on canvas
20 x 24
Bequest of Jane Oakley Hollingsworth
1987.025

William Hollingsworth
(1910-1944)
Black and White, no date
oil on fabric
24 x 28
Gift of Mrs. William Hollingsworth
1944.001

William Hollingsworth
(1910-1944)
Christmas Eve, 1942
watercolor on paper
15⅝ x 22½
Bequest of Jane Oakley Hollingsworth
1987.029

William Hollingsworth
(1910-1944)
Dance Team, 1933
lithograph
8½ x 6½ (sight)
Bequest of Jane Oakley Hollingsworth
1987.187

William Hollingsworth
(1910-1944)
Elevator, Tower Building, no date
oil on board
24 x 28
Bequest of Jane Oakley Hollingsworth
1987.065

William Hollingsworth
(1910-1944)
Family at Mealtime, 1943
oil on canvas
19 x 15
Bequest of Jane Oakley Hollingsworth
1987.042

William Hollingsworth
(1910-1944)
Playing Army, 1943
graphite on paper
10½ x 10 (sight)
Bequest of Jane Oakley Hollingsworth
1987.213

William Hollingsworth
(1910-1944)
The Alert, 1942
oil on canvas
32 x 26
Bequest of Jane Oakley Hollingsworth
1987.030

William Hollingsworth
(1910-1944)
Wet Hair, 1940
oil on canvas
24 x 20
Bequest of Jane Oakley Hollingsworth
1987.014

Robert Hubbard
(born 1945)
Road Cross #3, Hwy. 49, 2002
chromogenic color print
3 x 2⅜
Gift of the artist
2004.013

Birney Imes (born 1951)
Hollandale, January 31, 1986, 1986
chromogenic color print
16 x 20
Purchase
1986.009

Eyd Kazery (born 1953)
Ross Barnett, 1982
Neshoba County Fair,
1998
gelatin silver print
20 x 16
Gift of Christopher Haddad
1999.017

Jack Kotz (born 1961)
Heaven & Hell, Mathiston, Mississippi,
1987
Cibachrome
20 x 16
Gift of William Dunlap
1999.003

David Lambert (born 1961)
Dating Service, 1998
acrylic on plywood
34 x 28¾
Gift of the artist
2006.052

Ethel Pennewill Brown Leach (1878-1960)
Totin' Clothes, Mississippi, Oct. 1916,
1916
watercolor on paper
26 x 20
Gift of the artist
1916.002

Gwendolyn A. Magee (born 1943)
Five Years Hard Labor,
2007
textile
58 x 67
Purchase, with funds from Searcy Fund
2007.002

Ken Marlow (born 1960)
Still Life with Shallots,
no date
oil on canvas
9 x 15¾
Gift of Hassam and Speicher Purchase Fund, American Academy and Institute of Arts and Letters
1987.141

Tina Mason (dates unknown)
Hunter's Paradise, no date
oil on board
20 x 24
Gift of the artist
1954.010

John McCrady (1911-1968)
Rural Symposium, 1964
acrylic on board
20 x 31
Purchase, with funds from The Gallery Guild, Inc; McCarty Fund; Franks Fund; and the Heard family, in memory of Dr. and Mrs. Kenneth Heard
2004.058

Mary Katherine Loyacono McCravey (born 1910)
Choctaws, no date
oil on canvas
16 x 20
Gift of the artist
2003.041

P. Sanders McNeal (born 1949)
The Rehearsal, 1997
oil on canvas
36 x 60
Gift of John and Melody Maxey
2005.030

Ethel Wright Mohamed (1906-1992)
The Blue Bird of Happiness, circa 1979
silk and cotton
25 x 25 (sight)
Purchase
2000.005

Milly Moorhead (now Milly Moorhead West) (born 1949)
Schwerner, Chaney & Goodman, Aaron Henry's Drug Store, Clarksdale, Mississippi,
1983
chromogenic color print
8 x 13
Purchase
1997.099

David Rae Morris (born 1959)
Mural of Green Bay Packers quarterback Brett Favre at the Broke Spoke, Kiln (Favre's hometown), Hancock County, 1998
chromogenic color print
16 x 20
Purchase, with funds from Claire King Sargent and Henry B. Sargent
2006.064

David Rae Morris (born 1959)
Contestants for the Miss Catfish crown, Belzoni, Humphreys County,
1999
chromogenic color print
16 x 20
Purchase, with funds from Claire King Sargent and Henry B. Sargent
2006.066

David Rae Morris (born 1959)
Leon Gray, flagbearer for Martin Luther King Day Parade, Yazoo City, Yazoo County, 1999
chromogenic color print
20 x 16
Gift of the artist
2003.008

Frank Neal (born 1955)
The Existential Roofer: A Tribute to Giotto, 1981
oil and wax on canvas
44 x 52
Gift of the artist
1986.065

Elizabeth Pajerski (1915-2003)
Orchestra, 1971
black and white etching
15 x 17
Gift of the artist
1997.007

Tom Rankin (born 1957)
Deacon Fred Davis, 1990
gelatin silver print
10 x 10 (sight)
Purchase
1997.101

Tom Rankin (born 1957)
Handmade Gravestones, Mound Bayou, 1989,
1989
gelatin silver print
16 x 20
Purchase, with funds from Mary Mhoon Endowment
1996.071

Tom Rankin (born 1957)
Moon Lake, 1990, 1990
gelatin silver print
16 x 20
Purchase, with funds from Mary Mhoon Endowment
1996.072

Dale Rayburn (born 1942)
Sunday School Class,
1976
color etching
19 x 24¼ (sight)
Gift of the artist
1977.001

Sulton Rogers (1922-2003)
Crucifixion, 1989
wood with paint and cloth
12⅜ x 7¾ x 3¼
Gift of Warren and Sylvia Lowe
1993.016

Sulton Rogers (1922-2003)
Two Blues Singers, 1989
paint on wood
17 x 4 x 8; 16 x 4 x 7
Gift of Warren and Sylvia Lowe
1994.051

Lynn Green Root (1954-2001)
Happy's Room, 1996
acrylic on canvas
29⅞ x 40
Gift of Benjamin A. Root, Jr.
2001.060

Lynn Green Root (1954-2001)
no title, 1994
acrylic on paper
18 x 12
Purchase, with funds from Joshua Green
2003.095

Boyd Saunders (born 1937)
The Gathering, 1984
etching
16½ x 20½ (sight)
Purchase, with funds from Mary Mhoon Endowment
2002.022

Mary T. Smith (1904-1995)
no title, 1988
paint on wood
31⅜ x 24⅛
Gift of Warren and Sylvia Lowe
1993.020

Emmitt Thames (born 1933)
Flowers and Fruit, 1986
gouache on paper
20 x 14 (sight)
Gift of Richard and Valda Miller
2004.048

James "Son" Thomas (1926-1993)
Guitar Player, 1989
mixed mediums
7⅛ x 4½ x 3½
Gift of Warren and Sylvia Lowe
1993.021

Glennray Tutor
(born 1950)
Coffee Cup, 1994
oil on prepared paper
6¼ x 7¼ (sight)
Gift of Peggy H. Harris, in memory of her son, Tommy Ramey
2005.002

Glennray Tutor
(born 1950)
Still Life: A Season of Moment, 2003
oil on linen canvas
50 x 84
Purchase, with funds from Charles Holman Fund
2003.116

Kathleen Varnell
(born 1961)
Healing I, 2003
smokefired stoneware with earthenware slip
28 x 10 x 10
Purchase, with funds from Searcy Fund
2007.017

Miriam Weems
(born 1941)
Stars Under the Stars, 2001
oil on canvas
48 x 60
Gift of John and Melody Maxey
2005.034

Eudora Welty
(1909-2001)
Saturday Strollers, Grenada, 1935
gelatin silver print
18 x 10½ (sight)
Gift of AmSouth Bank
2001.049

Eudora Welty
(1909-2001)
Sunday School, Holiness Church, Jackson, 1935-1936
gelatin silver print
20 x 16
Collection of Elizabeth and Fred Thompson, Madison, Mississippi

Eudora Welty
(1909-2001)
Tomato packers' recess, Crystal Springs, 1935-1936
gelatin silver print
14 x 11 (sight)
Gift of Mr. and Mrs. Richard L. Miller
2000.013

Bruce West (born 1953)
Gravedigger, MS #1, 1996
chromogenic color print
7½ x 9¼ (sight)
Gift of the artist
1997.083

Bob Willis (born 1947)
Aux, 1994
wood
13 x 7
Gift of Lamar Life Insurance Company, by exchange
1995.024

Luster Willis (1913-1994)
no title, 1982
mixed mediums on paper
12¼ x 18
Gift of Warren and Sylvia Lowe
1994.047

Stephen Flinn Young
(born 1945)
Worth, 1982
mixed mediums
15¾ x 9½ x 2
Gift of the artist
1982.042

EXPORTING MISSISSIPPI'S CULTURE

Rebecca Alston
(born 1951)
no title, 2000
mixed mediums on paper
7 x 10¼
Gift of the artist
2003.026

Richmond Barthé
(1901-1989)
Feral Benga, 1937
bronze
20¼ x 7¼ x 7
Purchase, with funds from McCarty Fund and McCravey Fund
2002.016

Byron Burford
(born 1920)
Beauty Celebrates New Year, 1987
magna (solvent-based acrylic) on canvas
37¼ x 48¾ (sight)
Purchase
2006.067

Critz Campbell
(born 1967)
Eudora, 2005
mixed mediums
31 x 31 x 36
Gift of the artist
2007.033

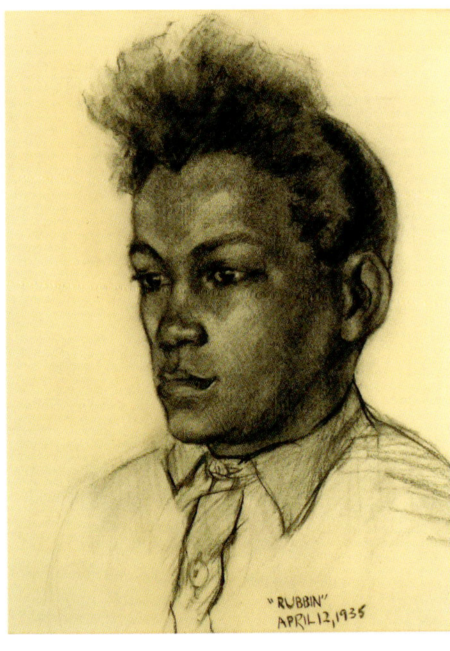

Helen Jay Lotterhos (1905–1981), *Rubbin*, 1935. charcoal on paper, 18¾ x 12½.

Kate Freeman Clark
(1875-1957)
Summer Landscape, circa 1909
oil on canvas
25½ x 29
Collection of Mr. Michael Wilkinson, New Orleans, Louisiana

Warren Dennis
(born 1927)
Firebuilder, 1988
oil on canvas
45⅛ x 56½
Gift of the artist
2005.023

G. Ruger Donoho
(1857-1916)
Blossom Time, Right of Path, Marlotte, circa 1911
oil on canvas
24 x 20
Gift of Velma Jernigan Rodgers
1981.272

G. Ruger Donoho
(1857-1916)
The Garden Steps, circa 1913
oil on canvas
16 x 20
Gift of W. E. Walker Foundation
1978.036

William Dunlap
(born 1944)
Leona Winor is 100 Years Old, 1971
polymer on linen
54 x 47¾
Gift of Norma Latimer Watkins, in memory of her mother Norma Latimer Watkins and

her aunt Hosford
Latimer Fontaine
1987.134

William Dunlap
(born 1944)
Old Masters Reconsidered—Good Company, 1971
polymer on canvas
50¾ x 50¾
Gift of Norma Latimer Watkins, in memory of her mother Norma Latimer Watkins and her aunt Hosford Latimer Fontaine
1987.135

Larry Edwards
(born 1931)
Amusement Park, Fires and Fireworks, 2001
gouache and pastel on paper
43¾ x 30¾
Gift of the artist
2004.001

Ke Francis (born 1945)
Tornado and Tuning Forks, 2001
woodcut
34 x 64
Gift of the artist
2007.015

Mimi Garrard
(born 1936)
Time Installation, 2006
DVD
Gift of the artist
2007.034

Sam Gilliam
(born 1933)
Birds Not Flying, 2005
acrylic on birch with piano hinges
53¼ x 48½ x 2¾
Purchase, with funds from Searcy Fund
2006.060

Randy Hayes
(born 1944)
Overnight Sensation, 1987
pastel on paper
64 x 52½
Purchase
1989.005

Randy Hayes
(born 1944)
The Fauna of Mississippi, 2006
oil on photograph, pushpins
40 x 50
Purchase, with funds from McCarty Fund
2007.005

Becky Hendrick
(born 1947)
Nature Morte, late 1980s
oil and acrylic on canvas
60 x 60
Gift of Children's Medical Group, P.A., in memory of Jim G. Hendrick, M.D.
2001.056

Valerie Jaudon
(born 1945)
Arcola, 1982
oil on canvas
81 x 120
Purchase
1997.005

Ed McGowin
(born 1938)
Banana Book, 1984
airbrush ink on board
29 x 41
Gift of William Dunlap
1997.023

Ed McGowin
(born 1938)
Dad Knew About Wine Chair, 1977
ink on paper
60 x 50 (sight)
Gift of William Dunlap
1997.022

Fred Mitchell
(born 1923)
Untitled, 1961
oil on linen
50 x 60
Purchase
2006.063

Alex O'Neal (born 1957)
Leon Koury's Backyard Messiahs, 2000
acrylic on canvas
95 x 112
Gift of the artist
2005.096

Mary Lovelace O'Neal
(born 1942)
Angel of the Hood, 1995
mixed mediums on canvas
84 x 60
Purchase
2007.018

Edgar Parker
(1925-1982)
Lieutenant Reynolds, no date
ink and graphite on paper
6½ x 3½ (sight)
Gift of Nell Parker Downing
1984.069

Edgar Parker
(1925-1982)
Self-Portrait, no date
watercolor on paper
8¾ x 9¾ (sight)
Gift of Nell Parker Downing
1985.041

Edgar Parker
(1925-1982)
Sleeping Rabbit, no date
graphite on paper
7½ x 9¾
Gift of Nell Parker Downing
1982.071

Robert Rector
(born 1946)
Untitled from the *Axis* series, 2004
acrylic on canvas
60 x 49
Gift of Eason and Ellen Leake
2004.057

James Seawright
(born 1936)
Carina, 2004
mixed mediums
9 x 12 x 9
Purchase
2006.061

James Seawright
(born 1936)
Hexflector, 1989
cast stone and mirrors
42½ x 47⅛ x 2⅝
Gift of Mary Jane Whittington
1991.384

Maltby Sykes
(1911-1992)
Pomegranate, 1954
color lithograph
10½ x 11¾ (sight)
Purchase
2006.048

George Wardlaw
(born 1927)
Guardian of the Light, 2004
acrylic on canvas
80 x 50
Purchase
2006.062

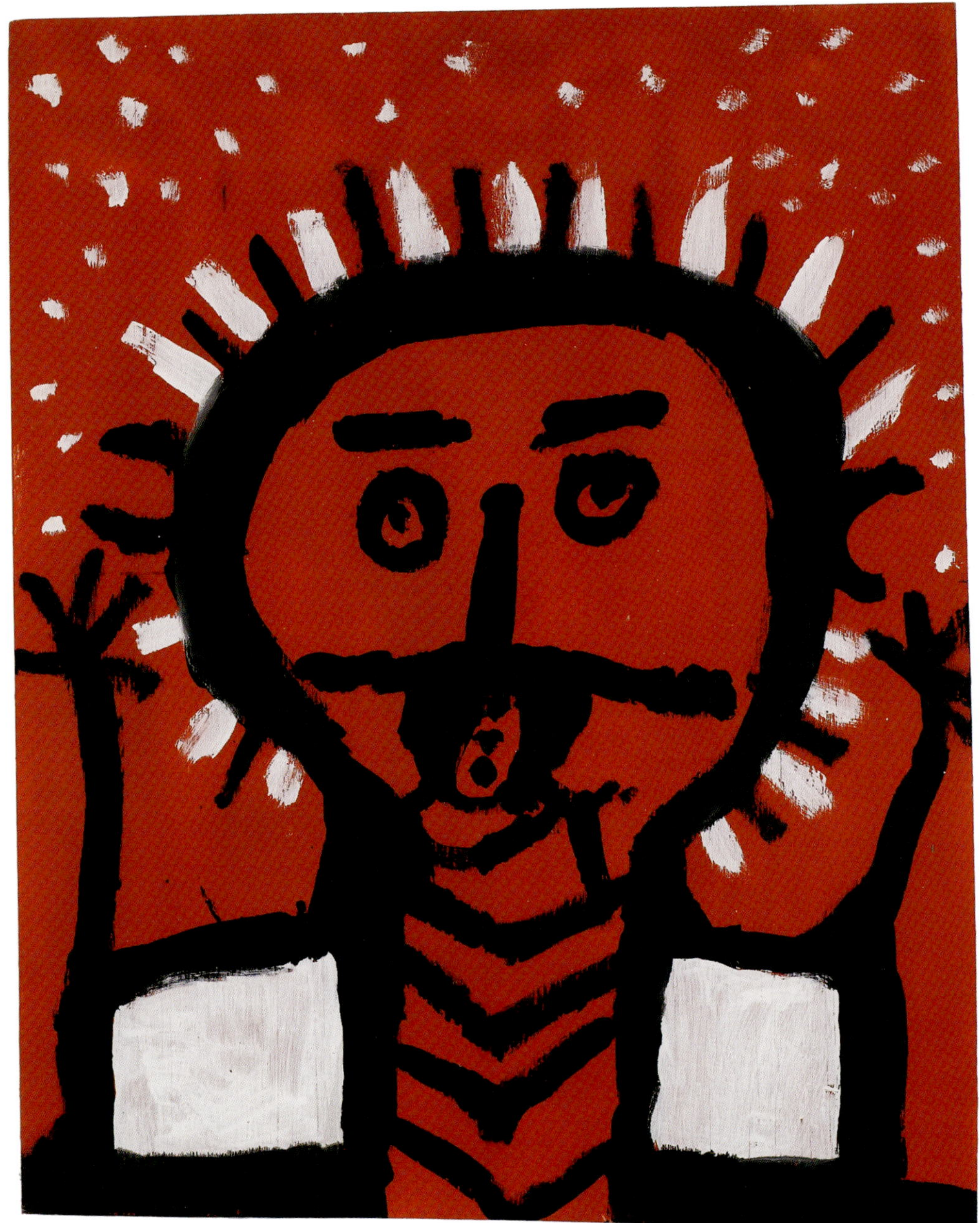

Mary T. Smith
(1904-1995), no title, 1988. paint on wood, 31⅜ x 24⅛.

Index

Numbers in boldface indicate an illustration on that page.